Joe Frank Harris

Personal Reflections on a Public Life

Joe Frank Harris
Governor of Georgia, 1983-1991

MERCER UNIVERSITY PRESS
MACON, GEORGIA

ISBN 0-86554-599-5   MUP/H451

The paper used in this publication meets the minimum require-
ments   of American National Standard for Information
Sciences—Permanence of Paper for Printed Library Materials,
ANSI Z39.48-1984.

Library of Congress Cataloging-in-Publication Data

Harris, Joe Frank, 1936-
    Joe Frank Harris: Personal Reflections on a Public Life / by Joe
    Frank Harris
        x + 280 pp.   6" x 9" (15 x 22 cm.)
    Includes bibiliographic references and index.
    ISBN 0-86554-599-5 (alk. paper)
    1. Harris, Joe Frank. 2. Governors—Georgia—Biography.
3. Georgia—Politics and government—1951- I. Title.
F291.3.H37A3   1998
975.8'043'092—dc21
[B]   97-47505
                                                         CIP

To my wife Elizabeth,
son Joe, and daughter-in-law Brooke,
and grandchildren, Catherine Elizabeth and Thomas Kimsey.

You are the inspirations for the priorities of my life:
To serve the Lord and to maintain a *good* name for my family.

"A good name is rather to be chosen than great riches,
and loving favor rather than silver and gold."
Proverbs 22: 1

Contents

Photographs

Unless otherwise indicated, all photographs are used courtesy of Governor Joe Frank Harris.

Foreword

It has been my privilege to know Governor Joe Frank Harris and his wife Elizabeth for a number of years. His personal invitations brought me to Georgia as the speaker for the Governor's Prayer Breakfast in 1987 and the Democratic Convention in Atlanta in 1988 to give the opening prayer. When the famous Georgia Dome was completed, it was my privilege to participate in the dedication and opening ceremony. Governor Harris then joined other Georgia leaders to issue a formal invitation to me at that time to hold a Crusade in Atlanta in 1995.

This book covers a long time span. It was in those eight gubernatorial years that some of the most dramatic and positive events in modern Georgia history occurred. A few of the contributions he made as Governor were the passage of a landmark education revision without a single negative vote in 1985; the securing of the Democratic National Convention in 1988; the building of the Georgia Dome; critical support of the visionary Billy Payne in the years before the '96 Olympics; and the building of 143 public libraries, while bringing over 850,000 new jobs to Georgia. Many know of these accomplishments, but little is really known of the personal history of the man who was instrumental in making them a reality.

What attracts me most of all to Governor Harris is his personal relationship with Jesus Christ. After being elected Governor of Georgia, Joe Frank Harris has proclaimed on many occasions that the greatest thing that ever happened in his life was not his election as Governor, but the time when he accepted Jesus Christ as his personal Savior.

I certainly recommend this book for your reading.

Billy Graham
Montreat, North Carolina

Preface

These recollections follow a chronological line, beginning in the Atco Mill Village where I was born, through many phases of my life, to my two terms as Governor of Georgia, and even beyond. It is an overview of *selected* events and includes many of the people who have shaped my personal and political history. There are many deserving individuals, staff members, and friends who were as significant and special as those mentioned here. I apologize to those whom I have inadvertently left out; your contributions to my life were just as important. A more in-depth, or even scholarly, perspective on these events should be the province of other, more objective observers.

This book was written to convey the "long view" of my life, in order that the reader might know where I came from and what my early influences were. Every decision I made in my public life was in some way a reflection of values I had been taught or experiences I had had or the lessons I had learned long before it *ever* occurred to me to enter politics. Once in that arena, whenever I found myself in a difficult place, I drew strength and, I hope, wisdom from my formative years with a loving family, and from the spiritual foundations provided by a deep and abiding faith in God and prayer.

In the years since leaving public life, I have found that I have been content with who I am and challenged with each new day. I also feel a certain contentment in knowing that while I was in office, I upheld the people's trust to the utmost of my ability.

I recall in these pages that on the day my successor was inaugurated as Governor, a friend of mine observed that I looked somewhat sad as I stood outside after the ceremony. I replied that my *only* source of sadness or concern was whether I had a ride back to my home in Cartersville!

I hope you enjoy my ride; I certainly have!

Acknowledgments

Writing a book is not something I had planned to do in my lifetime. Neither was serving as Governor of the state of Georgia. It is amazing how the Lord will close some doors while opening others when one is dedicated to God's service. Usually those doors are opened by other people the Lord is using, and you don't realize it until you have already walked through them. Without the support and help of many individuals, this book would not have been possible.

Dr. Carl Patton, President of Georgia State University, suggested that I write a book at the same meeting in which he invited me to lecture and share some of my experiences with the students. He never forgot his suggestion and allowed others at the university to support my efforts. Thomas C. Lewis, Vice President for External Affairs and my former Senior Executive Assistant in the Governor's office, kept the pressure on and even insisted that I ask Dr. Billy Graham to write the foreword. I am grateful to Cliff Barrows, T. W. Wilson, and Henry Holley, assistants to Dr. Graham, who helped make this possible. I am also eternally grateful for and honored by Dr. Graham's gracious words.

R. Cary Bynum, former founding director of the Georgia State University Business Press, asked probing questions to prompt my memory of these events. His professional experience and valuable advice were vital for this work. I have learned much from him and cherish our growing friendship. Russell Faulk provided the professional tape transcriptions while James A. Overbeck assisted with valuable early research. My heartfelt thanks goes to McRae F. Williams and Dr. Edgar C. Torbert, who provided administrative support; Dr. Ralph E. Russell, head librarian, and Dr. Carolyn L. Robison, associate librarian, Pullen Library, Georgia State University, for their cooperation.

I also wish to express my appreciation to Mercer University Press, in particular Dr. Cecil P. Staton, Jr., publisher, Dr. Marc A. Jolley, assistant publisher, and my editor, Dr. Andrew M. Manis, for their patience, understanding, and assistance.

Brothers
L-R Fred Harris (age 7) and Joe Frank Harris (age 5)

1

Atco Mill Village

I was born in the Atco Mill Village at 18 Wingfoot Trail, in one of the little wood frame houses there. When my parents met, and even at the time I was born in 1936, the village was not a part of the City of Cartersville. The city limits eventually expanded and took in the Atco Mill Village, but it remains a regular textile mill village today.

Atco got its name from the American Textile Company, which was the original operator of the mill before Goodyear came in. They had their own post office, general store, barbershop, beauty shop, their own clinic, and a school through the seventh grade. It was a self-contained little community. In years past, almost all of the employees had credit with the company store; you could pay with *chits*, and they would charge it against your paycheck.

People were employed or trained in the textile industry and followed the trend wherever the momentum might take them —moving around from mill to mill. Or they'd hit one, land, and stay there. That's how my mother and her family got to Atco. They were from Porterdale, Georgia, in Newton County. Because the economy of the mill down there had slowed, they were on "short-time," as folks used to refer to it in textile operations. Her family came to Atco Mill because that mill was operating at full speed and still employing people.

My dad's family had come to Atco for the same reason. When he was very young, they moved to Texas where they had a large acreage—and crops in the field. After his father died of typhoid fever, when Dad was three years old, his mother sold the crops to neighbors, put their belongings on the train, and rode back to Georgia. She knew she would not be able to operate the farm singlehandedly, particularly with a baby and three small children. About 1915, I guess, she came back home where somebody could help her exist!

In the early 1920s my dad's mother moved the family to Atco from Gilmer County. There were no jobs at all in Gilmer County at that time, unless you were a part of the sawmill or in logging, which had few jobs available and very few that paid a comfortable wage. One of her brothers-in-law was already at Atco. He had visited them back in Gilmer County and had told her that "If you come down, we'll get you a job." She packed up their things, went down to Atco, and got a job in the mill.

Since you didn't have to be any age—just big enough to work—my dad was working there by the time he was fourteen years old. Initially, he was doing *any* type of job in the mill, but then worked his way up into the machinery maintenance area. Later, he became the number one person in charge of the spinning department, which was his position when he left the mill to begin the concrete business.

The old Goodyear Mill consisted of three-story-high red brick buildings, similar to what you might envision *all* Southern textile mills looked like in those days. And as these communities go, Atco was a large village. I attended school there, too, the first four years. It was a brick school, a two-story building. The second story was a big auditorium and that's where all the village events were held. I can remember the smell of that building, particularly the auditorium. There was something familiar about it: I guess a school always smells like a school, and I can still remember that distinctive, musty smell.

There was a swimming pool right next door and the barbershop was next to the swimming pool. Adjacent to that were the baseball diamond, where the textile league played its official games, and the grandstands. They played good ball there. That was the field where one of the prominent professional players of that time, Rudy York, began his career. He went on to play for the Detroit Tigers and had a distinguished major league career, which included some home run records.

The old school in the complex was an elementary school that went through the first seven grades. The principal was a lady by the name of Jewel Gould. She was a very strict and stern disciplinarian. Kids would almost *tremble* when she walked up. Back then, the students in school respected the teachers and the people in charge, and, in later years, we were glad to have their discipline. They instilled something in you: moral standards, ethics, and values to live by. We've been fortunate over the years to be exposed to a lot of truly dedicated teachers who wanted to be educators. We have a lot of these people still in the systems today; I'm very grateful for them.

My father, Franklin Grover Harris, was eight years old when they came to Cartersville from Gilmer County. My mother, Julia Frances Morrow, was probably sixteen when her family moved from Newton County. They met in the church at Atco—or at least confirmed their meeting and conducted their courtship there. They were married on April 7, 1933, after a year-long engagement.

My father was a unique person. He was practically self-educated. He left school in the seventh grade to support his family. His father died when he was three years old, and his mother had not been in good health. His older brother had gone to live in Akron, Ohio, which left my dad to be the "elder son." He had a younger brother who, as an adult, went to live in Rockmart, Georgia, where he owned a funeral business. Then he had a sister who had died during his earlier years, soon after they had moved to Atco to work in the mill. So the household was made up of only Dad, his younger brother, and his mother.

At that time you could work in the mill at a preteen age; and while Dad had left school to work in the mill, that *didn't* end his education. He continued through correspondence courses and night school at Georgia Tech, staying at it for many years. He was good at math and an extremely hard worker.

Dad was also one of the most moral people I ever knew. If it wasn't right, then he was *not* going to be a part of it. He really set an example that I try to follow today. As far as a work ethic and doing what's right and serving the Lord is concerned, he was the greatest inspiration of my life—because that's the way he lived *his* life.

The Highest Priority

From the time he went to work in the mill, he began a program of self-education. Since his formal education had ended in the seventh grade, he took correspondence courses and attended all supervisory or training courses offered at the mill, ending up as an extension student attending classes at Georgia Tech. Early on, he had seen that the people with education were the ones being promoted or getting the good jobs. He couldn't qualify for many of those positions because he didn't have a college degree. So initially he had pursued *any* area of study as a way of converting it into what he needed to make a living.

One of my earliest memories was that he always planned on his children receiving a college education. From the time we were born, he started setting aside funds and buying war bonds for our college education. At one point he had to cash in those war bonds to go into the concrete business. But he was always driven to restore those funds to bonds—or some other savings—so that we would not be denied a college education. From day one he constantly hammered into our heads, "You're going to get an education." We just assumed that was the only way out; we had to do it. Years later, Dad served on the Cartersville School Board and was chairman for over ten years. A good education was always one of his highest priorities, a value I inherited and continued right on into the governor's office.

Making Music

Mother was a brilliant person. She only had a high school education, but she was very skilled with numbers. She could take a shopping list to the grocery store and know the totals before she arrived at the checkout counter. She'd have it in her mind how much money she needed to pull out of her pocketbook before she got there. Mom was dedicated to reading religious books and, of course, her favorite was the Bible. She was constantly in the books, reading and studying.

She was also very gifted musically. She had a natural talent and, with very little formal training, she taught herself to play the organ and the violin. Later, she took up the mandolin and could do a little "picking and grinning." She served as our church pianist for a number of years. She was in demand, particularly during the war years when there were few people around to play the piano for funerals. The local funeral home would call her, and many times she didn't even know the family of the deceased. But they needed someone to play and would send somebody to pick her up. As a kid, I went with her many times. I'd sit there on the bench until she finished playing piano for the funeral. Then they'd take us back home. I can't remember her ever accepting a dime.

We were all exposed to music. During my grade school years, I had to take piano lessons—but didn't continue them. In the neighborhood I grew up in, we thought it was kind of "sissy" to play the piano. I didn't want my peers to know I was learning the piano, and as soon as I got old enough, I refused to continue lessons and was able to devote more time to football and other activities.

Fred and Glenda

My older brother is called "Fred," but his name is Fredric Alan. Fred was almost two years older than me. Our ages were very close, and then our size became very close from the time I was six years old. Most brothers fight among themselves, and I could hold my own. But we were friends and shared a lot together. We bought our first automobile together—an old Model A Ford—that we'd saved up and purchased for $65! I didn't have a driver's license; I was only fourteen years old and he was sixteen: he would drive and I would ride in the back seat. We kept that car for a few years.

Fred committed his life to Christ about the same time as I did. So, we were dealing with a new beginning in our lives at about the same time. Many years later, we were in business together—from 1958 until we sold the business in 1980.

Our family had always wanted a little sister, and the Lord blessed our family with a girl on February 8, 1946. I remember, of course, because I had a paper route, and on the day she was born there was a flood in our community. With the abundance of rain, the creek between our house and the Atco Mill Village had overflowed its banks. On that day it had almost flooded the road. It was raining extremely hard, and I had to get those papers delivered. Mom was in the hospital expecting the baby. We finally got the papers out—and got there a few minutes after four in the afternoon, just about the time our little sister was born! That was a thrill for my whole family.

Her name is Glenda Chloe. I don't know where we got the Glenda or the Chloe, but we liked both names. (She has always been called "Glenda" and dropped the "Chloe.") She not only had the protection, but also the liability of two older brothers who really didn't know how to treat a baby sister. Sometimes I guess we were a little rough on her. Glenda survived, though; she was tough! She became a fine high school athlete and was on the state championship basketball team. Her team was a well-balanced group of girls who had come up together through the high school ranks. In 1964 they were state champions.

Glenda continued her musical education into college and became an accomplished musician. She's now the music director of our church choir and plays both piano and organ. I guess she inherited all the musical ability in our family. Of course, she didn't have to worry about someone thinking she was the "sissy" of the neighborhood!

Seeing a Need

Mom and Dad were two of the most generous, giving people I've ever known. They made a good pair, and even today we run across people who tell us—"Your Dad helped me with a loan," or "He helped my family when we had a problem." He and Mom assisted us or sent someone to school or paid tuition for someone. He was always helping ministerial students, for example, sending them on scholarships to Asbury College where he was later a member of the Board of Trustees. Even today there's an endowment there that provides scholarships in his and Mom's name.

I'm afraid I don't *think* like my father. A lot of times you won't recognize a need until later on. Then you think—maybe I should have stepped in here or should have done something there. Dad *immediately* sees a need and steps in! Even when we were still back in the mill village—raising and selling vegetables and chickens—Dad always gave away as much as we sold, usually to people in need or when there was a death in the family. Mother would always cook and send vegetables or a cake. She would bake pound cakes and put them in the freezer so she'd have them ready in case somebody died unexpectedly.

My mom and dad were married for over sixty-three years. Mom had been in a nursing home for a little over four years. She had hardening of the arteries and though it was not Alzheimer's, the results were the same and *dementia* had set in. She had not recognized anyone for some time and really did not know where she was. . . . Dad continued his regular visits. I felt that her state of existence was far worse than death. We knew she was ready to meet the Lord. . . . And in the early morning hours of July 22, 1996, she made her flight home to be with Him. My wife Elizabeth and I were with her when she slowly and peacefully quit breathing, and her wonderful heart did not beat again. In just a few months, Mother would have celebrated her eighty-fifth birthday.

Fatherly Advice

Dad has reasonably good health. He still lives in his own home—totally self-sufficient, not dependent on anybody for anything—and has one of the sharpest minds I've ever seen. He can recall just about anything that's ever happened from day one, much better than I can today. He plays golf a couple of times a week and can almost shoot his age! He'll score in the low 90's and occasionally get down in the 80's. He really enjoys it—along with the fellowship and companionship of the people with whom he plays, including his close friend Clyde Charles, a former mayor of Cartersville.

Regardless of the position one might hold or how successful one may be in life, you're always a son to your father. Our relationship continues today, but it might be unique in some respects: Dad was not only my father, he was also my boss for a number of years in our family business, and we had a good family working relationship.

After I was elected and became a member of the General Assembly, I can't recall many times over the years that he offered specific political advice. He was always ready to provide his personal feelings, or how something might fit, or his understanding of it. But he would never tell me—you need to vote "yes" or you need to vote "no" on this, or you need to take a particular position. He would give you his ideas, his feelings or assessment of a problem, which I greatly respected. I would make up my mind, based on my understanding of the total issue. The majority of the time, it would be pretty well in line with what his thinking might have been on various questions, since we embraced many of the same moral values and Christian principles. However, I can't recall a single issue that I had to deal with while I was governor that, after the fact, he said, "Son, you should have done this or you should have done that." He accepted whatever I did and supported it. Whether he *believed* in it or not, well, he never told me. . . .

2

An Early Work Ethic

We were known as "Atco Boys" and "Goodyear Mill Village Boys," even though we didn't live in the village when I started school in Cartersville. I had transferred to Cartersville in the fifth grade. That was the year my dad left Goodyear and decided to go into the cement business fulltime. If you were not a resident of Atco or an employee of Goodyear Mills, you weren't allowed to attend school in Atco, which is where I had gone my first four years in school.

When we transferred to Cartersville, we were almost like the kids from the wrong side of the tracks to the "in" group there. It was really a challenge. You had to prove you were worthy of fitting into their level. You were always working not only to get ahead, but just to survive—and prove you were as good as they were! And a lot of them—their parents—were a lot better off than our parents. I might have had some bitterness had I not accomplished some things as time went on. I made the basketball team, the football team, and was a class officer. And many of the people I thought might have created problems for me never became a problem.

We always worked. That was an ethic that Dad and Mom impressed on us—that "You've got to work to get ahead." Their parents had been raised with the same work ethic. They felt their children ought to be prepared to earn what they got. We were raised that way and worked hard all of our lives. And we needed to, really, because our family didn't have much money. We were common people, living from week to week.

When I was six years old we moved out of the Goodyear Cotton Mill Village at Atco and into a house on Cassville Road. Dad had saved money to buy that house all his life. It was still in sight of the mill but out of the mill village. On that property, we sold pecans in the fall, raised chickens and sold them—anything from which we could derive an income.

I began delivering *The Atlanta Journal*, the afternoon newspaper, when I was eight years old. In those early years, we didn't get to play ball or join our classmates in pickup games after school. Later on, when I was old enough, I was on a milk route and would get up at 3:30 A.M. and walk about a mile to meet the Jackson's Dairy milk truck and then carry the route. Sonny Jackson, a friend and classmate, whose family owned the dairy, worked the route with me. (Later, I roomed with him at the University of Georgia, and still later, as governor, I appointed him to the Board of Natural Resources.) Working the paper route would take a couple of hours or so. I'd get home in time to grab a quick biscuit, change clothes, and then take off for school. I would be in class all day, maybe football that afternoon, or work in a filling station and grocery store out near our home place. I would try and get there before 4:00 P.M. because the owner, Ted Craig, worked the second shift in the mill. I would run his business for him until 7:30 or 8:00 in the evening; then his wife, Marie, would come in and be there to assist. (The Craigs later worked for me in a motel that I built and in which I had a partnership.) Sometimes I'd work until closing time; a lot of times I'd go back and work for him on the weekends. It seemed like our whole family was always working.

Glass Bottles and Cold Weather

I think weather probably creates the most physical challenge in work situations, particularly during the winter months. I can remember that on the milk truck it could be so cold that our hands could hardly hold the milk. We had only glass bottles then—and we'd have to carry three to six quarts to many of the homes. Those bottles were heavy and the truck never really stopped; and while it was moving we'd run and set the milk on the porch, pick up the empties, and run back to catch the truck at the next house down the road. We'd grab another quart or two and jump off at the next one. Even though we'd try to wear gloves, we couldn't hold the bottles because our hands weren't big as an adult's—so we'd have to try to get the bottles between your fingers. I guess that's why I've got big hands today.

As I look back, I realize that while "weathering" the elements may have been one of the more difficult challenges in those times, we accepted it as if it was nothing out of the ordinary. We didn't have television as we know it today, and you didn't realize how other people were living. We just thought this was something you were supposed to do.

Early Commitments

I was about seven years old, I guess, and there was a revival meeting at our church. Back then there were "traveling evangelists" who came in to run the revival. The preacher who was holding this particular revival was also a magician. He would do youth programs and entertain the young people by getting their attention with magic tricks. These revivals were routine in those years—still are in some congregations. They were *events* in the church, intended as a time for people to make or renew their commitments to Christ. Back then we referred to them as "old-fashioned, old-time revivals," which would start on a weekend, usually on Sunday, and run a week or ten days, sometimes two weeks.

The preacher who was running the revival at the old Atco Church was named Ralph Johnson. The meeting had been going on for several days. Prior to evening services they would have a special time for young people of the church. During that time Reverend Johnson would do his magic tricks to keep their attention and draw a crowd, too. People would come to see what he was going to do next. This was in preparation, I suppose, for the altar time that occurred at the end the service: a time to go forward and pray for forgiveness of your sins—and accept Jesus Christ as your personal Savior. During one of those times that I realized that even though I had always attended church and been brought up *in* the church—I had not made a commitment to accept Jesus Christ as my personal Savior. I made that commitment; it was a very emotional time for me—and has remained *the greatest event of my life*.

We never missed a Sunday. As a family we were always in Sunday School and Wednesday night prayer meeting. Anytime the church doors were open, all of us attended whenever possible. During the war years, my Dad had to work on many Sundays because the mill ran seven days a week. He didn't get to attend during those times, although he would go on Sunday evenings, if he got off from work in time. Otherwise, we always attended church together.

Dad's Business Venture

When I was ten years old, right after the Second World War (1946), my father had just gone into the concrete business with a partner. He'd been an employee at Goodyear Textile Mills throughout his adult life and had moved up in their organization to become a supervisor in the spinning department, one of the largest departments in the mill. But because of the time that was required to move up in that organization, he may have felt that his future lay elsewhere; Dad was looking around for another opportunity. Why he would seek another opportunity is, even today, beyond my imagination. Usually, when someone's in a position with a future and being successful, you're comfortable staying where you are. But he'd had a dream or vision and saw something others didn't see at the time.

He joined with a friend of his and, by borrowing against their property, raised enough money between them to buy a dump truck and a "two-bag" concrete mixer. (The small mixer is pulled behind a dump truck and located on the job site. Material is shoveled in and mixed right there before being put into forms with a wheelbarrow by hand.)

They bought the dump truck and mixer at the surplus property sale, which was held after the closing of what was then the Bell Bomber Plant (now Lockheed). Still working at Goodyear, they brought the dump truck and mixer back to Cartersville and, as a side line, started pouring foundations for houses and other structures. Dad had envisioned that concrete blocks would be something that people would need because of the expense of brick and the scarcity of other building materials. So, they invested in a small handmade block-tamping machine and made blocks one at a time.

We had set up the machines and process in our garage behind our home on Cassville Road near Cartersville. Since we didn't have zoning laws then, we could build anything we wanted. There had been a dairy farm there before, and the neighbors didn't complain when we put a block plant in our garage. It was a very small operation, but that was the beginning of our concrete products company.

So, I grew up with business around me; and as the business grew, we moved it onto a more permanent site where it could expand—though that was not to occur for some years down the road.

A Lasting Impression

Since we lived a little ways out of town, we always had to ride a bicycle or walk wherever we went. But there was a time when some of my friends were able to buy motor scooters. I remember just going to bed at night and dreaming about being able to buy and have one of those motor scooters. We really couldn't afford it. I guess if we'd saved all the money we had and not done anything else, we probably could have bought one. But my dad had seen a serious motorcycle accident almost in front of our house; and it was so traumatic for him that he just wouldn't hear of us riding a motor scooter.

Another problem for me was that a friend of ours had a motorcycle —not a small scooter but a regular motorcycle, an Indian. (That was the major brand then.) He was a student at GeorgiaTech and asked if we could store his motorcycle in our garage while he was away, which we did. He said, "If you want to ride it around the yard or whatever—that would be fine." This was okay with Dad.

One spring afternoon there was a meeting of the Board of Stewards of the Methodist Church. Dad was one of the members of that board and when Mother said he had gone to the Stewards meeting, I thought the meeting was at the church. But the meeting was being held at a house between our home and downtown Cartersville.

After they'd had plenty of time to leave and get to the church (or so I thought), I decided that our yard wasn't quite big enough to hold that motorcycle and that I needed to ride it on up the street a ways. It had a loud exhaust, and that was music to a kid's ears. I was fourteen years old, didn't have a driver's license, and shouldn't have been on the street with a motor vehicle at all. But I wound that thing up—right up the middle of the street, meeting cars and passing cars, and I passed the place where Dad was meeting. They were standing out front and I knew he saw me go by.

I had two thoughts in mind: one was to go back home and face the music. The other was to see if I had enough money to buy some gas and just keep on riding as far as that motorcycle would take me. I circled on around town—miserable because I knew what was in store. And when I got home Dad was waiting on me. He had inquired of my Mom, "Did you send him somewhere?" which he knew she had not.

We had some big apple trees in the backyard. Dad believed in "capital" punishment and cut some switches off that appletree. Being the spring of the year the apple limbs were very soft, almost like a whip. I was a big boy—too old to cry—and here he was tearing up my rear end with those switches!

You don't forget those kinds of things. It made an impression on me. That was the last time I ever remember receiving any reprimand that severe. I learned that if you're going to take advantage of a situation and get caught doing something you're not supposed to do, you're going to have to pay the penalty. And I paid that penalty.

Athletically Inclined

We were all involved in sports from the time we were qualified to play. My sister, Glenda, played basketball; my brother, Fred, and I also played basketball, though I played more football. Dad was an excellent softball pitcher and competed in "fast pitch" softball. He was always athletically inclined and played when they had the old Textile Mill Association that would compete among the different mills in that region. Atco always had a good softball and baseball team.

When I was playing quarterback my senior year in high school, we had a nine and one season: we *lost* nine games and *won* one! In the region we were competing in then, the cities were a lot larger than Cartersville. We played Athens, Gainesville, Marietta, and LaGrange, who fielded teams of larger size and higher caliber. Most of those teams were undefeated when they played us—and undefeated *after* they played us. We really were no match for them. The combined scores my senior year were—Cartersville 103, Opponents 266!

But I remember that in one of those games (against Murray County/Chatsworth), I threw a thirty-five- yard touchdown pass. That was a memorable occasion. I had been tackled on every single play because our line just couldn't hold them. Their defense just filtered through—much too easily I thought—to sack the quarterback. On this particular play I had somehow evaded the sack and was running for my life. I circled around through the backfield two or three times, waiting on someone that I could "get hold of " with a pass. The receiver was Joel Cowan—who had already outrun my range by many yards and had turned to run back towards me. When I finally got the ball off, it was almost like a bad punt, kind of end-over-end, but with a high arc on it. Somehow or another, Joel ran under it, caught it, and was able to evade the defenders to score a touchdown—six points I'll never forget!

Joel Cowan, my receiver on the play, was president of our senior class, while I was vice president. Some twenty-seven years later, when I ran for governor, he became the chairman of my campaign committee, as well as my chief of staff during the eight years of my administration. Joel was also the developer of Peachtree City and is still a prominent resident of that community.

True Sand and Grit

My parents were very supportive of my involvement in football, though my senior year was tough. They attended every game; but some of the treatment I was receiving—being on a losing team—had to be quite trying for them. They were able to overlook it, and I got through it as well. But I remember one of our most difficult games was at LaGrange High. That was the big team; they were fast and had lots of excellent players. One of their running backs had been injured during the first quarter of the game . . . They felt somehow that the injury was intentional, though it of course was not. For the rest of the night it seemed as if they were intent on inflicting pain, suffering, and injury on as many of our players as they could. We were playing on an old baseball diamond with a sand infield, which was where I always seemed to be buried after handing off the ball. I would get tackled whether I had the ball or not. Two or three would pile on. This was in the days before you had faceguards and mouthpieces and were exposed to all the elements. They would just grab a handful of that sand and rub it in your eyes. After that game my eyes were so swollen I could hardly see for the next several days. I was just so full of sand and grit. The referees kept things in order as best they could, but there were several skirmishes on the field during the game.

After the game, we went to change clothes. The LaGrange players changed clothes faster than we did and came over to physically fight us before we got on the bus. So we had another skirmish right there! The police came and separated us; they put our team on the bus, escorted us to the edge of town, and told us to "keep rolling!" Usually, back then, we'd stop after the game and have something to eat, refreshments, or something like that. Arrangements had been made to have refreshments there in LaGrange; but we didn't get to stop and have them. We had to keep riding. Of course, during that senior year in football, we were working hard just to make it to the end of the year!

That was an occurrence that I'm sure was an embarrassment to the people there. It's a great community. A few years later I would spend a lot of time in LaGrange when I dated Elizabeth, who was attending LaGrange College. (I also did well in LaGrange and Troup County when I was campaigning for Governor.)

You learn a lot while competing in sports, and some of those lessons are still with me today. You learn never to quit; if you've got an objective or a goal in view, you continue to work. That's how I approached all my campaigns; we were always committed to *outworking* our opponents. If they were going to work twelve hours, we were going to work thirteen. That's something I guess you learn by experience: By working harder than your opponent, you *can* win. Now that does not mean *every* time! They can work hard, too. But at least you can get into a position where winning becomes a good possibility.

Leaving Home

When I'd ended high school in the spring of 1954, I didn't really have a decision in my own mind about what I wanted to do or where I wanted to go. Having been brought up in the church and a regular attender—and knowing that there could be a call from the Lord for some Christian service somewhere—I felt like I needed to be open to that. But the call didn't come, and I didn't feel compelled to do anything specific in that realm—except to go on with my life.

I'd become acquainted with Asbury College through people visiting and bringing special services to our local church. Some of the ministers in the North Georgia Methodist Conference with whom we were acquainted had attended Asbury College as undergraduates before coming down to Emory University for their Seminary degrees. So we were familiar with Asbury. No way could I have dreamed that Asbury College, so far from home, would invite me to return in 1983 as the speaker for their graduation ceremonies and award me with an honorary doctorate. (Other honorary degrees were to come from Woodrow Wilson College of Law, 1981; Morris Brown College, 1983; LaGrange College, 1987; and Mercer University, 1987 .)

But I guess I simply wanted to get out of state, get away from home. It's about 350 miles to Wilmore, Kentucky, located just south of Lexington. Actually, I had never visited the campus, never even seen it, until my dad dropped me off there the day I registered to enter the freshman class of 1954. I will always remember the emptiness and loneliness that I felt for the first few days. It would be several months before I could go home, and the only person I knew in the whole college was Eugene Bartenfield, my roommate and the son of one of our former pastors, from Dalton, Georgia.

This was an important year for me because I had the opportunity to make the transition into college life. Asbury was a small college with friendly students who made me feel at home and comfortable. We were all required to attend a chapel service a week in Hughes Auditorium. With assigned seating, one's absence was always noted. Many of my classmates resented this regulation, but I always looked forward to the many inspirational speakers and the spiritual programs. I realize now that these were valuable opportunities for me.

I received the following letter from Mother two days before I left for Asbury College in the fall of 1954:

My Dear Sweet Joe,

Must say the "lump" gets bigger as Sunday draws near, but tho' it stings to separate, I still am pleased that you chose to make something out of your life.

All these years we worked, we kept in mind that the days would pass, the time would come when you would then be grown, ready to go out either to make a man or break one. I'm sure you'll make it.

If I could make only one request in all the years of your life, it would be this—"Put Christ first in your life and keep clean." I'm sure you can and will do that, but if it takes slackness or backsliding to stay in college, then come home for I'd rather have you ignorant and unlearned and a Christian than all the education in the world.

Be sweet and kind and know that we will be thinking of you *all* the time and wishing for you the best of luck, with a prayer that you'll make good and will surely be proud of your accomplishment.

May God bless you and keep you ever to Himself, so close that the devil will lose in every battle.

> All My Love,
> Mother

3

New Destinations

I knew after I got into my first year at Asbury College that I was *not* going to be a preacher *or* a school teacher. I found that I was more interested in business. Asbury was a liberal arts college and didn't have a business degree in those days. Friends of mine from high school had gone on to the University of Georgia. I applied to UGA, was accepted as a sophomore for the fall quarter of 1955.

My brother Fred also became a student at UGA. He had attended the University of Tennessee on a basketball scholarship but lost his scholarship because of an injury. (He had injured his leg by slipping on some water on the court.) Fred had initially transferred to Georgia Tech and had, for one quarter, attended as a commuter student from Cartersville; he also dropped out a quarter. Then he decided that if *I* was going to UGA—he'd go there as well!

Fred was two years ahead of me, though there was not quite two-years difference in our ages. While we were at UGA at the same time (for about a year), we didn't room together. I roomed with a fellow I'd grown up with in Cartersville—Clyde 'Sonny' Jackson. As previously mentioned, his father owned the dairy farm I'd worked for when we were growing up.

The Better Part of Valor

I'll always remember one late afternoon when we were living in Clark Howell dormitory. I was walking out the rear door of the dormitory toward the parking lot. My brother arrived in his black and white 1954 Chevrolet with excess speed—whipped into that parking place, jumped out and started running towards the dormitory. Before he got there, another car pulled in and almost cut him off. A whole carload of boys jumped out and were chasing him! I tried to ask what was wrong, and Fred shouted "Y'all better help me!"

They immediately came up and I inquired "What's the problem here?" Apparently, Fred had splattered water on them with his car somewhere off campus, and they had chased him back to the dorm. One big fellow, a lot bigger than I was, immediately said that he was going to "get him" whether *we* liked it or not. I told him, "Before you get him, you're going to have to go through me." He said, "Well, that's not going to be a problem!"

We started to talk about the situation and before long got everything settled down. I've always felt that if you can get people talking, you can usually work out problems. We negotiated ourselves out of that situation. It's difficult, particularly when tempers are flaring and people are hostile. Things get very fragile sometimes. I believe that the skills I was developing back then helped me when I entered politics.

Fraternity Life

Fred had been a Lambda Chi Alpha at the University of Tennessee and transferred his affiliation to the chapter at the University of Georgia. I pledged the same fraternity, which made us not only "blood brothers,"but fraternity brothers as well. Fraternity life offered a circle of friends outside of life in the dormitory living quarters. But I guess the initial attraction to this particular fraternity might have been that I had a brother who was already there. You tend to try to accomplish some of the same things that other members of your family have been involved in—or even supersede what they might have accomplished. While Fred and I remained extremely close, my own association with the fraternity expanded to another group of people, a separate circle of close friends.

In looking back, I think it was an asset to me, one that even had implications for my political life. When I ran for governor, there were a lot of those same people that were out there campaigning and supporting Joe Frank Harris that probably would never have been there had I not been a member of their fraternal organization. It has been a lifelong association, and it's probably not for everybody. It was something you adapt to; for example, I've never had a problem with my own personal convictions in any situation in which I may have found myself. I think a lot of times fraternities are labeled with being just a vehicle for partying. There were a lot of very positive activities outside of the so-called "weekend parties." When I was at the University of Georgia, we may not have had many of the conflicts and troubles I've seen since in some fraternities. Occasionally, we would see problems, but not in the fraternity in which I was a member.

Unfortunately, Fred didn't have an opportunity to finish because he had transferred schools, thus breaking his deferment. The Korean War was over but they were still drafting everyone without a school deferment. Fred was drafted into the Army and began his service in 1956. He served two years on active duty in the military.

Filling in the Blanks

As a student at Asbury College, where I attended my freshman year, I had been able to accumulate about eighteen hours per quarter. When I arrived at the University of Georgia, I was able to transfer every single hour of my previous college work, though none of those hours fit into my new marketing major. This allowed me to transfer in as a sophomore and enabled me to finish college a quarter early.

There were still a number of electives that I was able to take, and I guess my choice of electives came as much from what was available (for the two or three hour courses) as from the subject. I ended up taking an agricultural engineering course, which included the elementary basics of surveying. This familiarized me with the instruments used for surveying and leveling a site on which one might construct a building. Later I was able to make practical use of this knowledge in our business—laying foundations for buildings and establishing levels for drain fields that we constructed.

I didn't know at that time whether I was going to pursue my marketing major in the private sector, in some department store, or where it was going to carry me. There was a home economics course available on clothing and textile design that was offered in the School of Home Economics. This, too, worked out to my advantage, providing information for later career situations. There were, as I recall, only two of us males in the class. It really gave me a background in textiles, and while I have never used it much, I was pleased to have the knowledge.

Even during my high school years, my interest had been in drawing and drafting. I had taken mechanical drawing and drafting classes and, later on, had utilized these skills in actually drawing plans for industrial buildings we constucted in Cartersville. In fact, I had drawn plans for a house that we built up on Lake Allatoona, which became a family place for many years.

The accounting courses I took became very valuable to me in business, because in our family business, the accounting and controlling end of it were my essential areas of responsibility. And when I arrived at the state level, it was a great education and preparation for understanding some of the nuances of the appropriations process.

I don't believe I could have been better prepared. The exposure I had to those courses during my high school and college years probably helped me, as much as anything I've ever done, earn a living—at least in the beginning of my career. When I look back and see all the opportunities I had to learn a little something about the various areas that I was going to utilize later in life, I feel like there might have been a plan. I feel fortunate to have had the opportunity to fill in some of the blanks along the way. I graduated from college in March 1958, about three months early, and went on six-months active duty in the U.S. Army Reserves.

Finding Time for Sergeants

I had actually joined the Air National Guard at the end of the Korean War. I recall that I had joined at that time because they didn't have anybody in it. They came to our high school recruiting, and a lot of my buddies and I joined the Air National Guard. I had been a member since the age of seventeen, until I went to Kentucky to Asbury College. Since I couldn't attend drill, they put me in the "standby" reserves, which made me eligible for the active draft. During my senior year in college, I was either going to be drafted or had to serve some active time in the military. This being the case, I transferred over to the Army Reserves and went through six months of active duty at Fort Jackson, South Carolina, and later Fort Knox, Kentucky.

One of the commitments the recruiter made to me when I joined the Army Reserve was that I could come back to the University of Georgia and get my diploma in June at the regular graduation. (They didn't have graduation ceremonies at other times of the year like many schools today.) On the Monday I was to receive my degree, I was scheduled to report to Fort Knox to begin armored training. I went on up to Fort Knox early and requested that the commitment the recruiter had made be honored in order that I could go back and get my degree—and return to start training a few days later. They laughed at me and said, "Who do you think you are?" They told me that no recruiter could make and guarantee a commitment like that.

I felt really low that I had worked so hard to graduate early—had joined the Army to satisfy my military obligation—only to discover that I couldn't go back and formally receive my degree. I had already made plane reservations—a flight from Louisville to Atlanta. I had also made up my mind that if they would not let me go officially, I would go anyway. I called my brother, Fred. He had gotten out of the Army only a few days prior to that. He pretty well knew what I was faced with. He had worked up high enough in the Army to know how to go about getting these things done, and he made a few phone calls on my behalf. I'm not sure today what he told them or who he talked to, but I did get a pass. I was officially allowed to leave and return to Athens to receive my degree. After I attended all the functions and activities at the university, I rushed back to Fort Knox and entered my basic armored training.

Tank training was ready to begin. The old Master Sergeant was pretty upset because I had known somebody who "pulled some strings"—in essence forcing him to let me go. When I arrived, my greeting from him was something to the effect that "As long as you're in this man's army, you're never going to get another pass!" He said that I could plan—for the duration of the training—on being there on all weekends as well. He added, "You've had your pass!"

In the first week of armored training they had announced that the proficiency test would be given on Saturday morning, covering the training we had received that week. The recruits, or "trainees," who made the highest grade on the proficiency test would be awarded a weekend pass. I had missed the first two days of training, but I picked up enough over the next two days to make one of the highest grades on the proficiency test. In spite of the Sergeant's threats, I did get another pass— the first weekend I was there.

The ensuing training period was a challenging time, but it was a good experience. I wouldn't swap anything we did during those weeks and months on active duty. (When I finished that training, I still had to serve five and a half years of reserve time, which I didn't complete until after I was married. Actually, I had already served eleven years of reserve time because I had signed up with the National Guard when I was seventeen. Since I couldn't transfer the earlier obligations, I had to renew for another six years—which included the time on active duty.) Fred had finished his military service about six months before I completed my active duty. In September 1958 I returned to Cartersville and joined him and Dad in the family business, Harris Cement Products, Incorporated.

4

A Tough Business

When we returned to the business in 1958, Dad was operating eight or ten trucks. They were very small and didn't have the volume or cover the territory that we were able to expand into later. Dad's cement business really began in the latter part of 1945 when he and a friend of his, a fellow worker at the Goodyear Mill named Harvey Silvers, pooled their resources and bought some used equipment. They had purchased from what we called then the "Bell Bomber plant"—an old Chevrolet dumptruck and a two-bag concrete mixer, which was one of those small mixers that you pull behind the truck.

The process was pretty basic: you shovel in the dry material, put in your bags of cement, add water, mix it for awhile and empty it out into a wheelbarrow. From there, you roll it to your forms, or whatever you might be using the cement for. But that was the beginning of the business, which they ran parttime since they were still employees of the Goodyear Mill.

In the late 1940s Dad left Goodyear to work the concrete business fulltime. His partner wanted to open a grocery store and wanted out of the concrete business. So Dad bought him out. They agreed on a settlement, and Harris Cement Products, Incorporated—manufacturing concrete blocks and ready-mixed concrete—was born. In those first years, the company remained very small; the volume was almost entirely generated locally—in Cartersville and Bartow County.

I guess you might say that Fred and I were "minor" partners, since we began working our way into the company when we were no more than ten and twelve years old. We worked summers, weekends, evenings, and nights—digging ditches and shoveling sand and gravel. We literally learned the business "from the ground up." But we grew into it and gained the knowledge that you've got to work hard to really accomplish anything; and we saw the fruits of those labors. We discovered what a little sweat and determination can achieve.

The business was very small when we came back into it in the late 1950's. However, we were blessed with regional growth over the next several years. Our father was president of the company and eventually became chairman of the board. Then my brother became the president. My area of operation was mainly in the accounting, bookkeeping, and financial end of it. Fred was in the sales and the promotion end of the business initially. Eventually, however—when we were able to add on sales people—he gravitated toward production.

The company grew and Dad remained very active—not retired by any means. But his role was not as demanding as it had been in past years. It was very satisfying for him because we had a good working relationship, and he filled in wherever the need arose. He was always a good advisor and resource even when he wasn't active in running the business himself. When Fred and I started operating the business ourselves, we were pretty much in agreement on most things and had a good feel for knowing our individual responsibilities. One of my roles was often to serve as an arbitrator who negotiated things like the purchase of equipment. All in all, Fred and I had an excellent working relationship, and that's a blessing, particularly in a family operation.

Initially, we didn't have a whole a lot of competition. When a competitor did establish a business there in Cartersville, the volume at that time was not enough to support two good-sized plants. He went out of business, and we ended up actually buying his equipment and starting another plant in Marietta with that equipment. We found that as independent operators we *could* compete with larger organizations. Some of the Cobb County operators, for example, would try to come over into Cartersville. However, the largest part of our market was in Cobb County. We might have expanded beyond that point, except that when you get beyond a twenty or twenty-five mile radius of your ready-mixed concrete batch plant, your haul time is too expensive. We tried to stay within a radius within which we could provide good service—as well as receive a fair return on our investment.

Exceeding the Specs

You've got a quality standard that you've got to achieve, particularly if you're involved in architecturally controlled jobs. These jobs required white sand, like you see most of the time at construction sites. It came from South Georgia. You could get wash-river sand, but it's not as white and doesn't have the sharpness that you get from what is called "bank sand." Most of ours came from Taylor County, and it would be shipped in by rail or by truck to that part of Georgia. Then the stone would usually come from a quarry that would be in the proximity of the batch plant. A lot of times it would be limestone or granite. Normally, you could use either one of them without any problem. The cement that came from nearby cement manufacturing plants in Georgia would be added to it. Quite a bit of the raw cement would be shipped in from Alabama and Tennessee into the Georgia market.

You would load cement, stone, sand, and water into the ready-mix truck and mix it up on the way to the job and, upon arrival, pour it out. Actually, you don't think of concrete "setting up" in that drum while it's turning, but after so many revolutions—it would start to set. You can't just keep turning it and keep it wet; you've got to get it out of the truck within a certain period of time. Of course, you've got to give it so many revolutions to achieve the strength, but after that, the strength factor will go down. Thus, the more turns, the *less* your strength; also, the more water you add beyond a certain point, the weaker the strength.

There are standards of strength that must be maintained, and we felt fortunate that we never had problems meeting those expectations. The reason was that we always tried to exceed the specs. If the concrete was supposed to pass 2,500 pounds per square inch, then we would make sure that we had enough ingredients to test in excess of three thousand pounds per square inch. It was our experience that your reputation precedes you wherever you go; it's your best advertisement. If you're able to put out a quality product and provide good service, you can compete with anyone, anywhere.

A Down Side

Anybody who owns and operates equipment and machinery in business expects to encounter accidents and problems. Probably, the most gut-wrenching experience that you could have happen in the concrete business is when one of your truck mixers turns over. You can't take a wrecker out and just pick up one of those trucks. It takes an extremely large crane to right one, because even if you attach cables to a wrecker and try to pull it over, the center of gravity is so heavy—with that concrete lying on the ground—you will more than likely tear your equipment to pieces. Even with a crane, you can almost always kiss that equipment goodbye. If a truck turns over, it's usually damaged beyond repair by the time you *do* get it back up.

When we would get a call saying that one of our trucks was in an accident, the first thing that would pop into our minds was, "I hope someone is not injured." Because of that excessive weight, a lot of damage could be done, particularly if it's in the wrong setting. We had our own wreckers—and people in our organization who were skilled and experienced through trial and error—in dealing with those kinds of problems. We'd get them on the site as soon as possible. We would usually cut the drum (the barrel containing the concrete) off the mixer. Normally, we'd have eight yards of concrete in the truck; that's quite a large tonnage. Very seldom could we mobilize and get a crane to that wreck site fast enough, before the concrete could set up in that drum. Even so, we'd try to cut the drum off the chassis, and then get a water truck there to pressure-wash out as much concrete as we could, depending on the location.

Fortunately, we had very few injuries over the years, but we did have the normal loss of equipment and the accidents that you would expect in operations with a lot of exposure and mileage. We hoped our drivers were skilled, and in most cases, they were. We always tried to have a good training program. Evidently, we must have been fairly successful, because we had a minimum of wrecks and problems—and we were still able to afford the insurance!

A Complete Job

While we were growing up, we were regular employees of the company, and when we got old enough to drive and have licenses, we were operators of the equipment. From your front-end loaders to the mechanized equipment, right on up to the tractor-trailers and semis, we operated it all. Had to.

When we sold the business in 1980, we had expanded our plants into Cobb county, operating seventy-five trucks with about one-hundred employees. The scope of the business was such that we had ready-mixed concrete, a manufacturing facility for concrete block, and also a pre-cast concrete business. We also manufactured septic tanks, drain tile, and pipe. Then we would pour specific architectural concrete for special purposes. We also constructed industrial buildings and had some buildings that were leased commercially. We did some subcontracting work and had concrete finishing crews that would place and finish and do a complete job with concrete.

The cement business is heavy and dirty. Nothing's lightweight around construction; it's a tough business. Invaluable are the experiences you gain and the kind of things you learn about life in a setting like that, or any small business operation. Those lessons stay with you forever.

5

Elizabeth Carlock Harris

In June 1960 Reverend Ernest D. Carlock came to Carters-ville as the pastor of Faith United Methodist Church, which was my home church and where I am still a member today. At the time of their move, only Reverend Carlock and his wife, Minnie, were living at home. Their two oldest children, Fran and Winton, were grown and married with two children each. Elizabeth, their youngest, was away in college. Born when her mother was forty years old, she was "a surprise."

When the Carlock family came to Cartersville, Elizabeth had just completed her junior year at LaGrange College. She had been a popular student there, and was later elected "Miss LaGrange College" by the student body. That summer, she was interning with Tennessee Gas in Houston, Texas. Her major was General Science and Secondary Education; she was looking for experience within that area—and didn't return home until time for fall quarter, which began in September.

We had known the Carlock family over the years because we had attended the Indian Springs Holiness Camp Meeting down at Flovilla, Georgia. Dad had always been active there and was a member of the Board that helped promote it. Her father had also attended for many years, but I had really never crossed paths with Elizabeth because she was four years younger than I—a *big* difference at that age. I had completed college and active military duty and was back in Cartersville in business with my father and brother at Harris Cement Products. I didn't have time to worry about looking for a mate—or didn't *think* I had time. I was twenty-five years old, which is not that old, of course; but when you're going through it, you feel like you're already getting over the hill!

On the Sunday she came into the 11:00 A.M. church service, her sister was visiting the family and they all came in together. I was seated toward the rear of the church and, as I recall, they chose a seat maybe a row or two ahead of mine. I had spotted her when they came in and got a glimpse of her—and had a good view of her for the balance of the service. She was very attractive, had beautiful brown eyes—just a gorgeous young woman, really. Naturally, a young man of that age is attracted to a good-looking girl, so after church I struck up a conversation with her, talking mostly about my new white Oldsmobile 88 convertible. I've often said that she may have been more attracted to the car than to me, but I'd like to think that wasn't the case. That evening we did talk a while and I learned that she was leaving early the next morning to return to LaGrange College. It would be a while before I would have a chance to see her again, though she did return a week or so later for an event at the church. That was the beginning of our courtship.

Meet You at the Sundial

I realized that there was more here than just a casual date when I asked her to go to a Georgia Tech home football game. Tech was not far from Cartersville; we'd always attended Tech games. (I didn't harbor any of the hostility toward Tech of some other University of Georgia graduates.) I invited Elizabeth to meet me at the Tech stadium for a game—probably in late September or October 1960.

She was coming up from LaGrange, and I was coming down from Cartersville. But where were we going to meet? That's a tough question when you've never been somewhere with someone—and you're trying to point out a convenient place on a large campus. I had remembered that there was an old sundial in the quadrangle at Tech—and I tried to describe its location. She knew where The Varsity, the best known drive-in restaurant in Atlanta, was on North Avenue and knew where the stadium (now Bobby Dodd Stadium) was located. So I talked her through the directions to the sundial.

I was there early, waiting for her to arrive, hoping that she could follow my directions and find that sundial. Sure enough, I spotted her. She was just as beautiful as I had remembered. It was a cold day, and she had on a beautiful tan coat. She was very fashionable and very impressive. There was an immediate spark between us, a spark that has continued to this day.

We had dinner that evening at Mammy's Shanty, a well-known eating establishment on Peachtree Street. In our conversation we found that we had a commonality of past experience, almost identical at times, so far as our families and religion were concerned—and in many other things. Our budding relationship was growing very comfortable.

Later on, I discovered that for our date she borrowed a coat from one of her classmates. For a preacher's daughter who didn't have much money, this was typical. She was having to work her way through LaGrange College with the help of student loans. (We had to repay those loans after we were married, an obligation I didn't realize I had *before* we were married. Of course, she didn't realize that she had to help me pay off the notes on that Oldsmobile 88 either.)

With many telephone calls and letters, along with weekend trips home over the fall and winter, we came to believe that our lives were meant to be together. Neither of us remember an exact moment when I asked Elizabeth to marry me, but in March I definitely remember having to ask Preacher Carlock for permission to marry his daughter.

Then on April 7, my parent's wedding anniversary, we got engaged. On June 25, 1961, we were married in the Faith United Methodist Church in Cartersville. Her father gave her away and then walked around the altar to perform the ceremony.

Bridge to Aragon

It had been the practice of some of my friends that when one of our group got married, the others would go along and harass them on the first night of the honeymoon. We were determined that we were going to prevent them from interrupting us during our first wedding night. So we devised a plan that one of my closest friend's father helped to carry off. Sonny Jackson, who had also been my roommate at Georgia, was the friend—and his father, Louis, who would never have been suspected of being part of such a scheme, agreed to participate.

When we left the church—instead of getting into *our* automobile, or someone else's that would have seemed more appropriate—we circumvented the crowd and got into the back seat of a car driven by Louis Jackson. When we left the church, we had a full procession of all the people who wanted to follow us. We took a route through downtown Cartersville and then beyond the city limits. Near the Jackson dairy farm on the outskirts of town there was a one-lane bridge over a little creek. Louis pulled up onto that one-lane bridge and stopped. None of the cars behind him could get past, and we had another car waiting on the other side of the bridge—driven by Sonny Jackson. My brother, Fred, was waiting at another one-lane bridge several miles down the road—just in case someone made it through the blocked bridge. No one did, and we didn't need to change cars again.

Sonny drove us to Aragon, Georgia, about twenty miles from Cartersville, where we had left my car the day before. We'd parked it in the garage of a friend of ours, Tom Davitte. He had "protected" my automobile for us. But had the crowd somehow evaded that blockade and caught up with us again, we had yet *another* bridge to block them between Cartersville and Aragon.

We made our exit and got away and drove to Columbus, Georgia, knowing that if we went down Highway 41 toward Florida (the route most people traveled enroute to honeymoons or vacations), they might try again. (My friends and I had hunted people down along that route before.) Therefore, we needed to take a route that was not on the normal path. The day we were married, on the way to Columbus, I asked Elizabeth if she had any spending money. She said, "Yes." I asked, "How much have you got?" "Two dollars," she replied. Wondering if that was all the assets she had brought into the marriage, I asked, "What else do you have?" "Well," she said, "I've got a typewriter." So I've always joked that I married her for two dollars and a typewriter.

We spent the first night in Columbus, Georgia, from which we drove to Miami to catch a plane to the Bahamas for the remainder of our honeymoon. We had heard from friends that tourists could get accommodations in Nassau without making reservations. When we arrived at the airport, there were a close to a dozen hotels that had representatives there *bidding* for your business. We found the one that we thought would be most satisfactory and that fit our pocketbook. I sometimes say that when we met she told me that if I'd marry her, she'd make a governor out of me. And the truth is that if she *had* told me something like that, I would probably have *believed* it.

When we got back to Cartersville, we didn't really have a *home* to go to; but we had decided to spend the summer at Lake Allatoona—at a cabin I had built with my brother and dad. I had drawn the plans and built it in my spare time, completing it some time the previous year. Just a few days into the summer, Elizabeth began experiencing some severe stomach problems. She had first experienced these physical problems during her senior year at LaGrange College—and had gone through some preliminary examinations and had been treated for an ulcer. This diagnosis later proved to be an error. The pain would come and go; but she didn't really discover what it was until just before we were married.

Elizabeth had a cyst on her ovary. We had to admit her to the Floyd County Hospital in Rome (Georgia) within three weeks of returning from our honeymoon. Removal of one of her ovaries was deemed necessary, and the surgery was performed by Dr. Lester Harbin. We soon learned that the surgery had also cut our chances of ever having children in half. We of course worried that we might never have any children.

Elizabeth spent that summer recovering from the operation. She was scheduled to teach Advanced Science at the junior high in Cartersville that fall. School superintendent Jack Acree, a longtime friend of our family, hired her. By the beginning of the school term, she still hadn't completely recovered from the surgery.

Surgical methods in those days were almost crude by today's standards, and she started that career probably as physically weak as anybody could. Nevertheless, she persevered through her recovery and grew to enjoy her opportunity to teach. She kept at it, loving the challenge of the classroom and her students, and taught for almost three years—until our son came along.

6

Our Brightest
and Darkest Year

We had hoped to have children, but we really didn't expect it. However, the Lord decided that Joe Frank Harris, Jr. was going to be our child! He came into the world on March 22, 1964—almost a miracle birth—and our family was complete. We were never able to have another child. The Lord knows how many children a family can handle, and maybe that was *all* we could handle. We would loved to have had another child, but it was God's will. We accepted that and were blessed to have Joe.

He arrived five weeks early. During his entire first year we didn't realize that one of the reasons why he was crying so much was that the little fellow couldn't see. He was starting to eat solid food—keeping his head down because he couldn't focus properly. After he started walking, he would run into the corner of the table. He fell easily and couldn't catch a ball. You'd hand him a ball, he'd reach out to get it, but his hands wouldn't come together.

We carried him to an ophthalmologist, who indicated that he would probably grow out of it. But the problem grew worse, and Dad suggested that we take Joe to see Dr. Jess Lester, a long-time friend and opthamologist, for a second opinion. He discovered immediately that there was a muscle problem in Joe's eyes and that he needed to go through an *orthoptics* rehabilitation program, doing prescribed exercises to strengthn the muscles and possibly avoid surgery.

Joe was over a year old before he ever slept a full night. I would try as much as possible to relieve Elizabeth because she was with him twenty-four hours a day, and that was a lot of emotional and physical pressure on her. Looking back, we didn't really know enough to feel that Joe was in any danger of losing his eyesight, but as new parents, we were greatly concerned. We were also worried that the condition might affect Joe's learning ability.

When we first began the orthoptics treatment, we made frequent trips to Atlanta. The sessions were spread out over a fairly long period of time, but were very intense. He had to wear a patch over one eye for a certain period, then move the patch to the *other* eye—to try to coordinate his vision. He then had to wear thick glasses, which was disturbing to a small child. In the end we were able to discover his problem and he was able to overcome it without surgery.

When Joe was still a small child he had a reaction to aspirin he'd been taking for a flu-like problem. This generated what doctors felt was Reyes Syndrome, a serious childhood disease of the brain that can be fatal. We honestly felt that we would lose him. Though I'm not a very emotional person, watching your child in the throes of one of those seizures can be a very emotional experience. That's the time, too, when you realize the power of prayer. And it's a comfort to realize that you're not there *alone*, that there's someone else you can call on who's *also* in the healing business—who handles these kinds of problems—and you are able to turn it over to God. The Lord *did* answer those prayers and Joe was healed. Since then he's been healthy for most of his life.

Joe got into athletics during his junior high years and became a very good athlete, even played football. He also became an honor student and was able to qualify for the honors program at the University of Georgia. He went on to become a lawyer. He's in his early thirties now, married to Brooke, and with a new daughter, born in July of 1995. Her name is Catherine Elizabeth.

One Forward Step

When we were married, Elizabeth and I were determined that prayer was so important in our lives that we would make it a basic part of our family. We established in our home what we call a family altar. This is a period of time when we pray together. It's difficult to have hard feelings about someone with whom you're sharing prayer. You might have had ill feelings during the day, but when you get down to praying for each other and praying for your own future, those problems become a lot less important. It's easier to work out solutions when you have a common thread that runs between the two of you. The birth of our son tied the three of us together, and that extends on into his marriage and family today.

That family altar was established during the time when we recommitted our lives—our family and our future—to whatever the Lord wanted us to do. It was kind of scary, because you can't just give *part* of your life to the Lord; you've got to give it all—one hundred percent! You can't reserve even a small part for yourself; you can't say "Lord, I'm going to keep *this* because this is what *I'd* like to do." That might not be in line with the Lord's will for your life. You've got to commit it all. As a family in 1963, we committed our future to the Lord.

I was fearful that I might be called upon to enter the mission field—to do something that I might feel uncomfortable trying to do. Looking back, if I'd known it was going to be in politics, I guess I really would have been scared! You can always come home from a foreign mission field; but politics is something that you can't turn loose. It's almost like being electrocuted: you know it's killing you, but you've got hold of a hot wire and can't let go!

You don't have a red flag or light that turns on and says "Turn around" or "This is the direction." It's a feeling of peace or a gentle nudge in your heart that lets you know that this is something you need to do. Or, at least, you need to make *one more step forward.* And if that's not the direction you're supposed to go in, I've always felt that God would block it or change your direction. That has also happened to me many times. When you feel that you're moving in the direction that the Lord wants you to move in, you feel an awful lot of satisfaction. I've been able to look back and realize that I was not only accomplishing some things for Joe Frank Harris and the state of Georgia, but I was also serving the Lord as well.

Hearing the Call

Crest Auto Parts became the place for young people like me, who were active and interested in our community, to meet and discuss issue of concern. Owner Gene Tilley had always had keen insight and understanding of the "hot-button" issues. With his encouragement, and with the active support of Sonny Jackson and Bobby Joe Womack, I was selected to be the "first sacrifice"—the first of our group to try for an elective office.

When these local business leaders asked me to consider running for state representative, I didn't know how much time would be required. I didn't know what you had to do to campaign or how much it would cost to qualify. I didn't even know what the job paid, if anything. My only experience in politics had been in Governor Carl Sanders' campaign two years earlier, tacking up posters and attending a few meetings, but not enough to know what was required. I was ignorant of the whole process.

Elizabeth and I had made the earlier commitment that we would be open to any service that the Lord might have for us. We thought this could be one of those causes. Looking back today we realize that it truly *was* that kind of call, though we didn't know it at the time. We had a lot of anxiety and many questions when they asked me to consider running. I didn't want to refuse without giving it proper consideration. So my answer was that Elizabeth and I would pray about it.

I went home that day in April 1964, and I'm not sure but that Elizabeth thought I had lost my mind! Our son Joe had been born just a month earlier, but several weeks early. His systems had not yet fully developed we were concerned for his health. Then, a couple of weeks after Joe's birth, Elizabeth's father had major surgery at Emory University Hospital. While he was in the recovery room, Elizabeth's mother fell and broke her hip. The hip had to be replaced and she developed a Staphycoccus infection. She was in isolation at Emory Hospital for over six months. When Elizabeth's father got out of the hospital, we brought him back to Cartersville to stay with us. I was also trying to do my job at the concrete business. On top of all this to consider running for political office *did* seem crazy.

A few weeks after her dad had come to live with us (at that time he was the pastor of the Temple United Methodist Church in Temple, Georgia), he recovered and was enjoying being there with his grandchild and wasn't in *any* hurry to go back home. Finally, it got to the point that I had to suggest to him: "Preacher, I've got my hands full now, and I think maybe you could contribute more if you relieved us of this burden." He understood. He was a tremendous person and had total love and respect for our family. And he did go on home (though it was a few weeks later than we had anticipated he *would* go home).

The Door Was Not Closing

We still had Elizabeth's mother to think about. We could not visit her in isolation without putting on a gown and mask and going through all the procedures. (Staph infection was a much more serious condition in those days.) Elizabeth was having a difficult time traveling from Cartersville to Emory to check on her mother and also taking care of a crying baby. This was during the time when we were deciding about the possibility of entering the political arena.

When the group came back to the office after a few days, I guess they were anticipating that my answer would be "yes." They had already solicited about forty people for contributions. (I think the largest was about one hundred dollars, most of them were around ten dollars.)They had made out a check for $250 to the Bartow County Democratic Party for the qualifying fee. At that time, you qualified with committees in the counties. In the meantime, I had *not* experienced the feeling that the door was closing—or that the Lord was not in support of what I was undertaking. So, rather than turn them down, I said we'd hold the check and make a bank deposit for the campaign. Still, I had no idea what was required in terms of money or time and didn't really have time to find out. Finally, I said, "Well, if you really feel that strongly that I could succeed in this kind of venture, then maybe this is what I'm supposed to do."

So, the next day I made an appointment to see a local attorney named Percy Bray who was the secretary of the county Democratic Party. I wanted to qualify for Post Number One and gave him my check. In those days we had two representatives in Bartow County, a county of 28,000 population; but Fulton County, with the largest population in the state (556,000), had only *three* representatives; so, we were very *mal*apportioned. (Reapportionment came the following year.) In my lifetime no person served our county as representative for more than two terms, or four years. The person that I was about to qualify to run against had only served one term. He was right in the middle of his so-called "four-year contract" in the minds his supporters. Bray quickly pointed out that I must have made a mistake, that I needed to run for the *other* position, because that person had served the traditional two terms. I had to tell him—no—that my opponent was going to be the incumbent, Jake Cullen. That's who I intended to run against.

Bray said, "Well, maybe I'd better hold your check for a day or two so you can study about it a little longer. Then, if that's what you want to do . . . well, you give me the signal and we'll qualify you and let it go." But I insisted, "No, my mind's made up. That's what I want to do, and this is the position I want to seek." He took my check, but he *didn't* say, "You're qualified and ready to run"—giving me all the blessings that you'd expect at the time.

I left his office and went down to the local newspaper, *The Daily Tribune News,* to see its editor, Milton Fleetwood. He was an authority figure as far as "newspapering" goes in North Georgia, well respected by his peers. "You're a fine young man," he said, "I've watched you grow up, and I think you've got a great future ahead of you." "But," he added, "are you really sure this is what you want to do? Maybe I 'd better hold your announcement for a few days ." That was *two for two* right at the outset! Both reluctant to say "Yes, you're running . . ." and turn me loose! So, I told him "Mr. Fleetwood, I hope you'll go ahead and announce it. My mind's made up and that's what I want to do. I'd like for people to know I'm a candidate."

He did go ahead and make the announcement the next day, but it was not very prominent, kind of *small*, in fact, almost like an afterthought. But that was the beginning, and looking back, we realized the Lord *did* open a door. This was an opportunity, and it was preparing me for larger things to come.

If We Could Live Through That Year

The primary was on September 9, 1964. We struggled with one thing right after another. Elizabeth's mother was still at Emory Hospital when the primary was held. She'd been there that whole spring and summer. We were still dealing with Joe's health problems; he was over a year old before he slept through a full night. Our business was beginning to expand very rapidly. We were in the process of opening up a new operation in Cobb County, our first venture outside Bartow County. So the pressures of everything I was doing were probably as great as they've been in my lifetime.

We felt that if we could live through that year and be successful, then we could probably take on *anything* that came along. In looking back, it was a real challenge. But then the Lord gives you the strength to handle anything that's before you. He saw us through.

Canvassing the Neighborhoods

Campaigning was something I had never been exposed to before. Everything was totally new and it was kind of experimental. I had promoted our business and dealt with marketing that enterprise, but promoting and marketing yourself is different. I had a lot of advice from mostly older people who had been politically involved before. They told me, "Now, son, if you're going to win, this is the kind of thing you're going to have to do: You're going to have to go house to house, knock on every door in Bartow

County. You're going to have to meet every shift change of all the businesses and stand there at the gate and let *all* the people know that you want to be elected."

Advice on how to win never ended. One morning, a few minutes after 2:00 a.m., a ring of the phone startled my tired body that had only found the bed after midnight because of a late night of campaigning. Cobb Green, my elderly friend from near Adairs-ville, who took politics very seriously, was on the phone suggesting that I call someone that should be supporting me. My response was, "I will give him a call the first thing in the morning. I don't think he will appreciate being awakened at this hour." Without any hesitation, Cobb responded, "Oh no, you need to call him now. He will remember it!" I was too tired to make the call right then, but I did call him the next day. (But I never told Cobb that.)

All of the seeds were being planted. And based on what I felt were the past experiences of people who had been successful, I started out doing all of these things. Much of it was quite useful. But I learned that if I'd spent my time knocking on all the doors in Bartow County, I would have been wasting my time because there were not enough people at home when I was knocking. You only have a few hours each evening that you can really find people at home. They're usually busy; they're having dinner or coming in from work tired. They don't want to be bothered. It's a tough proposition, but people in a community have got to know that you want to be elected bad enough that you're willing to do that. They've got to know that you're working—and *willing* to work. You've got to have a feel for what's necessary within your legisla-tive district and the issues that people believe are important. Also you have to learn how they're going to decide between you and your opponent.

I spent a lot of hours canvassing the neighborhoods. Elizabeth joined me and did an awful lot of door-knocking. Even some of her friends helped with the canvassing. We learned to hit a few neighborhoods in one part of the county and go immediately to another neighborhood hoping to let people see that we were working hard to cover the whole county. It was a learning experience, and what we were able to learn during that first campaign served well for all the other elections that I had in the General Assembly.

I had the opportunity during these elections to run both opposed and unopposed. I'll take the *un*opposed anytime; that's the best way to run! We gained some good experience during that first campaign, because we were running against an incumbent, Jake Cullens, who was generally well-liked in the community and extremely well-financed. We had no idea of what kind of money would be required. Back then, the amount was negligible compared to what is needed today. Media costs were just so much less. Of course, you didn't have the saturation that you have now—with local cable television, radio stations, and newspapers. In our county, we had only two newspapers and one radio station; the cost factor was just not that great. Still, you had expenses, and you needed to raise funds for the campaign. We learned a valuable, quick lesson in politics: When people contribute their money, no matter how small the amount, their support and personal involvement usually follow.

When the votes were counted, we had enjoyed a good margin of victory. All the projections were that if we were to win at all, we were just going to squeak by. We didn't exactly "squeak by.'" There were fourteen voting precincts: We took all of them except two—a pretty good win in our county!

We had a campaign headquarters in the Old Cile Hotel building near the courthouse, which is now the site of the Cartersville City Hall. After we won that evening, we had cokes and refreshments and what was almost like a street party there in downtown Cartersville. Even then, we didn't have alcoholic beverages involved in our campaign, so we didn't have any problems with the celebration. It was a feeling that I had never experienced before! I felt like I had been anointed in my own community, elected by people who knew and were willing to trust me. And while some of my critics had thought I was too young to do the job—still wet behind the ears—I had been chosen to do that job. I took the responsibility very seriously.

Locating an Opponent

The second time I had opposition was after I had been in the General Assembly for four years, two terms. That year, I did not have Democratic opposition. However, before qualifying ended, there was a conversation among some of the regular morning coffee group at the local drug store. They were talking about how in Bartow County, for many years, no one had ever served over two consecutive terms without opposition. State representatives might have been re-elected, but they were challenged by someone at the end of that four-year period. The conversation was that Joe Frank Harris had been down there for four years, and nobody had opposed him during the last term. It was time someone challenged him, they thought. They had a hard time, I was told, locating an opponent for me, but they finally found one in my old high school principal, John I. Parker. I never knew him to be a Republican *or* Democrat, but I guess he decided he wanted to be a Republican. At any rate, he was my opponent.

That year my legislative district had been reapportioned. It had been expanded into Cherokee and Pickens Counties, along with Bartow County, where I also had to campaign. Because I had opposition, we worked hard during that election. Had he *not* been on the ballot against us, I probably wouldn't have gotten into the new territory and made myself known as well as I did. We won by a large percentage, receiving over *ninety-seven* percent of the vote in all three counties, a landslide in our favor.

The next time I had opposition was after I had been in the General Assembly for ten years. This was at a time when an opportunity in the United States Congress was about to open up. At least some of the people in our seventh district thought there was going to be an opportunity for someone. The incumbent had had some problems and rumors were that he might not even offer to run. And if he did, he seemed very beatable. I had been in the General Assembly for ten years, and I needed to make a decision about whether I was going to stay there, step *up* to another political opportunity, or get out altogether. Of course, that was always an option. I became the target of many people seeking a candidate. We prayed about it and groups of people came to meet with me: Individuals who had heard that a run for Congress might be a possibility suggested that they would like to support me financially.

The truth is, I never really felt that office was the place I needed to move; I just didn't feel like the Lord had opened that door up for me. So I chose not to run. Just prior to the qualifying time, I called those who had been contacting me and gave them my decision. I did not know that I was going to have opposition for my House race. It was generally known that since I didn't run for Congress, I was going to run again for the House.

Early one morning in 1974, I was shaving, getting ready to go to work and had the local news on to see what was happening. I heard that Jeff Davis, the son of our Superior Court Judge, J. L. Davis, was on the way to Atlanta that morning to qualify to oppose Joe Frank Harris for his seat in the legislature. I just finished shaving and told Elizabeth what I had heard on the news—that Jeff Davis was going to run against me and that perhaps we had made a mistake and *misread* what we were supposed to do. Maybe I wasn't supposed to run again for the General Assembly; maybe I was supposed to run for Congress. Without any hesitation at all, Elizabeth just came right back very firm and very strong in her conviction that we had made the *right* decision and that this was what the Lord had led us to do: to run again for the General Assembly, win, lose or draw! This was what we were supposed to do, and this was our decision; we were sticking with it. I won that race with over sixty-five percent of the vote for the *sixth* term, defeating Davis, who eventually became a Superior Court Judge.

7

The Budgetary Process

When I was elected to the Georgia General Assembly in 1964, and took office in January, 1965, the Speaker of the House was George T. Smith, who had been selected by the Governor Carl Sanders. The committee chairmanships were appointed and the members of the committees were recommended and approved by the Governor. Back then there was not the separation *nor* the independence between the legislative and executive branches that exists today. After I arrived, and while learning the process, I observed that the General Assembly was operating pretty much as a rubber stamp for the governor and his administration. Whenever the Appropriations Committee met, it was just a formality. The recommendations would be passed out and ready for consideration by the full House in just a few minutes time—no debate, no discussion, no questioning the reasons behind any of the recommendations.

All of that was in the process of changing, however. I didn't realize it was going to change as rapidly as it did. Very shortly thereafter, on 10 January 1967, Lester Maddox was elected to succeed Sanders as governor. He was elected by the General Assembly, though the majority vote in the general election did not go to him. Howard H. "Bo" Callaway actually received more popular votes than did Lester Maddox. Ellis Arnold, a former governor, was also one of the candidates. Thus, a majority did not go to either one. In the absence of a run-off provision, it became the responsibility of the Legislature to make the choice. This occurred during my second term in the General Assembly. I didn't have a problem because the district I represented was overwhelmingly in support of Lester Maddox. I was spared the dilemma of some legislators who might have been Democrats representing an area carried by Republicans.

During the time before the actual confirmation by the General Assembly, which came the first week after the session started in January, George L. Smith, became the House Speaker for another term. We met in January, and the slate was presented. Maddox Hale was chosen as Speaker *pro tem* and the committee members were selected. I made a pitch to Speaker Smith to be a member of the Appropriations Committee, knowing that my seniority of only one term would make my selection remote. I was surprised, however, when he did choose me—and this was the beginning of my work in appropriations and with the State budget. At about the same time, the House declared its independence, instituting a new agency to do its own budget analysis called the Legislative Budget Office. Previously, only the administration and the governor had determined the budget, without imput from the House.

The budget was my specialty. As previously mentioned, in our family concrete products business I had always had the accounting, controlling, and bookkeeping responsibilities. My background and financial expertise transferred over into state government and proved to be excellent preparation. My interest in working with the state budgetary process was helped along by Pete Hackney, who was selected as the first director of that office. He was extremely knowledgeable and had one of the sharpest minds I've ever seen. With his photographic memory, he could look at a group of numbers and remember them, not just for a day or two, but for years! He had total recall for appropriations numbers. We might have had an appropriation that we didn't use, or one that we had requested—or, perhaps, something may have been wrong with an appropriation. Pete could remember it in detail. With his help and training, plus my actual work in the budgetary process, I learned a great deal.

The total state budget at the time I was elected to the General Assembly was less than $500 million dollars. When I left the governor's office in 1991, the budget for Corrections alone was more than that. But in 1965, the total State budget had not yet reached a half a billion dollars. Of course, the population of the state was barely four million people. We were just beginning to grow with the intensity we see today. I kind of grew up with the budgetary process, and it was probably the best place to learn for someone who might wind up as governor. I cannot value this experience enough—both my work with Pete Hackney and my exposure to the budget process.

The Green Door Committee

It was in those days that the so-called 'Old Green Door Committee' originated. The initial 'Green Door' members were James "Sloppy" Floyd, Chairman of the Appropriations Committee, George Busbee, who was selected the majority leader in the General Assembly, and Tom Murphy, who later became Speaker of the House. A t that time Murphy was Governor Maddox's floor leader in the House. I was allowed to sit in but was not an official member. I didn't hold any official position in the House. I guess they recognized my interest in the budget from some of the questions I would ask. They were cultivating some of the younger members, too, and they gave me a tremendous opportunity.

A couple of years later, after I became a member of the Appropriations Committee in 1971, George L. Smith died and left a vacancy for the Speaker post. Tom Murphy had moved up, in the meantime, to be Speaker *pro tem* of the House. It was a natural move for him to fill the position of Speaker. George Busbee was majority leader, and a lot of pressure was brought to bear for him to run for Speaker against Murphy. I guess he knew in his heart that he probably wanted to run for governor some day and that it would behoove him *not* to run for governor as Speaker of the House. So he declined and remained the Majority Leader.

Speaker Murphy and I had been friends since my coming to the assembly. I was supportive of his campaign to become Speaker and helped him win. He appointed me to the first vacancy to open up in the leadership of the Appropriations Committee, which was the Secretary of the Committee; I served in that capacity for several years.

Where the Action Is

Very shortly after the election the Democratic Caucus of the House of Representatives always met to choose the nominee for Speaker of the House and the other caucus officials. Later, there would be a training session for the new legislators at the Continuing Education Center of the University of Georgia in Athens. Many of the instructors were experienced members of the General Assembly along with the faculty of the University. We had just completed the training session in Athens when Murphy called me on the phone and indicated that I had enough seniority to be one of the committee chairs. There were several openings. However, I had spent most of my time with the appropriations process and at that time was serving as secretary of the Appropriations Committee. I told him, "Mr. Speaker, I'd rather be a member of the Appropriations Committee than be a chair of some of the other committees. Appropriations is where the *action* really is." I added, "That's where I'm comfortable, and that's where I'd rather stay."

Sloppy Floyd had been the longtime chairman of the Appropriations Committee and was still chairman. The vice chairman was also coming back. The Speaker said, "If you are willing, I'd like you to stay on the Appropriations Committee as Secretary and be one of the conferees on the budget between the House and the Senate." I agreed.

The year that I became vice chairman, he said almost the same thing, that I had been in the House for ten years and that I had enough seniority to be chairman of some of the other committees. "But," he added, "I would like for you to stay on in the Appropriations Committee as vice chairman." Floyd was having some health problems, and Speaker Murphy wanted me to be in a position to fill in for him if it became necessary. Therefore, he said he'd like me to move up to vice chairman and added, "Of course, you would still be on the Conference Committee." That was a prestigious position to have, to be one of the conferees on the budget. I indicated that I was still "happy to serve" where I was needed.

In December 1974 a few of the House leaders—myself included—were scheduled to meet down at the capitol with Sloppy Floyd and Governor-elect George Busbee. He was working on his budget recommendations, and we were all to meet and discuss his revenue estimate. Speaker Murphy, Marcus Collins (chairman of the Ways and Means Committee), and Clarence Vaughn (majority leader of the House), were also to be at this meeting. Floyd did not arrive for the meeting. Eventually Pete Hackney came in and announced that Floyd had been found dead that morning at the Georgian Hotel.

We were all stunned and found it hard to believe. After we talked about the situation, the Speaker asked if I would meet him over in the Speaker's office for a few minutes. (We had been meeting across the street from the capitol in the old Health Building.) After I got to his office, he asked me to consider being chairman of the Appropriations Committee. He said, "I don't want to make any announcement until after the funeral is over and all of that is behind us, but I need you to start planning."

A mean SOB . . .

He *then* said "I do have some reservations: Your personality and the kind of person that you are . . . , well, you aren't very mean. To be chairman of that committee," he advised, "you've got to be a mean SOB. . . ." Only he didn't use the initials; he used the language. He said, "I'm not sure you're *mean* enough to do the job."

I replied, "Mr. Speaker, if you want me to do the job, I'll do it. Joe Frank Harris will do the job. I can't fill Sloppy Floyd's shoes, or anybody else's, but I can fill my own." I told him that I thought I could do it without having to be that mean *or* an SOB. In looking back, I feel like I was able to do that—not only to meet expectations, but hopefully exceed them. He had given me the opportunity, and I'll always be grateful for that. Frankly, I never thought in my wildest imagination that I would soon be elevated to chairman. Doors had opened for me to gain even more experience, and to move into a position to later be considered for governor.

Rheumatoid Arthritis

Things were really going well and life was bestowing all the wonderful things that young couples dream about. We had a wonderful young son, my business was profitable and growing, my political career was moving forward, and we had many opportunities for both of us to witness for and serve the Lord. In fact, Elizabeth, at this time, was serving as the president of the Rome District United Methodist Women. Just then , we received some devastating news. Dr. Lamar Cousins, a personal friend and family physician, gave us the sad and shocking news that tests had confirmed his diagnosis that Elizabeth had rheumatoid arthritis. We had never expected this is to be the explanation of the excruciating pain she had been experiencing over several months.

The pain had become so severe that Elizabeth's normal daily routine could not be accomplished, including the requirements for our child—meals, washing and ironing clothes, along with her other duties. Because we didn't know the cause of her problem, we were praying for answers. When an answer did come, we were not prepared for the severity of it.

Dr. Cousins explained that rheumatoid arthritis was the most debilitating form of arthritis, and it could cause a loss of mobility. We couldn't believe what we were hearing. He told us that this was an *autoimmune* disease—one in which the immune system attacks itself. Researchers suspect that this is caused by an unidentified virus. Frankly, we really didn't understand what we were in for at that time, and looking back now, I'm glad we didn't. However, since we had identified the problem, our prayers were concentrated on *healing* from the Lord.

After several years of anti-inflammatory drugs and multiple doses of cortisone, along with a nerve block, Elizabeth had no relief and we continued to worry. Dr. Cousins, a rheumatologist, decided to prescribe *gold shots*. This is a series of injections of metallic gold in a salt solution. I joked with Elizabeth at the time that with all the gold that was given to her, she would certainly become a twenty-four carat; gold was selling on the market for the highest price in history at over $850.00 an once! Understandably, my attempts at humor did not lessen her continuous pain.

During this period of continuous treatments the constant pain actually changed her vivacious personality, along with her looks. Her faced would swell and look very puffy; she gained weight that had never been a problem before. Finally, after several years of trying everything the medical profession could prescribe, Elizabeth attended a special healing service at the Indian Springs Holiness Camp Meeting. There was a special prayer for her while she was anointed with oil as described in James 5:14. Even though her healing was not immediate, she gained an inner peace that she was in God's hands. Even if her body had not received healing at the time, her mind had been healed. She was better able to cope with the devastations of arthritis.

Several months later in January 1981, a crisis developed during the first week of the General Assembly Session. I was Chairman of the Appropriations Committee and had to be in Atlanta full-time during the session. I left on a Sunday afternoon, and I remember feeling that it was not a good time for me to be away; something just wasn't right. As had always been our custom, I would call home every day, and when I called on the first night of the session, I could tell after a few words that I needed to rush home. When I arrived, I thought Elizabeth was dying. I had never seen her this way, and I knew something had to be done quickly.

Early on, someone had suggested the Mayo Clinic as a possibility. I now felt that she needed to be admitted there as soon as possible. I knew it would be hard for me to take time off as Chairman of the Appropriations Committee during this critical time, but I was ready for whatever it took to find some relief for Elizabeth.

With Dr. Cousin's permission, we called the Mayo Clinic in Rochester, Minnesota, for an appointment. I described Elizabeth's condition and after a few minutes one of the physicians was on the line with the word that we shouldn't wait for the normal appointment. We should get up there immediately. Many times, prayers are answered and we don't realize it. In looking back, I realize that the Lord made the immediate appointment available at Mayo and answered another prayer when Ann Cummings, one of Elizabeth's long-time friends, volunteered to make the trip with her. We were then able to get airline reservations that allowed Elizabeth to be at Mayo the very next day. This had to be an answer to prayer!

Again, the examinations by the physician and all the diagnostic tests confirmed what Dr. Cousins had found several years before: Elizabeth had rheumatoid arthritis, but the news was not all bad. In fact, we couldn't believe the *good* news. They had found that her problem, which had become so severe and difficult, was a reaction to her *medication* (gold shots) and that the *arthritis* was actually in remission. The Lord had miraculously healed Elizabeth, and we didn't even know it! When Elizabeth returned, we had a real time of thanksgiving and praise for the prayers that had been answered. Little did we realize that God was freeing her up physically for the campaign and the days ahead.

8

Asking for the Ride

I had never been obsessed with politics, much less with running for governor of Georgia. Serving in an elected position was not something I needed to spend a lifetime doing, and I felt in my own mind that maybe eighteen years was long enough. Maybe it was time to quit and let someone else serve. Maybe it was time to go home and devote myself to business and making a living for my family. I can't point to one particular instance that impressed me that running for governor was something I had to do. It evolved with time. We were as willing as ever to serve where the Lord wanted us to serve; I would never say *no* to an opportunity, because you don't know where it may lead. Something a friend said a long time ago has proven to be wise: "If you're not willing to travel, don't ask for the ride." I had asked for the ride, and I had to be ready to travel.

Early in that ninth term in the General Assembly, we had to decide whether or not to run for governor. Pressure from friends and people I served with kept coming, urging us to us to hang with it—to move forward and seek the next level. In 1981, the year before qualifying, after the General Assembly had ended, we decided to give it a chance. I wanted to see if my conservative philosophy, particularly on fiscal issues, would be something that people throughout the state could identify with.

I started accepting speaking opportunities all around the state. From March of that year until December, I spoke over one thousand times and drove myself to every one of them. There was one three-month period (during that time) that I was on the coast twenty-six times—Savannah, Brunswick, Jekyll Island, and other places—back and forth between there and Atlanta. I would be there for a speech in the evening, drive all night, change shirts, shave and then go to other speeches in Atlanta; that afternoon, back to the coast. It was both a physical and mental challenge to

see if you could do it physically, and also to see if you had
anything to offer when you met people in their own communities.

A Quilt of Many Patterns

It is opportunities like this that enable you to you to see, feel,
and smell some of the problems people have to deal with. You
could identify with them, and it is really an education. Of all the
experiences during the campaign, and over all the years of being
in politics, this was probably the most beneficial for me. I had
never really traveled to those communities, other than just
occasionally passing through. I realized that the state of Georgia is
a quilt of many patterns: the mountains to the north, the piedmont, the flatlands and coastal plains in the southern part;
different cultural heritages and the different dialects of the English
language in our many regions. I found that the common thread
running through it all was that our great state is part of a great
United States, with God-fearing people proud of their families and
their communities—red, white and blue Americans with great work
ethics and worthwhile goals in their lives. Those visits to their
communities and the feedback they were giving me told me that
they were looking for someone who would not only represent them
and their interests—but would be sincere and honest about it.
That's why I ran for office.

You find areas across our state in which people have not had
the opportunities that some others have had. In our minds those
may be depressed areas with few of the "extras" found elsewhere.
But they have a lot of pride in what they do have, and they were
seeking to improve their lot in life. It's disappointing to realize that
you can't just recover those areas and make everybody whole. I
think it gave me an added incentive to try to improve education
for their children and grandchildren, to start the evolution toward
being better able to compete and gain the affluence of other parts
of the state. What came out of the meetings with those people was
that the secret to helping them was their own education. Obvi-
ously, a quality education program was needed; but it was not

something that was going to happen overnight. There is no such thing as a "quick fix" in education.

Had We Made a Mistake?

While traveling the state, having private conversations with people, you can feel whether or not you're being accepted. When you leave, you hear them saying that they understand you may run for governor and "if you do, we want to support you." Some offered personal campaign contributions, which I couldn't accept because I didn't have a campaign committee and was still not certain I was going to run. I tried to keep as many of their names on a mailing list as I could; if I did run I could get back to them. There were a lot of commitments and offers of financial support and this was encouraging. While it was a minuscule amount compared to the total that we needed, it was still a beginning. A little later I notified the people on my mailing list that I *was* running and that they could now make their contributions, only to see it trickle in. Now I realize that sometimes it comes in later. That was a trial period early in our campaign. We had to weigh whether or not we had made a mistake and, if we had, to get out. Again, the Lord removed the obstacles and the door was opened a little wider.

The opportunities to speak started to really come in on their own. It was not something I was soliciting. I'm not sure even today what generated those opportunities. But they came in the form of everything from civic clubs to ribbon cuttings to anything where people gathered. The number of invitations mushroomed. I think sometimes that an incident that occurred a couple of years before this may have enhanced the situation: A friend from Hawkinsville by the name of John Henry Anderson had served with me in the General Assembly. John Henry was about my age and had been in the General Assembly two years prior to my arrival in 1965. We became friends because I was the second youngest member of the House. Some of the older members of the house kept referring to us as "the young Turks." In those days, in a legislative setting, young legislators were supposed to be seen and not heard for many years. We tried to abide by the rules, but John Henry was a close friend and had some business cards printed up that said "Remember this name—Joe Frank Harris." No phone number. No address. I kept running into those cards all over South Georgia. People would meet me, pull out a card and say, "You're Joe Frank Harris." He had been passing those cards out for months before I knew he'd had them printed.

Things like that were happening and multiplying, getting my name out. People who believed in me and were supportive were doing things on their own that I didn't even know about. This helped bring it all together.

Asking for Prayer

I felt that religion was an area a lot of people could identify with and was something we had in common. There were also many skeptics. When I got into the campaign, I would usually say in my speeches that "I need your help, your support, but I also need your prayers." I was sincere; I did need their prayers. I believe in prayer even today. I received mail from people who were skeptical of my talking about prayer, even including the word "prayer." One lady from Savannah wrote, "I support your improvements in education . . . and your platform for making prisoners work . . . and economic development for the state with no tax increase . . . but I'm fearful that you are a religious fanatic, because you're always asking for prayer. . . . You always end up mentioning God." Sometimes you wouldn't hear these views directly; it's what people would say to their friends.

My own friends would tell me that I was going to create a problem with my religion. If anything, I think it was an asset. I was always conscious that people can spot a phony a mile away. You've got to be what you are. If I'm religious in my own home and in my own community of Cartersville, then I don't need to change my stripes somewhere else. I think people respect that, even though they may not agree with you. You don't wear your religion on your sleeve. People will judge your actions by your life and what you're living in front of them, not what you're trying to impress them with—or tell them you're doing. And I certainly didn't want to do anything that would bring discredit to my commitment to the Lord.

The Point of No Return

The decision to run for governor was not an easy one. It wasn't made hastily or overnight. It was something that gradually evolved after I had been in the General Assembly for many years. However, it was during Governor George Busbee's second term, which began in 1979, that the pressure began to build from friends and people in the General Assembly letting me know that they felt I ought to consider it.

I never really considered who else might be running. To me, that was never a factor. I never felt, and certainly don't feel now, that I was anointed to be governor. A lot of people talk in terms of, "The Lord sent me to run for governor, or the Lord made me governor or ordered me to be governor." I have always been skeptical of politicians who equated their own ideas, and sometimes their own selfish motives, with God's directive. Still, I did feel that it was God's guidance, direction, and help over the years that allowed me to be in a position to run. Ultimately, after I made the decision, I felt that in order to remain in God's will and do what I should be doing, that I should make the race. In preparation for that run for governor, I had been chairman of the Appropriations Committee for a number of years and had grown up with the state budget. When I first entered the General Assembly, the total state budget was less than $500 million; at the time I considered running for governor—it was approaching $3 billion. There had been an almost unprecedented increase in the population of our state in the 1960s and 70s, and it was quite an educational opportunity to have been involved in the budgetary process during those years. It gave me some insights into the internal workings of state government that I couldn't gained elsewhere. Having the background in business was another good preparation. State government is a big business, and it takes the same kind of operational procedure to be successful there. It was the accumulation of these kinds of things that made people who were interested in someone with these qualifications feel that I should and could get elected.

Elizabeth and I were constantly praying about this. We felt that if it was the Lord's will, then He will continue to open doors. We were looking for the door to either be closed, or we were prepared to continue moving. It even seemed like the doors were perhaps opening wider as we went along. Still, we did not make the decision to run during those early days. As had been the case when we ran for the General Assembly so many years before, we were simply praying for the door to stay open and our hearts to be willing if the opportunity came.

As I traveled throughout the state I continued to receive encouragement from my speeches. People would come forward and say, "Well, I hope you'll run for governor," and "I really liked what you said about education," or "I liked what you said about the prisoners working," or ". . . about the management of the State's resources. . .," "operating the State government and not raising taxes, . . ." and things like that. Some support even came from my opposition to gambling.

I began to feel that people would be supportive of my values and philosophy of operating state government—that I offered the people something they could relate to. I felt that if I could convey this message widely enough, I could run a viable campaign. We were actually getting to the point of no return. So many people were encouraging me to run that it became almost a matter of pride; there was nothing to prevent our running.

Another important factor, which I guess figured into it at least subconsciously, was that our concrete business had been sold in 1980. I had no conflicts or any problems or any personal businesses that would prevent my devoting all my energies not only to a campaign but to the office of governor. I was as free and clear as I had ever been in my lifetime to pursue something like this and had none of the restrictions or restraints that people sometimes have. I felt like maybe the Lord had put me in this position and allowed these things to happen so that I could be able to accept this kind of challenge. Hindsight being twenty/twenty, you see that the door was opening wider, a little at a time. But many times along the way, you got the feeling that it may actually be closing—and that this was as far as you were supposed to go; you had to constantly reassess where you were and whether or not you could actually finance the campaign. When you paid your fee and put your name on the dotted line, then there was no turning back; I mean it was full speed ahead, wide open day and night.

I was committed to the idea that none of the other candidates would ever outwork me. Looking back, I don't think they did. If they had, they probably would have been elected instead of me. But we had none of this hindsight in those days. Early in 1981, Elizabeth and I decided to undertake the race.

9

A Statewide Campaign

During the early stages of our campaign, before a committee had been formed to enable me to accept campaign contributions, I personally paid all of my expenses to travel the state to test the waters and give me the feel for the requirements of a statewide campaign. I traveled alone and drove myself to over a thousand speeches during the nine months after the 1981 Legislative session ended. All over the state, I received encouragement and offers of support. The names and addresses of these people received a special notation in a list of prospective supporters that I compiled and kept at every appearance.

In the fall of that year, based on the promises and support I had received, a campaign committee was organized and registered with the Secretary of State. Joel Cowan served as the chairman, and Gracie Phillips was selected to be treasurer. Then, Tom Daniels, who had been one of Governor George Busbee's senior staff, was brought on board to begin building the foundation for our "venture of faith." The campaign office was opened in Cartersville at 314 West Main Street in an office building I owned with my brother Fred. Immediately volunteers began to arrive in surprising numbers to support our efforts.

The failure of promised contributions to come in became the first real crisis of our campaign, and it shocked us into re-thinking where we were headed. We had to re-assess our decision and consider that perhaps this was not what the Lord had in store for us. Maybe this was not what we were supposed to do. I kept thinking, "If this is the Lord's will, then why aren't the contributions coming in?"

Elizabeth and I prayed: "Lord, if this is what we're supposed to do, we need a confirmation. We need some signal that we will know that you want us to continue in this race." We even placed a deadline on our prayers. We needed a positive answer within three weeks or we would be forced into withdrawing, folding our tents, and getting out of the race.

The Beginning of the Future

With the final week about to arrive and the first two weeks of our deadline period past, I received a call from Glenn Taylor. Glenn lived in Atlanta and had a large farm near Cartersville where he enjoyed spending time and raising cattle. He even moved to "the farm" a portion of his Bankhead Enterprises, which manufactured transportation equipment and trailers to haul new automobiles. During the construction of this plant, our business had furnished all of the concrete and I had come to know Glenn as a customer. Later, I became better acquainted with him and his wife, Bea, after the annual Euharlee Farmers Club barbecue. Our county agent, Walter Culverhouse, invited Elizabeth, me, and the Taylors to enjoy homemade peach ice cream at his home.

The phone call was short and to the point, as is Glenn's custom: "If you are going to be in town on Saturday, I will be at the farm. Can you come by?" It just so happened I was coming in that Friday night and leaving Saturday afternoon. I tried to get home at least one day during the week or weekend to get a clean shirt, and take care of everything before heading out again. I went out to visit him at his farm house, which was just being completed, and he invited me into the kitchen where we could "Sit down and talk a minute."

He began: "I know that none of the special interest groups are going to be supporting you. The liquor industry is not going to support you because you are a teetotaler." He went down the list of various groups that he felt wouldn't be supportive of my campaign because of the moral standards that I upheld, the values I embraced, and the record I had already established. He knew that money was not going to be as easy to raise for me because my potential contributors would be limited.

"I know you're going to have a little problem raising money," Glenn continued, "I'll do what I can. I like what you stand for, and

I believe in your campaign. I won't be able to give you that much money personally, but I've got some friends whom I can contact." He went on to list ways in which he could be helpful to our campaign.

I'm not an emotional person, but I could hardly finish the conversation with Glenn that day. It had really choked me up. When I returned home Elizabeth anxiously asked "How did it go?" I was so choked up, I couldn't answer her. She knew that Dad had just left five or ten minutes before and immediately thought something had happened to Joe or that I had seen a wreck down the street. She had not seen me that way since Joe was a small child suffering the seizures associated with the Reyes Syndrome. Finally, when I had gathered my composure, I told her what had happened. She was just as excited as I was, because we knew that this was the confirmation from the Lord and really was the beginning of the future in the governor's race. We weren't going to have to withdraw.

Everything Glenn Taylor offered to do that fall day, and then some, became a reality. He personally wrote to every employee who had worked at Bankhead and lived in Georgia, which was approximately two thousand people. He spoke to people in his clubs, his church, and everyone he came in contact with, and gave many of them tickets to our fundraisers. Along with being one of our best contributors, he attended every finance committee meeting and became the leader by example. Now this was hardly the end of the obstacles, problems, and difficult decisions that we had to make in the campaign. But it was a sign that the door was opening a little bit wider and to keep on moving.

Not an Embarrassment

When I was elected Governor, I appointed Glenn a member of the Board of Natural Resources. He never asked for anything; I mean, never, ever had he asked: "Can you do this?" Or, "Would you do a favor for me?" Nothing ever personally for himself, never in all these years. And when I appointed him the first time, he was reluctant and didn't want to serve: "Because," he said, "the kind of business I'm in," which was asphalt paving, construction, metal fabrication, things like that, ". . . we're exposed to environmental rules and regulations. There could be a problem or an accident, or something, that could embarrass you and your administration. I would rather not serve . . . ."

I said, "Mr. Glenn, there's not one person whom I can choose—who could bring experience, honesty, and integrity to any of these positions—who wouldn't, somewhere along the line, generate some kind of conflict. That's where you've got to use your discretion. If anything ever comes before you that may be a problem, it's up to you not to participate in that activity. I would much rather have somebody that I've got trust and confidence in filling this position than to have to rely on somebody that I really don't know."

When it came time for his reappointment in 1990, he came back in and said, "Well, we've been lucky to serve this first term and I haven't embarrassed you. I'd rather you choose somebody else now." Glenn Taylor never did embarrass me, and he never will. He was reappointed for a second term.

After I left the Governor's office in 1991, Glenn contacted me one day and wanted me to have lunch with him down at the Capital City Club in Atlanta. He was there with Frank Felder, who was the president of Bankhead Enterprises, the number one person in his organization, and laid out the proposal for me to become a member of their corporate board. Glenn had become such a trusted advisor and personal friend, I was glad to accept without hesitation.

Checking the Polls

A typical day would be from early to late, going from the earliest time that you could get up and meet with somebody—or find an audience to promote the campaign. Your day would be totally consumed with one stop after another, one city after another, moving many thousands of miles up and down and around the state. At each stop you had to be fresh, you had to look sharp, you had to try to be sharp, and you had to have something coherent to say. You couldn't just have a speech for North Georgia and a speech for South Georgia. You had to have a unified appeal that most of the people could relate to. It was also one of the most physically draining times of my life. In sports and in business, you could always call "time out" or rest. But in a political campaign of this magnitude, there are few times out and not much rest.

I never felt intimidated by the other candidates, because I felt I had a more immediate knowledge of the workings of state government than my opponents. I always felt that if I could articulate my message to enough people, they would accept it and be supportive. That was my goal. We wanted people to take our candidacy seriously, and yet we were operating a campaign on limited funds, stretching them as far as possible.

Polls are expensive, so we didn't spend any money on polls up-front. Almost all of the other candidates were utilizing polls, and even some of the news media were conducting polls of their own. After making a thousand speeches in 1981, having been in the General Assembly for almost eighteen years, serving on statewide boards, and participating in many business and religious organizations across the state, still the highest I rated on any of those polls was three to five percent. With the kind of exposure we'd had over so many years, one would think people would have remembered my name.

In retrospect, I can see that these numbers were not all that unusual. Unless you'd had some notoriety or notice of an unusually negative nature, you're not going to have a very high percentage of people remembering you just out of the blue. One of the candidates, Bo Ginn, had been in Congress for a number of years and had a wider constituency than I did throughout Middle and South Georgia. Another candidate, Billy Lovett, had been on the Public Service Commission for years; and Norman Underwood had served on the Court of Appeals and had been in Governor Busbee's Administration for a number of years; Buck Melton had been the mayor of Macon. Another candidate, Jack Watson, had been a

Georgia lawyer and with the Carter Administration in Washington. They had all had a good bit of publicity, most of it quite positive, and one or two of them were rating sixteen to twenty percent better than us in those first polls.

Choosing Good Horses

We hovered for quite some time at three to five percent before we started to move. When we did start moving, we could feel the change even before the polls registered it. Somehow, you had a perception; you knew it was coming. The broadcast and newspaper media are, of course, a potent force, and if you can gain access to them effectively and with enough repetition, you can move name identification along very quickly. We were able to do that with the assistance of Deloss Walker of Walker and Associates, a public relations group from Memphis, Tennessee, whom I had met through a mutual friend (Mitt Connerly, from Carrollton) when I was considering running for governor. At the time we signed on, Deloss had handled some fifty political campaigns and had won all but two of them. I had noticed that he had placed what we felt were some very skillful ads in his handling of Fob James's gubernatorial campaign in Alabama..

Deloss was the only public relations person with whom I spoke during the course of the entire campaign. I was impressed with him from the start. He would not commit to anyone until after an initial interview and after he had spent some time with you in your home and community. If it was not a compatible situation, then he would move on and pick a candidate with whom he thought he had a better rapport. For some reason he was impressed with our campaign and took us on. I was very encouraged and felt that we had gotten over a serious hurdle now that we had a quality person who could help us put together a viable media campaign. In our ads Deloss managed to capture the positive image we felt was right for us and that could relate to the people.

The only advice that I did not accept from him was his insistence that my name was too long and too "Old South." His argument, which had some merit, was that "Joe Frank Harris" was too long for a bumper strip. "Joe Harris" would be much shorter and less expensive. My response was that I had always been "Joe Frank" and had been elected nine times with that name on the ballot; I was not going to change it just to run for governor.

He also suggested an innovative technique that had not been utilized very successfully in other campaigns. We were able, however, to make it work in Georgia. We set up a statewide radio network and let the local communities pay for the air time. Someone locally would raise the money to buy radio time in daily thirty-minute or one-hour segments just before the Primary. We repeated this process before the primary runoff and for the general election.

During the course of the campaign, we would go to WGST in Atlanta where we could simultaneously broadcast to over 125 stations throughout Georgia. The program time was being paid for locally; all we were paying for was its origination in Atlanta. I would sit there and Ray Moore, a former TV anchorperson in Atlanta for many years who was then working for Georgia Tech, would act as moderator. Ray would field the questions live on the air and pass them on to me to answer as best I could. Questions were phoned in from everywhere in Georgia. Deloss Walker also participated and assisted as master of ceremonies. It became very successful.

We learned later that people were listening every day; they'd find out what time we were airing locally and tune in to hear our views on a number of problems and issues that concerned them. I didn't have all the answers and would admit it. But I think they determined that we had a willingness to try to find the answers and that we were going to work hard to do the best we could for Georgia.

A Major Mountain to Climb

From the first polls, all the other major candidates were registering well ahead of our less than five percent and had maintained their status during most of the campaign. During the last several weeks, we could feel the momentum shifting. We were consulting what we called our "old backyard indicators," which were really unsophisticated telephone calls within the communities, a "Who's your choice for Governor?" kind of thing. It was surprising how close to the real polls those surveys came. We were using them to follow up in communities where we'd had a campaign function or I had visited to gauge what, if anything, was happening. We could see that the "temperature" was going up and that our momentum was increasing.

Our gubernatorial campaign placed our Atlanta headquarters in the old Dunfey's Hotel overlooking Northside Drive and I-75. Our first major fundraiser was held there the week before the legislative session in 1982. Everyone discouraged having a hundred-dollar-a-plate event so soon after Christmas. However, we needed to begin raising the funds and creating support for our campaign. Since an event of this type usually was not held at this time, we felt that we had to have at least five hundred people there or the press would really crucify us.

The ballroom at Dunfey's could be partitioned off to accommodate the numbers we projected. We learned from an earlier experience that a political event was always more successful—the participants more impressed and excited—when the room is crowded and overflowing. A small crowd in a large room just does not make the impression of a large crowd in a small room.

Just as we had expected, the advance reservations were coming in very slowly. As an added obstacle, the weather was projected to be very cold with rain turning to sleet. It seemed that anything that could happen to prevent our success was happening. However, on the morning of the event, the phones started to ring with additional reservations. Before noon on that day, the hotel was asked to remove the partition and plan to serve many more than the five hundred we had been expecting. There was still a lot of doubt and once again a test of our faith. What if all of these people that made reservations didn't show? If they did not come and bring their money, we would be stuck with a huge tab at the hotel. This was yet another time when we had to trust the Lord and believe we had not come that far to be left hanging.

The weather did turn bad, but the crowd started to arrive well in advance of the dinner. As was our custom, there was no alcohol served during the reception, but people crowded in and enjoyed a lot of good fellowship. Panic struck all of us when a steady stream of people receiving their name tags let us know that they "knew you needed a good crowd tonight" and brought a few more than they made reservations for. When the meal was finally served, the ballroom had been filled, tables set up in the foyer, and even the restaurant space upstairs had been utilized to accommodate the over 1,500 people who attended. We were grateful the fire marshals were not present because we were over the legal capacity.

Jackey Beavers, a pastor and the noted songwriter who wrote "Some Day We'll Be Together" for The Supremes, was on the program to sing and get the spirit of the crowd up just prior to my remarks. He changed some of the words to the song, "Praise the Lord, He Can Work Through Those That Praise Him." Later, he became a member of my Senior Staff and a spiritual inspiration. Some had suggested that it would not be appropriate in that setting for Jackey to sing. I disagreed and he sang wonderfully. The spirit and enthusiasm were extremely high, and the roof almost lifted when Jackey got to the second verse and began to sing:

> Praise the Lord,
> Joe Frank Harris will be the next governor.
> Praise the Lord,
> Joe Frank Harris is his name.

Our prayers had been answered; another door had been opened, and our skeptics were wondering what was happening.

Life on the Other Side

That location had been a special place for us, so we arranged to have people gather at the Dunfey's Hotel on 10 August 1982, the evening of the Democratic Primary election. With good indications from the our polls, we were optimistic that we were going to make the run-off that night. Some of the real polls indicated that we were going to be much further behind. When the returns started coming in, places in Middle and South Georgia, where we had no idea of our strength, were indicating good support for us. In fact, the numbers had us ahead of most of candidates Norman Underwood, Jack Watson, Billy Lovett, Buck Melton, Mildred Glover, Henry Jackson, Tom Irwin, Mac McNease. Only Bo Ginn was outpolling us. We could tell that his momentum had stabilized. We were just hoping that we could be the one in the run-off with him.

As the night progressed, the enthusiasm escalated. The crowd was just overwhelming. But I have to say that my excitement was, I guess, a little subdued. Early on, I had convinced myself, had prepared myself mentally, that regardless of what happened on that night life was going on. All the way through, Deloss Walker, who had been involved in many campaigns, had warned the campaign to be as prepared to lose as to win. "There's life on the other side of this campaign," he had said. "This isn't the end of it, and it's not going to wipe you out." Now it *would* have wiped me out financially, I guess, but not emotionally.

The results came in that August night and, sure enough, we had made the run-off with 24.84 per cent of the vote. Congressman Bo Ginn had a larger percentage with 35.11per cent, so we were still the underdog. He was able to raise more money and had some larger contributors. (See Appendix A for election results of both gubernatorial races.) However, we had a larger pool of contributors and we felt that was a good sign. Most of these contributions were very small amounts but they were coming from a broad spectrum of people who were putting their money where their mouths were. In the end it's better to have more contributors than the largest contributions.

I didn't get as caught up in the excitement as one might think a candidate would. I was excited and pleased, but I wasn't overcome with excitement. In the back of my mind I could see that while we did make the run-off and were going to be there, I still had three more weeks of intense campaigning and an awful lot of money to raise. All the things that were necessary on the other side of that night were, I guess, heavier than the excitement.

We expressed our appreciation to the people gathered there that evening and challenged them to "hit the streets tonight" and work even harder. We still had a major mountain to climb.

10

A Wing and a Prayer

We had a tough time trying to raise enough money. We had gotten estimates and thought we could run a whole campaign, win the Democratic primary, and go to the general election for two million dollars. We had raised and spent that amount just to get into the run-offs. Now we needed several hundred thousand dollars within a three-week period just to keep pace with the competition and get our message back on the air. Bo Ginn was well-financed and able to use the media quite effectively. In fact, he was putting up two or three TV spots to our one. We knew we had to raise some additional money very quickly. We were very busy campaigning and didn't have time to back off the campaign trail to put together more fundraisers.

There is so little time in a run-off, it just seemed almost an impossibility. We realized that we had to borrow the money to stay afloat. There is no credit on TV ads; it's cash up front. Deloss Walker and his group were having to manage all this, but they couldn't buy ads or place them until we had the cash to put in their hands. So Joel Cowan, who was the chairman of our campaign, had made arrangements with our banks. Some local people in Cartersville and others around the state would sign some notes for up to $5,000 a piece. If I hadn't been elected or couldn't raise the money to repay it, then they would have been responsible. But those amounts couldn't cover anywhere near the needed amount.

I remember receiving a call from Joel. I was out in the state campaigning, and he said "I think your schedule's got you in Cartersville tonight. I need you to run by the bank in the morning and sign a note." "How much is the note?" I asked. It was a line of credit established at the bank for between a half and three-quarters of million dollars. I was going to have to be a personal endorser for that note, and I arrived home that night with my head spinning.

You get to that point in a campaign when, almost like a religious conversion in which you cannot hold back part of your life, you have to be totally committed. But I got some advice from Harry Jackson, the mayor of Columbus, Georgia, and a long-time friend, who had spent a lot of his own money running a losing statewide campaign for governor in 1974. Early on, he advised, "Don't spend your own money. If you can't raise it, then get out."

That kept echoing in the back of my mind. I had already committed a considerable amount, campaigning for almost a year and a half at my own expense, furnishing my own gas, my own automobile, and paying the initial fee to the public relations firm out of my own pocket. I wanted to be sure that I was going to be a candidate before I formed a committee, and, of course, I couldn't raise any money until the committee was formed. I knew that to sign a note for hundreds of thousands of dollars would really put my name and my future on the line. Had I lost, I probably would have been working for the rest of my life to repay that debt. But I would have paid it.

I got in that night and Elizabeth and I prayed about the situation. I don't think we slept at all. The thing that kept going through my mind was the faces of so many good people whose paths I'd crossed over the years, who had contributed what they could afford to support me. If I didn't go ahead and risk it all, then I would not have honored their commitment to me.

The next morning we were still praying about the matter when it was time to go by the bank. I felt that even if I lost everything I still had to sign that note, to finish the campaign, and try to do it honorably. So I went to the bank and signed the note and went on with the day's obligations. Now the funds were there to go ahead and purchase media time.

The Right Words

There were so many times during the course of the campaign that you would get to a point of exhaustion or disappointment or discouragement, or all three at once. Elizabeth's discernment was almost uncanny. She was able to give the kind of advice and help that was needed and could convey it in just the right way. She would have that word of encouragement or she would remind us of our obligation not only to the Lord, but to the people who supported us. I felt that this really was inspired by the Lord, because she had that kind of nature: a very optimistic, caring person who always had the right words at the right time. She didn't always use the same words or have the same response, but it would be the appropriate response. As a result the campaign workers always felt energized and enabled to move on to the next level.

I think it's very meaningful when you have a partnership, a home life, and a working relationship with someone over many years and are supportive of each other in both your opportunities and obligations. I think we were both always willing to sacrifice if necessary for each other. While I believe she has done a lot more sacrificing for me than I was ever able to do for her, it really has been a partnership, one for which I'm eternally grateful.

A Crash, Not a Landing

During the course of our marriage, Elizabeth and I had kind of an understanding that after 11:00 p.m., we wouldn't discuss anything negative or bad. We had always tried to honor that. On one particular night during the campaign I was on the way back to Cartersville in a borrowed plane from a trip out in the state. We had been flying in planes that people would lend us and sometimes they would lend you their planes with a pilot. At other times, we had to hire a pilot to fly their planes. Bill Roquemore, from Lanier County, who had a grass and golf course business in Lakeland, Georgia, had loaned us his twin-engine Beechcraft plane. My pilot was Mac Williford who operated an air-freight business from the airport in Cartersville. This was a slack time for him, so he was my pilot for most of the campaign. He was an excellent pilot; he'd have to be, because I'm here to tell this story.

We probably would have been landing in Cartersville around midnight. Wayne Reese, who was traveling with us, had been an intern for me when I was chairman of the Appropriations Committee.* That night, we stopped at the Fulton County-Charlie Brown Airport to drop Wayne off . We took off from the Atlanta airport to fly the few minutes to Cartersville. Just as we were landing a few minutes prior to midnight and the plane was almost ready to touch down, two deer jumped up on the side of the runway. They both ran across right in front of the plane. Mac Williford, the pilot, had enough presence of mind to try to pull up, instead of letting the plane land and hit the deer. In the process of pulling back up, we were so committed and losing air speed so fast that the plane's landing gear was almost on the ground. Then we heard a big thud. It was almost like we had hit a large rock on the runway. Actually, we had hit one of the deer. We both thought it was the nosewheel because of the way it felt.

Immediately after he pulled the plane back up, we were back in the air. There was no way of knowing the extent of the damage because we couldn't see the landing gear, and the panel light was showing the landing gear down. Mac said, "Let me see if it will retract. If it will, then maybe everything's okay." It wouldn't and we knew we had problems. I was seated beside him in the copilot's seat. His immediate reaction was to turn to me and ask, "You didn't have anywhere else you needed to go, did you?" When I shook my head "no,"' he added, "We'd better fly back to Atlanta, because they've got some emergency equipment there. We may need it. It'd be safer to try to land there than it would be to try to land here at the Cartersville Airport."

As we flew back to Charlie Brown Airport, he contacted the tower and told them that he thought we had a problem. They

---

*Wayne Reese had traveled with me almost every mile during the whole campaign. An able aide and assistant, he was a highly intelligent person who added a lot of perspective to the many issues we faced through out the state. Today he is a practicing attorney in Atlanta.

instructed us to fly by the control tower and said, "We've got some lights we'll put on the plane and see if the landing gear is down." If they could detect any damage they could tell us that, too. We made several passes back and forth by the control tower. They said, "All three of your wheels are down. If you think it's the nosewheel, come on in for a nose-up landing." That meant, of course, that he would keep the nosewheel off the ground until the plane had gotten on the ground and slowed its speed. Then, if the nosewheel had collapsed, the damage might not be as severe, or we might be able to survive it at least. They also wisely suggested we fly around for a little while longer to burn up some of the fuel. We did that for a short period of time, though we really didn't have much fuel. We'd already been on a long flight and had just enough to get us to Cartersville with the proper reserve.

When you get into this kind of a possibly fatal situation, you think you'd be scared to death. I have to tell you, I was not. My prayer was: "Lord, if this is it; if the campaign is over, and we're not going to make it out of this landing, I'm just grateful for the opportunities I've had." I felt that if I died that night, I was going to heaven anyway. That was okay. Of course, I hated to leave my wife and young son and my family, but I had a real peace about it. I guess if I had died that evening, it would have been a calm experience. It was not something that I was panicked or nervous about.

When we touched down Mac immediately cut off the engine so that the props wouldn't be turning. This reduced the possibility of damage and fire. He was ready for whatever came. Speaking as a layman, not as a pilot, it appeared that he had everything in perfect readiness. The plane, instead of rolling straight down the runway on two wheels, made a severe jerk to the left, and we realized it was really the landing gear under the left wing, not the nosewheel that had been damaged. Well, it jerked us almost off the left side of the runway. Then, for some reason, it immediately swerved back to the right. At that moment I knew this was a crash, not a landing. I thought it was going to flip over, but it kind of hopped up and bumped and tilted and teetered and started spinning around and around. We spun on across the runway on out into the infield. When we did finally stop, the plane was covered with dust, dirt, grass, and whatever we had churned up when we were spinning off into the infield.

The minute it stopped moving, I flipped the door open on my side and jumped to the ground. The pilot looked out and said, "How did you get out so quick?" I assured him that I didn't have any hesitation in getting myself out. All I could think about was that there could be a fire or an explosion. But I realized that the prayers for my safety and protection that so many people had been praying during the campaign had not only surrounded me but had also shielded and protected us in that airplane that night.

We came out without a scratch, but the plane didn't look good. We later learned that the collision with the deer had broken the stabilizers and the wing's landing gear was flopping around loose, going in whatever direction it wanted. Fire trucks, emergency equipment, and many people came out to provide assistance. Since I was not injured and didn't need the emergency assistance, I had someone drive me up to the hangar to make a phone call. I knew it was getting late and that Elizabeth was expecting me back in Cartersville about midnight and would be worried. When I reached the phone, I called her but didn't tell her we'd crash landed and really damaged the plane. I told her we'd had a mechanical problem with one of the tires on the plane and that I'd be there in a little while. Immediately, I called Wayne Reese and asked him if he would come back and drive me to Cartersville, which he did.

The next morning, I told Elizabeth what had happened. She said that I didn't have to tell her, that she already knew what had happened. She didn't know the details but had a heavy feeling that something bad must have been going on. She was there praying for me at home, too. All of our prayers had been answered.

The Race Goes On

Bo Ginn had entered the campaign as a frontrunner when he made his announcement. He was well known across the state because of his many years in the U. S. Congress and earlier as a member of Senator Herman Talmadge's staff. As a member of the House Appropriations Committee, well respected by the national Democratic leadership, he would have been in a position to become national Speaker of the House. For many months prior to his entering the race, it had been rumored he would leave Congress to run for governor.

In a private conversation with him at a fish fry near Millen, his home town, he indicated to me that he felt he could best serve the state by remaining in Congress and not sacrificing his many years of experience and seniority in that arena. I congratulated him on his decision, because I felt that whoever the next governor of Georgia might be, it would be an asset to have his help in Washington. But less than two weeks after our conversation, he called a press conference to announce that he had decided to leave Congress and become a candidate for governor. His announcement left me with the loss of a number of commitments of support that had been made by many of his loyal friends who thought he was not going to run.

As the runoff went on over those three weeks in August, my opponent's apparent advantage began to slip. In fact, you could feel the same kind of momentum that had carried our campaign out of the Primary had remained with us into the Primary Runoff Election . On 31 August 1982, we gathered once again at Dunfey's Hotel as the votes came in. It was a hard-fought, though decisive, result 410,259 votes for Bo Ginn and 500,765 for Joe Frank Harris.

Even though we had come out of the run-off victorious, we didn't have a solid Democratic backing. In fact, none of my opponents in the gubernatorial campaign endorsed my candidacy for governor. For whatever reasons, we didn't have their endorsements and, looking back, it's probably just as well. You can't really transfer support to someone else. You may endorse someone personally, and that means you can transfer one vote if you're committed to support that person. But to try and bring your supporters over is hard to do. People have minds of their own.

They like to feel they've made their own decisions and that someone else is not pressuring them to go in one direction or another. It would have been comforting and a great boost psychologically if all the candidates had said "Yes, we're for him; he's going to make it, and we'll help him all we can." The failure to win those endorsements became another difficulty we had to overcome.

Our Republican opponent for governor, Bob Bell, had been in the State Senate for a number of years before the governor's race. I'd served with him in the House of Representatives before he was elected to the Senate where he served several terms. Bob and I had always had a friendly working relationship. Our philosophies were not that different; I was a more conservative Democrat than some of the others during that time, therefore a real solid distinction was not drawn for many of the voters. Our campaign had the momentum going into the race and in the end they were unable to match that momentum.

We had been outspent in the Primary, outspent in the Run-off, and now our opponent had outspent us in the general election. The Republicans had not had a very competitive or costly Primary and since that money was still there they were able to move it over to the General Election and have a well-financed campaign.

Bucking Disclosure

There had been a political standoff surrounding financial disclosures for many years. My own decision not to disclose my personal finances during the campaign centered on several pertinent questions: What are you going to disclose? How are you going to do it? And, if you do disclose, what format will you use? The thing that most of the candidates tried to do at that time was "leverage" their opponents into exposing their income tax returns, which, in my opinion, really doesn't tell much about a person's finances. For example, it doesn't tell you where the money comes from. It doesn't tell you how it was generated. It doesn't even tell you who that candidate might owe. It was not a very good disclosure method, if that was the criteria. I was committed to passing laws in Georgia that would give us some semblance of uniform disclosure. This was passed during our Administration and has even been improved upon since then.

That method was not there during the campaign, and I guess I'm a little stubborn sometimes when I make up my mind on issues or anything else. When I'm firm and solid in my belief about something, then I'm not going to be moved or swayed. I probably could have lost the whole race because I bucked the disclosure challenge. I kept crossing paths with people who told me that they disagreed with my approach and that maybe I should go ahead and disclose. But they also said that if I had the guts to hang in there and stand up for what I believed in, then they were going to support me.

There was absolutely nothing for me to hide about my finances. In fact, it could have been an asset to show that with honesty and hard work a small business person could be a success. My real reason for not yielding was that we had just sold our family business in 1980 and it was widely known that the ownership was split between my father, my brother, and myself. My disclosure would have indirectly disclosed them. They were not the candidate for governor and did not deserve to be exploited just because I had entered the race.

I guess it probably washed itself out as to whether it was negative or positive. I did make a determination that I would place my assets in a blind trust, which I did. The assets stayed there until the disclosure laws were passed. When this occurred, we brought them out of the blind trust and complied with the requirements of the disclosure. I did what I said I would do.

In looking back, the blind trust perhaps gave me a peace of mind, because I did not want any personal investment or business connection to conflict with any decision which I had to make while serving as governor. My directions to my blind trustee, Bill Gaston, who was a Certified Professional Accountant (CPA) with George A. Pennington and Company, were not to invest any of my assets in any business or corporation regulated or doing business with the state. This eliminated all of the banks and many of the Georgia corporations that have done so well and would have been good investments at the time. Because of this, my net worth really suffered while I served as governor.

My Relationship with Speaker Tom Murphy

Most of my opponents during the primary and even in the runoff, and particularly in the general election, tried to target Speaker Tom Murphy and make that a negative. In some cases, it may have been, but then Speaker Murphy and I had served together in the General Assembly. He had appointed me to the Appropriations Committee and supported my efforts to run for governor; he had also been a long-time personal friend. I felt that if I had to sacrifice my friends just to get elected, then I wasn't going to be much of a governor. "You've got to dance with those that bring you." People can spot a phony two miles away, and I was not going to disrupt a long-time friendship for a political opportunity. Neither was I going to bite the hand that fed me.

The Equal Rights Amendment

I have always supported equal rights, whether it's male or female, black or white, or whatever. That was not the problem. The problem I had was with the specific amendment and the general tactic of amending the Constitution of the United States. I will always remember that my last year in the General Assembly, just prior to my running for governor, was when the amendment was voted on again. I had opposed it in the past, and it really upset some members of the General Assembly that here I was about to take on a state-wide campaign not supportive of their equal rights. I had to vote against it in the General Assembly that year because that was my own personal conviction.

Tom Perdue, who later became my initial Chief Administrative Officer and was very helpful in our campaign at the time, drove all the way to Cartersville and had a very vigorous conversation with

Elizabeth. He indicated that my opposition to ERA was a "litmus" test imposed on me. Some of my campaign staff, along with Tom, felt that if they could get to her, then it would change me. I think there was an understanding at that meeting that it was not only my conviction, but this was our conviction. This was the way it was going to be. If that was going to eliminate my opportunity to be elected governor, then so be it. That was the position I had to take. In looking back, after all these years, I'm not sure that had the Equal Rights Amendment passed we would have had any more or any faster progress. Barriers have certainly been removed, and the problems that existed then are a lot less. Even though there is still work to be done, we've seen some positive developments.

Two Other Questions

Foremost in some people's minds, just as it is today, was the direction in which our state and nation were headed in reference to crime. Of course, we all strive for safe places to live and work; we want our state to be safe. I guess the two most asked questions during the time I was campaigning in 1982 were, one: Do you believe in capital punishment? Invariably, everywhere you would travel or hold a forum, this would be one of the first questions to come out. The second question was: Are you a lawyer? This was not long after the Watergate fiasco in Washington, D.C.; people were very skeptical of lawyers and felt like we had too many of them in elected office. They wanted to be sure that I was not. I *was* in favor of capital punishment and I was *not* a lawyer.

The Seventy-eighth Governor

By the general election on 2 November 1982, there was really no question. All the polls were overwhelmingly in our favor. I guess we entered into the night expecting to win; but, again, I still had that same reservation: Anything could happen. The office of governor belongs to the people, and they've got to make a choice. I always knew that I might not be the one that's chosen. It was kind of a sobering evening. We realized we had given it all we had and we could also lose it all. However, any trepidation about the election vanished as the results flashed up on the screen. Our efforts in the race against the Republican candidate, Bob Bell, had paid off with a gratifying 62.8 percent of the vote.

My feeling was certainly one of appreciation. The people attending that victory celebration had stood by me and worked extremely hard. A lot of them had contributed way beyond their means because they believed in what we were trying to do. We were willing to do what the Lord wanted us to do, and now we were being honored. I had been selected and was going to be the seventy-eighth person in the history of our state to serve as governor. It was also a realization that the campaign was over. I had told the people what I wanted to accomplish and what I thought I could do. Now I had to deliver.

It was an unbelievable feeling; even now I wake up some mornings and wonder if it was a dream. Was I really able to accomplish all the things that I intended to accomplish? You realize how you've been blessed and how, again if you're willing to make that first step and willing for the Lord to use you the possibilities of where you can go and what you can do are unlimited.

11

The Governor's Office

On Inauguration Day, 11 January 1983, we chose to return the swearing-in ceremony to the Capital steps. Governor George Busbee had moved both of his inaugural ceremonies into the Atlanta Civic Center. In early January, the weather is usually pretty bad and almost always cold. In fact, we had a bit of a minor confrontation with Speaker Tom Murphy because he liked to be inside and didn't want to subject the members of the House of Representatives to the weather. I guess I'm a little traditional and the state has historically held its inaugurations outdoors on the steps of the Capitol. The Speaker's objection was overcome by a special assignment given to Elizabeth. It was not only a matter on her prayer list; she also made a personal visit and in her loving way, convinced the Speaker to endure one more inauguration in the open.

We didn't want to spend the money that had been spent in the past building a large wooden platform. Steve Polk, who was the director of the Georgia Building Authority and a very resourceful and innovative person, had an old double-wide trailer platform that he pulled in, which made the platform space adequate enough. The platform was placed just in front of Tom Watson's statue. However, in order that "Tom Watson" wouldn't "interfere," the statue itself was enclosed in blue cloth with a big Georgia state seal on it. In years past the platform had been behind that statue, requiring that a large structure be built. The upshot was that we were able to get all of these preparations done effectively and a lot less expensively than in past years.

Praying for a Good Day

I'm not sure that we were ever able to "convince" Speaker Murphy, but eventually he supported our decision to move the ceremony outdoors, and of course he did attend. But for several weeks prior to the ceremony, he expressed his displeasure and couldn't understand why I had made this kind of decision to be out in the weather. Elizabeth, however, was in charge of the weather, and she had been praying for a good day.

Actually, that morning we did something that had not been done before. We had a prayer and dedication service at the Trinity United Methodist Church on Washington Street near the Capitol and invited all the General Assembly members and state officials. During that service, which included a sermon by Commissioner Andrew Miller of the Salvation Army, we dedicated our coming four years to the Lord and asked His blessings on our Administration. It was a spiritually satisfying time for us all and started the day off right. Afterwards, as we moved to the formal inauguration ceremony outside, the sun was shining and it was not really that cold (though a little chilly perhaps).

We started the ceremony just prior to noon and tried to time it so that the oath could be given as the clock struck 12:00 noon, when I officially took office. I've had an awful lot of emotional experiences over the years, and fond memories, but that was one of those incredible, indescribable feelings. I felt every syllable of my inauguration address, which opened: "This day began as a venture of faith for me and my family many months ago. Being governor of Georgia is a tremendous honor and an awesome responsibility that, with God's help, I accept."*

I knew that for the next four years I was going to be in charge of implementing the dreams and future plans I'd had for the state of Georgia. I also had a certain satisfaction in knowing that the long campaign had been successful and that eventually we would

---

*For the full text see Appendix A.

even be able to repay our campaign debts. But any feelings of satisfaction that I might have had were quickly diluted by the realization of the enormous obligation and responsibility that was before me. That really puts the occasion into a proper focus on inauguration day. Still, it was one of those experiences that you carry for a lifetime.

The Rest of the Day

I think another sobering moment came when, after the inauguration was completed and the swearing-in had taken place, the National Guard presented its traditional nineteen gun salute. They brought in cannons for the occasion, and while they did not of course use live ammunition, some people thought that Atlanta City Hall had been hit. There have always been a lot of pigeons around, and when the guns went off the birds went crazy. You'd have thought doves had been released at the opening ceremonies of the Olympics. The guns kept booming, rattling windows across at City Hall. (I think a few of the windows over there had to be replaced.)

That afternoon, after a brief family luncheon, I went into the governor's office and executed some orders that officially started the Harris administration. Then, I signed some other executive orders that were already prepared and appointed some members of the many boards. Next, we swore in the constitutional officers in the House chambers who were elected along with me. After that, I had a lot of formal duties to carry out, which stretched late into the afternoon.

The Governor's Ball that evening was held at the Atlanta Civic Center. There were bands and other entertainers and singers. Most of the entertainment was in the auditorium; the other part of the facility (later occupied by ScienceTrek museum) was all set up with food and a space for those who wanted to dance.

We did receive criticism from some of the media because we didn't serve alcoholic beverages at the Governor's Ball. Again, that was our conviction. In spite of that, everyone seemed to have enjoyed themselves; it was a festive time with plenty of quality entertainment, fine food, and good fellowship. The weather, which had stayed nice during the day, turned inclement that evening. A cold front arrived and with it came sleet and even some snow later that night. But it had held off for the inauguration ceremony, and for that we had both the Lord and Elizabeth to thank.

As the day ended, I did feel like we had arrived at a certain juncture, but that we had an awfully long way to go a tremendous responsibility ahead of us. Had I not had experience in the General Assembly and experience with the budget and had I not known many of the leaders in state government and not worked with them for many years, and had we not had mutual respect for each other, it would probably have been a very lonely time for me. I can't imagine just walking off the street without having had any experience at all and realizing "Well, I've got this responsibility now." It has been done many times, but it was reassuring to me to realize that I was well prepared to be governor on my first day in office. I campaigned on that message among others—that my experience would make unnecessary any "lag time" or on-the-job-training. I pretty well knew what to do.

Quiet Satisfaction

There were a lot of people who sincerely thought I could win, supported me, and felt very confident and very optimistic. Then there were those who sincerely supported me and felt I could make a race of it, but who doubted that I could win. They didn't really convey this until after it was over, then a lot of them pulled me aside and said something to the effect that "I supported you and contributed and attended the events and helped in the campaign, but I never thought you'd be able to do it." I have to admit that this provided me an awful lot of satisfaction. Some of those people were there from the very beginning when we could probably have held our campaign rallies in a phone booth. That's how many supporters we had in some of the towns I visited. But the people who did support me took the abuse from others who questioned what we were doing and chided them for supporting an unknown who "couldn't get elected anyway." Our supporters were able to go back to them and say "I told you so." That was probably one of the greatest feelings and moments of pride for me during the whole course of the campaign—to be able to give the people who had believed in me, had worked hard, and had been willing to pay the price for victory a chance to gloat.

We still owed a million dollars for the campaign, which was the money I had signed the notes for plus some initial funds that had been spent but hadn't yet been raised. I had a little bit of satisfaction knowing that if there was any way to raise that money, I would have a better opportunity of doing it as governor than as a defeated candidate. I had to feel good about that. I think it was proof that anyone who can qualify to run and get their name on the ballot has the potential to mount a campaign and be a winner. Now, that does not mean that anyone who gets on the ballot is going to be a winner. Funds are very hard to raise; but I don't think anyone is eliminated just because he or she is not endowed with money or great wealth.

Another source of satisfaction had to do with my parents. Mother and Dad had always been tremendously supportive of anything I've ever done. Of course, they were there, participating in the events of the inauguration. True to form, though, they always wanted to stay a step or two in the background. It's not Dad's nature to stand up and beat his chest and say "Look, that's my son." He was very reserved about it, but there were several opportunities during the inauguration that I really sensed my parents' pride, even without their saying a word. Mother, however, was not content to express her pride silently. A few days before going to Atlanta for the inauguration, I received a letter from her that read:

December 28, 1982

My Son,

Almost forty-seven years ago, as I held a little brown-eyed, dark headed baby boy in my arms, the second precious gift from

God, and felt that sincere love as only a Mother can, little did I know or dream how that life would turn out. As I saw that little timid, quiet boy grow—dreams to be a fireman, a policeman, all the things little boys dream . . . . but the big one was to be a "captain in the Army." Remember the little army uniform? Then, your drawing board—in the floor with paper and pencil—but big dreams that the talent to draw would pay off in drawing plans for real buildings, etc., in later years. The little boy that made friends then and love people. Remember the bicycle that was given to you at 5 years of age and the Norsworthy couple drove a hundred miles to bring it to you? That was real friendship. I'll always remember the little boy who always said to me when we dressed to go out, "Mother you look so pretty!"

Another mental picture I have is the two little boys out collecting *Preacher money* and was so happy to do it. Any way the *Wesleyan Christian Advocate* got your picture and did a "write up" on you and it went over the State. Was that your first Campaign start?

From age five that little boy wanted a little sister and finally would not tell what he wanted for Christmas, only a baby sister. That prayer was answered, and he loved and cared for her even in her 13th year to loan her his car one day—tho she didn't bring it back on time—remember?

Then through High School and to College and I remember putting a note in your shoe and in it I wrote: please keep your good name and if you have to lower your standard, quit and come home for I'd rather you were ignorant and good than to be highly educated and lose your good name and your soul. You went and had fun (too much at times) but no scandal and desired to keep the good name, going to church regular tho a college student, having given your life to Christ and joining the church at an early age and have not only grown in knowledge but have grown in spirit being led by His Spirit and not ashamed of your religion and your stand for Christ, nor your humble beginning the hard work and sacrifices through the years which has proven a blessing, the deep understanding and love for others and I pray, tho the honor is yours and the prestige is there, that you will never lose your love and devotion for others desire to help the old, the weak and afflicted for love and humility are God's greatest gifts, I think.

Your hometown for these almost forty-seven years will greatly miss you, and I shudder when I think of *me* and how I will miss you all, but at last I rise to say Bartow County has been highly honored to have you grow up here and didn't know it. And the State is about to share the high honor of getting a Governor that not only has knowledge to guide the State, but salvation and dedication to pray for them and I say thank God for His love and guidance through the years and we cannot fail Him now!

> Courage dear, do not stumble,
> Tho' your path be dark as night.
> There's a light to guide the humble,
> Trust in God and do the right.

God bless you!

> Love,
> Mother

Of course, I had satisfaction at having been successful in this campaign, but it was so much more meaningful that it was something that made my parents proud. I think any child wants that kind of feeling somewhere along the way. I feel fortunate to have experienced it.

All in the Family

Going into that first term as governor, I think I was probably as prepared physically and mentally as anybody could be and so it was not a big shock to me. But I knew the schedule was going to be tremendously intense and that my family was going to be deeply affected by it. There was no way after you run a campaign and gain that degree of exposure throughout the state that you can ever really go back to where you used to be. Win, lose, or draw, you still couldn't return to that "unnoticed" status again. I was fully exposed and my life as a private citizen was gone.

There are several major concerns that I think anyone would have who is about to assume a position of that magnitude, intensity, and responsibility. My foremost concern was, of course, being sure my relationships with my family were maintained and that I didn't get so consumed in my role as governor that I didn't have time to be a husband and father. I intended to see that these relationships were maintained and with the good Lord's help, they were. I am very blessed to have a wife who was willing to make the kind of major sacrifices that it took not only to campaign but to serve and fill the responsible place that she did as First Lady. Not only was Elizabeth my sounding board and closest advisor, she was the person responsible for all the functions and duties at the Governor's Mansion—awesome responsibility.

Being governor also affects your children. However, I think we were able to utilize the time we could set aside, which wasn't that much, as quality family time. We had grown accustomed to this kind of life over the eighteen years I had been in the General Assembly. Also, in the days when we were operating a business, we didn't have a lot of vacation time, and had often tried to incorporate vacation with legislative functions that would include family. So we had already become accustomed to doing those kinds of things together, and after I became governor, we naturally tried to continue to find some quality time just to be a family.

Growing Up in Politics

Our son Joe was just entering the University of Georgia, and he naturally felt the impact of the position I held and the notoriety I received. If you've done something to please people, they often indicate that to your children. Conversely, when you've done things people don't agree with, they indicate that also. Your children have to be able to handle that. We were very blessed that Joe had grown up in politics. He was a baby, just a few months old, when I first qualified to run and was elected to the General

Assembly. He was able, however, to develop an understanding and a knowledge that were helpful to him. I don't know of any young son who could have handled it better than Joe. He made us proud all along the way and never did a single thing that brought embarrassment or reflected poorly on our administration or that was picked up or reported in the press. This has not been the case with a number of people who have occupied these kinds of elected positions over the years. This was an area that I was very careful and very concerned about.

Joe made it through college, then law school, and went into law practice. Thus far he has been successful in all of those areas including marriage. He married the former Brooke Gurley while he was still living in the Governor's Mansion. The wedding reception was held there as well. It was a beautiful event and one in which we were very pleased and proud to participate. Today, Joe and Brooke are the parents of our two grandchildren, Catherine Elizabeth and Thomas Kimsey Harris. They have added a new title for me, 'Grandfather,' and an additional joy to our family.

We were very fortunate that our family really was not infringed upon to the point that it affected our private lives. Now, this was not something that just came naturally; it was something we were willing to work hard to protect because it was just too important.

12

Hit the Ground Running

After I had been governor for several weeks, a letter came in the mail that had a twenty dollar bill enclosed. The letter started out "Dear Governor, several years ago I didn't pay all my income taxes that were due. Recently, my conscience has been bothering me and I can't sleep. Enclosed please find this twenty dollar bill as payment on the taxes that I owe." The letter was unsigned. Down at the bottom, it said "P.S. If after sending this twenty dollars to you, I *still* can't sleep, I'll send you the rest of it." I don't recall receiving the rest of it, but we did deposit the twenty dollar bill in the proper place.

It is an awesome responsibility when you realize that the buck stops with you. It can be a lonely place at times. You're isolated and insulated, to some degree, by the protocol of the office and the necessary security. I guess if I had not had the reassurance of knowing that there was a higher authority, that the Lord was there with me, it would have gotten a lot lonelier. I believe in prayer and exercised it many times every day. I remembered something I had read many years ago that Abraham Lincoln had said that he often found no other place to go except to his knees. I'm glad I had that One to turn to, that place to go to. It made me realize that I was not there alone.

I guess our administration was somewhat predetermined coming out of the campaign, because that's when our priorities were established the priorities upon which we campaigned, received the majority of votes, and got elected. You could almost boil it down to two basic issues: Education was my first priority and it was number one on everybody's mind. Next was the state's economic development, because we were in a slow economic period and people were apprehensive about it. They were not only looking for more jobs in the economy, they were also looking for a little job security of their own.

There were, of course, other issues on the table. One of these was the issue of prison space and other problems in our prison system, e.g., getting the Federal government and courts out of one of our state prisons. (They had taken over and were actually dictating operations of the prison down in Reidsville, a problem left over from the previous administration) The prison system was another of our priorities, and it had to be dealt with effectively.

Our state had seen considerable growth. The population of the state had grown from four to 5.5 million people over the eighteen years that I had been in the General Assembly. Already I had a good deal of "hands-on" experience in state government and had been involved with the issues. I knew the people there and the leadership that had remained, as well as the personalities with whom we were going to have to work if we were to be successful.

As I had campaigned on that experience acknowledging the fact that I could be a governor the first day I entered office without a "training period," I felt I would know what to do. I could hit the ground running and that was basically what we did operating and moving state government forward without any lag time or lapse in the operations of ongoing programs. We didn't have to gain momentum to reach a reasonable speed of operation. It was wide open from the very first day.

When I was inaugurated, the staff appointments had already been decided. We knew who was going to be in what position. There had already been quite a bit of planning, and those chosen were ready to move forward. In a special sense, I had organized the governor's office as you would a corporation. I looked at myself as the chairman of the board and chief executive officer of the State. The president of the corporation was like my senior executive assistant: This was the person just under me who would exercise and carry out the authority of the governor's office; it was to the senior executive assistant that I would delegate authority to carry out the policies that were established. The parameters were set just as in any corporate or business operation.

The vice presidents were similar to senior staff members. They had their assigned "territory" and the agencies with whom they would be working. Constituent responsibilities were going to remain where each of these people were assigned. They were ready and eager to operate in that fashion. Everyone understood his or her responsibilities, what authority they had, how to exercise it, and how to stay within the boundaries of the policies (and politics) that had been established by the governor's office. We were prepared, and I think the productivity and results of our staff and the people that had arrived with me attest to that fact.

A Few Hitches

During Inaugural Week almost everything becomes a minor crisis because it's usually not something you've dealt with before, and the staff has not had hands-on experience in the governor's office. There was a bit of a feeling of panic: Are we doing this right or is this the way we're supposed to respond or handle this?

There's always something unique that you remember about almost any speaking engagement. I have to watch out sometimes, when I'm giving a speech, because I talk with my hands and am apt to knock a microphone off a podium. My first crisis after being sworn into the governor's office was that the wind blew away some of the pages of my text as I delivered the inaugural address. Frantically, I was able to hold on to most of them and made it through the speech. Fortunately, it was a short inaugural address. You don't want to bore people with a long speech, especially when they're out in thirty-degree weather.

Then, a bigger crisis occurred. That very first week, the governor's car was stolen. That created a crisis, particularly for Captain Jerry Wheeler, head of my security. I was speaking to a group of attorneys at one of the downtown hotels. I never will forget that after the speech the security person assigned to me that day came up and said, "governor, I need to tell you something." I thought he was going to tell me we were running late and needed to hurry back to the capital. Very apprehensively he told me our car was gone. I couldn't believe it. Here I was being protected by security and somebody had stolen the car from security.

Actually, we had driven up to the front of the hotel, and the doorman suggested that our driver pull the car up and that we go on in and find our places, which the driver did. The keys were left in the car. Before the doorman could get to the car, someone else walked up and drove it off. The State Patrol's radios, the telephones, and other security equipment were all in the car. Every day that passed with the car still missing was an embarrassment.

Finally, the local police found it parked in a housing project not far from the hotel. The only thing missing was the battery. All the radios and equipment were intact. The people in the housing development said they thought the car looked "out of place" but surely belonged to somebody who lived there. The license plate had numbers for security purposes, but the average person wouldn't know that it was different from a regular automobile. We put in a new battery and after a thorough inspection it was ready to go. The entire incident caused me to have some second thoughts about my personal security, and I couldn't help but think that the public must be having second thoughts, too. But we survived that crisis. I threatened security that I was going to take a 'log chain' with me, find a fire plug, and hook up the car the way you used to tie a horse to a hitching post. That way, no one could take my car. Eventually, we were able to laugh about it. A lot of kidding went on about that and more than a few jokes stemmed from this incident.

Life in the Mansion

During that first week, I guess the most frequently asked question was how long did it take us to get used to living in the Governor's Mansion? My answer to that question was that on the first night we were there, I guess I stayed awake maybe fifteen or twenty seconds making that transition; after that it was no problem. We had actually moved in about a week before the swearing-in ceremony. It was good of Governor Busbee to give us that time in order that we could get acclimated and move in our personal possessions. We returned the favor to my successor Zell

Miller and his wife, Shirley, when we left office. (We vacated a week before, and allowed some time so that renovations and repairs could be made, and the Millers would not have to move in on inauguration day.)

All we needed were our clothes, and we just moved right in. It's a beautiful home, and we felt very fortunate that the state of Georgia has that kind of facility. It's a real tool for economic development and for entertaining, particularly foreign dignitaries. Protocol is so very important to many people. Georgians do not have to apologize at all for our facility. I don't believe a single invitation was ever extended during the whole time we lived in the Mansion that people didn't respond to or accept.

The Governor's Mansion serves the state very well. At the time it was built (in 1967), I was a member of the General Assembly, and it was probably one of the most controversial projects that I experienced during that period. The funds were allocated and set aside to build the Mansion. At the time almost everyone who had been denied an appropriations request for a project or an improve blamed the Mansion project for getting their money. The average person on the street finds it difficult to sympathize with spending a couple of million dollars to build a home for the governor. Not many people in Georgia have homes that cost several million dollars. But it is important to remember that the facility belongs to all the citizens of Georgia. It represents the state in a multitude of ways and, of course, the property it sits on (eighteen acres) was practically donated to the state. We probably never could have allocated the money to build it had it not been for that gift and many others. Governor Carl Sanders and his wife, Betty, deserve much credit for building such a magnificent facility. The Mansion was dedicated in January 1968.

I will always remember our first Christmas there. We established the practice of having a "tree lighting" event with a big Christmas tree and decorations and inviting the public in for the ceremony, initially to the front steps and lawn. We had a choir or choral group perform and someone to read an appropriate biblical passage and give the devotional or an inspirational Christmas message. At the high note of the carol, *O Holy Night*, the tree was lit and everyone would be invited inside for refreshments and a reception. Depending on the weather, sometimes hundreds of people would turn out.

When they entered the Mansion and enjoyed the creative and elegant decorations, we would invite them into the ballroom on the lower floor. This is quite a nice space for entertaining and having state dinners and the like. It is an excellent room for receptions and special occasions.

That first Christmas, Elizabeth and I were standing at the entrance, greeting people, shaking hands as they arrived. A small Brownie Scout troop came in with their leader. One little girl in particular, who had a gap where her front teeth had been, walked up to me, looked up and smiled, said "If you're as rich as they say you are, how rich are you?" I knew she was looking at the beautiful Mansion, the white columns out front, and the antique furnishings inside, and she thought they all belonged to me. I tried to explain to her that "this home does not belong to me, it really belongs to you and all the people of Georgia." When I told her this, she looked quite puzzled, as if to say "Well, I don't live here. This can't belong to me. My parents are not residents here." She looked over at her leader for clarification and the scout leader said, "Don't worry, Governor, I'll explain it to her. Everything will be fine." About an hour later, when we were still in the entranceway saying goodbye to people as they were leaving, the little girl walked up to me again, extended her hand one more time and said, "Governor, you take care of my house now, you hear?"

There's a hidden agenda involved in the operations of the Mansion that the public doesn't really know about. In fact, it's almost like operating a hotel. It's such a public place, and even the private residence on the top floor is not really very private. You constantly have staff moving through. The custodial people are all state prisoners. You're protected by security twenty-four hours a day but have prisoners working and moving freely throughout your home. This was an adjustment, but it works well. You understand very quickly what's required and how to deal with those things.

In our case, it was the governor's wife who assumed responsibility for running the Mansion. There were sometimes several functions a day at the Mansion, and often large numbers of people that have to be fed, entertained, or both. The house and grounds must be properly maintained for these occasions and the staff must be supervised. Elizabeth, had to learn how to become a manager, a role to which she was not accustomed. She had never before "hired or fired" anyone, much less supervised a staff of people. It was quite a rude awakening for her, but she did an outstanding job. She had grown up in a Methodist parsonage which was a good experience for her because she had always lived in houses where everything, including furnishings, belonged to someone else. She had also married into a business family and understood the "bottom line" that said if you can't afford it, you don't buy it. If the money's not allocated, then you don't spend it. She had to live within those regulations and fiscal restraints established by the General Assembly and did very well indeed.

A Potpourri of Projects

Elizabeth had several projects that she initiated that not only added a lot of character and quality to the Mansion but made it more pleasing to our many visitors. She would actually give me trees for my birthday. These trees were planted on the Mansion grounds, and many of them are still thriving today. She wanted the Mansion to have the fruit trees and the kinds of trees that are representative of our state. The word went out and donations of trees came in, and she planted many kinds of trees. Vegetables, especially tomatoes, green beans, corn and okra, and even blueberries were found growing in the Mansion gardens. One year the peach crop was so great, she recruited every available staff person, troopers included, to peel peaches for the freezer. These were enjoyed at many an elegant dinner.

Jim Gibbs and Steve Murray with Gibbs Landscaping contributed considerable knowledge and expertise in helping to rejuvenate the landscape and bring back into proper alignment some of the shrubbery which had become overgrown. They also helped with tree plantings and beautifying many overgrown areas particularly around the tennis court. Callaway Gardens, especially Executive Vice President and Director, Dr. Bill Barrick, the Garden Clubs of Georgia, the Rhododendron and Rose Societies, and many other organizations an individuals gave donations and gifts of plants and helped with hours of labor to add to the beauty of the grounds and the Mansion.

The Rose Gardens were Elizabeth's favorites. It was a special friend, Pete Pike of Pike's Nurseries, who donated over four-hundred rose bushes, including most of the different varieties dominant in Georgia. These were labeled and designated with their proper names to assist our visitors. Not wasting a thing, she would also take the spent rose petals, dry them in the Mansion boiler room, and make potpourri to be tucked into elegant needlework or lace sachets that were representative of the sweet smell of our peach state. These special touches of Georgia would be given to the wives of the foreign dignitaries and others as we traveled abroad or exchanged gifts with them when they visited Georgia. This was another operation that took time to prepare but created a lot of good will. Elizabeth loves people and this was reflected in the way she handled a multitude of situations.

As members of the General Assembly for eighteen years before we were elected to the governor's office, we had been to the Mansion many times over the years. But we had never been there alone to walk around and see what was really there, the kinds of antiques and other furnishings. We found that the Mansion had been blessed with probably the most representative group of Federal period antiques of any collection anywhere, particularly in the South. Their value has increased tremendously over recent years. Some of the paintings and furniture are of extremely high value now. It is amazing how the value increased from the time they were contributed or donated to the state. A lot of it was purchased very reasonably when the Mansion was built. However, the value now of just the furnishings is in the several millions of dollars. Of course, the value of the whole facility has increased tremendously since it was built. It is prime property, located in the middle of Buckhead. It couldn't be replaced today monetarily. Getting an appropriation approved by the General Assembly today to build a Governor's Mansion at that level of expense would be impossible.

No More Books "By the Yard"

On the first evening we were there, we were walking around together after dinner, just looking at the beautiful antiques. We ended up in the front-room library. I started looking at the books on the shelves and didn't recognize many titles. Neither did Elizabeth. We inquired about it later and found that many of the books were actually purchased "by the yard" just to fill the shelves and look nice. They didn't really have any real application to Georgia.

Elizabeth's idea was that wouldn't it be great if we could fill all those shelves with first editions by Georgia authors, or books about, or representative of, or pertaining to the state of Georgia. Shortly thereafter, Celestine Sibley (a friend from our early legislative years and a respected author and columnist for the *Atlanta Constitution*) wrote an article making reference to Elizabeth's idea, and soon the books started coming. When they did, we started moving the other books off the shelves and replacing them with books which had some reason to be there. It has now grown into an excellent collection. Sandy Candler and others worked part-time cataloging all of these books. A little later the catalogue was put on the computer. It can be accessed through the Georgia archives and its reference department. Elizabeth's determination has brought in hundreds of volumes practically all first editions, many of them autographed by the authors. The value and size of this collection has grown since we were there. I hope it will continue to develop into the next century.

13

Our Highest Priority

The attitude of the average person is that when someone enters the governor's office, they just walk in and take power. I've never looked upon it as "taking" anything. My estimation is that you've got to *earn* the power of that office. The people have given you the opportunity to enter the office. However, to earn it, you've got to have not only a staff capable of exercising the authority, but programs with which people can identify, along with an understanding of the needs they want to see addressed during your Administration. Of course, education was one of my top priorities established during the campaign.

As a candidate for governor, I had called a press conference at the Capitol. A press conference called by a candidate is usually not very well attended. There are a dozen other candidates all competing for attention, all with access to the Capitol. But I always remember the remark I made that day, which was that "A student in Georgia, a young person in Georgia, certainly has a right to a quality basic education."

A Right to QBE

My reference was in support of the idea that they should have the elementary opportunity to learn how to read, write, comprehend, and communicate—the foundation that you can build on in continuation of the learning process, which is a lifelong pursuit. Out of such an emphasis on quality basic education came the program passed by the General Assembly after much study by the Education Review Commission, which had been established in January 1983.

I was determined that any revision of the educational system was not going to come from just the professional educators. This had been done in the past and had proven to be inadequate. There had been several revisions about every ten years regardless of who might have been in the governor's office. We started with the Georgia Minimum Foundation Education program, or MFPE, and updated it during the Sanders Administration. Ten years later, during the Carter Administration, we came back with the APEG or Adequate Plan for Education in Georgia. I wanted something a little more than the minimum. I wanted something that was not only adequate but something that could build more quality. Thus, we came up with the QBE or the Quality Basic Education program.

I had determined that since it would last ten years or longer, the review commission should come from a cross-section of the state. We called it our Educational Review Commission. It was made up of thirty-five people. We appointed black, white, male, female, professional, non-professional, just plain laborers, house-wives, and others to serve on that Commission. Subsequently, I was able to sell my dream to Ed Harris (no relation to me), who was the partner in Price Waterhouse, an accounting firm in Atlanta. He accepted the chairmanship of the commission.

The Review Commission spent hundreds of hours reviewing all the laws pertaining to education as of that date. They tried to project what our needs would be twenty or thirty years in the future. Then they put together a funding formula that would suffice and avoid court challenges which so many other states were experiencing because of the inequities within the funding formulas between the more affluent and more impoverished areas. Our formula was devised by the Review Commission. They also revised the core curriculum. We had some systems around the state that didn't teach enough academic courses. The existing curriculum was not structured strongly enough, and students were not being properly prepared to enter college. Others had such a broad-based curriculum that they couldn't do a good job with all of it. Or they were offering too much. Hence, we tried to arrive at an average or standard for everybody that included the seventy-six competencies and skills that are designed to help all learners think clearly, be effective citizens, be employable, and be lifelong learners.

No Negative Votes

The Education Bill weighed in at about one hundred and fifty pages when it was presented in the General Assembly. While it was being prepared to be introduced in the House, I'll always remember that when the bill was printed Speaker Murphy made one of his somewhat "determined"' visits to the governor's office. When he came in, I knew he had something very important on his mind, and I invited him to have a seat. At first, he had very little to say, though I knew he wanted to discuss the education bill, because I recognized it in his hand. He walked over to the coffee table in the office and threw the bill with a loud thud on the coffee table and said, "I don't know who you've been listening to, but if you think you're going to pass that bunch of trash through this General Assembly, you've got another thought coming!"

I had to treat him with due respect and, of course, he had been my friend for years and still is. There were many things about which we disagreed, but usually we could find a common ground and continued being friends. But that was the way he had of expressing to me that support in the House was pretty weak. There were some who still had serious questions. He wanted to be sure that those questions were cleared up, and we were prepared to do that. I tried to explain that to the Speaker and don't know how well I did that day. Speaker Murphy has always been an important player in the process of trying to improve education. Eventually, with his help, we moved that bill not only through the House but through the Senate, through the Conference Committee reports in both houses, where it was considered a total of four times in the two bodies without a single negative vote. Now, in the history of Georgia, I don't think anything of that magnitude has ever had that type of success! This has to be my proudest moment of legislative victories. The Quality Based Education Act was signed on 16 April 1985.

There are several reasons for that. I mean, even in a motion to adjourn, you're always going to have people voting "no" or expressing opposition to most any motion. There are very few times that anything will pass without a single dissenting vote at every step. I look back on this with great satisfaction, knowing that it was accomplished not only through our hard work and that of the Educational Review Commission, but also through another group that was formed during that time, Georgians for Excellence in Education, headed by John Clendenin who was the chairman of the board of Bell South and supported by the Georgia Chamber of Commerce.

The business community joined in support of this "blue ribbon" group. They not only helped raise money to campaign for the revised education program for our state, but they helped to carry the campaign around the state, from bumper stickers to posters and placards to speakers who would take assignments and go into the communities and explain what was happening and what we were trying to do by soliciting and eliciting the support of all Georgians. It was almost like a regular political campaign that generated enthusiasm and took on a life of its own. I think most of the General Assembly members were really fearful of going back home, having voted against something as "apple pie and motherhood" as that revision in education! Basically, I felt we had one window of opportunity, and maybe we helped to create that window by laying the groundwork. People were receptive and ready for it. We moved into the vacuum with something to offer and they accepted it.

Teachers in Georgia have always been underpaid in comparison to our region and the nation as a whole. We were in the process of trying to address that deficit and during our Administration we were able to increase teachers' salaries every single year. We had an almost seventy percent increase (which led the nation) during the time that I was governor. The ranking of our state moved considerably forward in comparison to other states. In fact, we moved from forty-seventh up into the twenties in comparison with teachers' salaries and resources in other states. We put over two billion new dollars into education during that period of time, building or improving over eleven hundred schools across our state. My plan for education was outlined to the General Assembly on 16 January

1985. Never before in the history of the state had the governor of Georgia appeared before a joint session to make an address exclusively on education.

Capitol Celebration

The unanimous passage of our education reform (QBE) and the enthusiastic support of all across the state dictated a special signing ceremony and celebration at the Capitol on 16 April 1985. All of the education leaders along with the members of the General Assembly, joined the Education Review Commission on the steps of the west entrance to the Capitol in the same area where my inauguration was held. The size of the crowd spilled off the Capitol grounds out onto the street. In fact, it looked almost like a rerun of my inauguration because many of the same faces were there along with the balloons, bands, and a festive atmosphere. In my remarks, just prior to the signing of the huge bill, I stated: "From this day forward there will be a new standard of education achievement, a new standard of performance, and new budgetary support." I further declared that, "A quality education is the basic right of every child in Georgia no matter where they reside and we have taken steps to ensure this in the future."

I can look back and realize my optimism on that day was well founded, because progress has been (and continues to be) made. However, this progress has been at a much slower pace than I had hoped for. We had a long ways to go, and still do, but I can remember how far we have come.

Highlights

QBE was a commitment to excellence that not only included an educational opportunity for all students but mandated a new funding program focusing on student success. While helping students perform better in the classroom, there was a uniform environment for students statewide. For the first time in our history, a full-day kindergarten was available to all students to improve "school readiness" determined to be one of our most important educational needs. Criterion-referenced and Basic Skills testing along with norm-referenced tests would provide teachers, parents, and the public with information about the achievements of Georgia's students. In order for the teachers to be professionally certified, they were mandated to pass the Teacher Certification Test, demonstrating proficiency in the subjects they teach.

Teachers Are the Key

Regardless of how well you build a facility and the kind of materials and surroundings you can provide, unless you've got a quality classroom teacher who is able to communicate with students, you're not going to be successful. I felt from my own personal experiences over the years that whatever we could do to enhance or enable a quality, experienced teacher to be in that classroom, this would be the secret of our success if we were going to have any success. We moved immediately to raise beginning salaries in order to attract a better qualified teachers and also to provide a means of testing those teachers. Having a college degree didn't automatically mean they had the ability to be a good teacher. This brought more responsibility for those qualifying for jobs. Teachers are the key and the experience they had before arriving in the classroom, their commitment after they get there, and the experience they receive in the classroom are also critically important.

Quick-start Training

While education remained our number one priority, our second highest priority was economic development, or as we liked to call it, "jobs for Georgians." When you've got money as salaries or wages flowing to an individual or into a community, you've got people who are not only tax-paying citizens, but people who are becoming more educated themselves. They are able to afford better opportunities for their families and higher standards of living, housing, automobile, travel, and recreation. So if you've got a plan for education, and you're able to bring in the kind of jobs that will help to fund that plan, you can move forward. I have always felt that our average SAT scores were directly related to the incomes of families.

We had determined in our Administration that as much as possible we were going to target and assist those areas that needed help the most. We learned early on that no matter how much you might try at the state level, you cannot bring an industrial prospect to a local community and close the deal. You can carry the prospect to the local community, but they have to close the deal. Unless they've got a unified group, including their schools, governmental agencies, chambers of commerce, and average citizens all working together, there is no way that you can introduce a prospect to them and be successful. "Unity in the Community" became a code word of our Administration. Often delegations from across Georgia would visit the governor's office complaining that we brought their neighboring county or neighboring city an industry but had not secured one for them. We would have to spend a few minutes explaining that we didn't really bring them anything except an opportunity for them to make the sale, which they did. We assured them that we could bring the same kind of prospects to their community, if they could handle it and take the order when it got there. Some cities and counties are simply more skillful and able to put together this kind of unified effort, taking the order or making the sale when the opportunity came. This did not keep us from trying to work with these other communities and help them develop successful tools. We spent an awful lot of time trying to do that and overall we were very successful, because a large majority of the new jobs we helped create were outside the metro area where it really counted.

Usually, a criterion is already established when a business prospect is looking for a location. They want natural and environmental resources that are necessary for their operation, like water and sewage, electrical current, natural gas, among others. If that's available and ready in a community, you eliminate those things as a negative. Of course, good schools and good transportation are important. They often want railroad access and good roads but not necessarily interstates. They would also need an available, trainable work force, and the "Quick Start Training Program" to address that need, which was improved and expanded during my Administration.

Our state developed what is probably one of the finest programs in the United States for attracting prospects and training their people, once they chose Georgia. We sent our representatives around the world, if necessary, to learn what kind of training their industry would require in a community. We would then go back to our technical education, and "Quick Start" professionals to design the kind of training program either on site or in facilities that were available in the local community. The locating industry had the option of choosing the applicants who were best qualified for their purposes. We came up with the innovation that if these people, after they were hired, were not proficient or could not perform up to reasonable expectations, then we would re-train them at no cost to the company. This did not happen to my knowledge, but it sounded good. This was an alternative that proved to be a good sales tool, almost a money-back guarantee.

We had a commitment in our Administration that we would not chase just "any smoke stack" coming down the pike or bring just any kind of industry to the state, regardless of expense or future problems. We were trying to be as selective as possible, and not simply court every prospect who would seek out Georgia. If their industry didn't fit, we would try to find the ones that would be compatible.

Providing an Oasis

We built 142 new libraries, and these were not small libraries. This was a new program that resulted in the building of more libraries than at any other period in the history of the state. Many existing library facilities were also improved or expanded. The average cost of each project was over one million dollars each. When you put a million dollars into a library in a small community, I believe you've built something that is going to remain there forever. I can't remember a library ever being closed. It would be expanded, but you would never see a library just shut down. It is an oasis for learning in that community. It also becomes a facility where people can gather for civic and other meetings. The program became a very solid investment for the state a legacy that I'm very proud was left by our Administration.

On accepting an award from the Georgia Council of Public Libraries on 8 September 1988, I said, in part,

> When I ran for governor in 1982, I put education at the top of the agenda. The accumulation of information, the acquisition of knowledge, and the application of that knowledge to solve problems or enhance life are principal functions of our education system. Libraries offer a great range of resource materials that greatly enrich education and increase the knowledge and understanding of all Georgians.

"The Wedding"
Faith United Methodist Church, Cartersville, Georgia, June 25, 1961
L-R Elizabeth Keeney Carlock, Joe Frank Harris

Joe Frank Harris
78th Governor of Georgia

Victory Celebration
November 2, 1982 Atlanta, Ballroom Dunfey's Hotel
L-R (front) Elizabeth Harris, Joe Frank Harris, Joe Harris
L-R (rear) Speaker Tom Murphy, Lt. Gov. Zell Miller

Visit in Governor's Office on Inaguration Day
January 11, 1983
L-R President Jimmy Carter, Governor Joe Frank Harris

1983 Inaugural Ball and Gala
January 11, 1983
L-R Frank G. Harris (Father), Glenda Gambill (Sister), First Lady Elizabeth Harris, Governor Joe Frank Harris

Entering the Governor's Office for the first time as Governor and First Lady
Inauguration Day, January 11, 1983, L-R Governor Joe Frank Harris, First Lady Elizabeth Harris

1987 Inauguration
January 13, 1987, Oath of Office Administered by Judge Robert
Benham, Court of Appeals, Now Chief Justice of Supreme Court.
L-R Judge Robert Benham, Joe Harris, Elizabeth Harris,
Governor Joe Frank Harris

Welcome to Georgia!
L-R President Ronald Reagan, First Lady Elizabeth Harris,
Governor Joe Frank Harris

Visit with President and Mrs. George Bush
September 1989
L-R Governor Joe Frank Harris, First Lady Barbara Bush,
President George Bush

**Reverend Billy Graham, 1987 Governor's Prayer Breakfast
Speaker**
L-R Reverand Billy Graham, First Lady Elizabeth Harris,
Governor Joe Frank Harris

1988 Democratic National Convention Reception
L-R Governor Joe Frank Harris, First Lady Elizabeth Harris

**1988 Democratic National Convention Atlanta
Committee Co-Chairs**
L-R Michael Lomax, Chairman, Fulton County
Commissioners, Joe Frank Harris, Governor, State
of Georgia, and Andrew Young, Mayor, City of
Atlanta

First Lady Elizabeth Harris in a Brumby Rocker at the Georgia Governor's Mansion

Legislative Dinner
1990 State Drawing Room, Governor's Mansion
L-R First Lady Elizabeth Harris, Governor Joe Frank Harris

1986 St. Patrick's Day Parade
Savannah, Georgia
L-R Governor Joe Frank Harris, First Lady Elizabeth Harris

The Parents and Son of Governor Joe Frank Harris
Family Dining Room, Governor's Mansion, March 21, 1987
L-R Joe Harris, Son, Frances M. Harris, Mother, and Frank G. Harris, Father

Sharing the 1996 Olympic Dream with Billy Payne
L-R Joe Frank Harris, Elizabeth Harris, Billy Payne, President and Chief
Executive Officer, Atlanta Committee for the Olympic Games

President Bush honors Atlanta Olympic Committee at White House
1990, L-R Dr. Harvey Schiller, Executive Director, United States
Olympic Committee; Andrew Young, Chairman, Atlanta Organizing
Committee; Governor Harris; President Bush; Billy Payne, President,
Atlanta Organizing Committee; Anita DeFrantz, Executive Director,
Los Angeles Amateur Athletic Foundation; Robert Helmick, President
of the United States Olympic Committee.

His Majesty, The Emperor Akihito and Empress Michiko
Tokyo, 1986

World Heavyweight Boxing Champion
1990
L-R Evander Holyfield, Governor Joe Frank Harris

The World of Coca-Cola Dedication
1990 With the Children of the World
L-R Governor Joe Frank Harris, Roberto Goizueta, Chairman
and CEO Coca-Cola, Don Keough, President Coca-Cola,
Maynard Jackson, Mayor, City of Atlanta.

Harris Administration Senior Staff
L-R William Suttles, Rick Stancil, Tom Lewis, Governor Harris, Gracie
Greer Phillips, Jackey Beavers, Rosemary Preston, John Sibley, Stanley
Gunter, and Nellie Hoenes. Not pictured: Mike deVegter, Susan Kahn,
Lewis Massey, Barbara Morgan, Tom Perdue, Steve Rieck, Mark Sanders,
Rusty Sewell, and Bill Tomlinson.

Georgia's First Family
State Drawing Room, Governors Mansion, 1990
L-R Governor Joe Frank Harris, First Lady Elizabeth Harris, Brooke Harris,
Joe Harris

**Enjoying the beauty of the North Georgia Mountains near Sky
Valley**
Fall 1989
L-R Governor Joe Frank Harris, First Lady Elizabeth Harris

The First Family
1987
L-R Joe Harris, Governor Joe Frank Harris, First Lady Elizabeth Harris

Harris Family
Thanksgiving 1990

Dedication of The Governor Joe Frank and Elizabeth Harris Boulevard
Georgia National Fairgrounds & Agricenter, Perry, Georgia
October 8, 1997
L-R Brooke Harris, Joe Harris, Catherine Harris, Elizabeth Harris, Joe Frank
Harris

The inscription on the bust reads as follows:

GOVERNOR JOE FRANK HARRIS

Joe Frank Harris served as Governor of Georgia for two terms, from 1983-1991.
His administration is noted for improvements in education with the Quality Basic
Education Act and for economic development with more than 850,000 new jobs. He
played a key role in the successful bid to hold the 1996 Summer Olympics in
Atlanta.

Before his election as Governor, he served 18 years as a member of the Georgia
House of Representatives. In his last eight years in the House, he served as
Chairman of the Appropriations Committee, a position in which he became the
acknowledged expert on the state budget.

The Harris Administration was marked by his strong moral stands arising from
a deep religious faith and belief in the power of prayer.

THE GOVERNOR JOE FRANK AND ELIZABETH HARRIS
BOULEVARD DEDICATION
October 8, 1997

In recognition and appreciation for Governor Harris' steadfast support of the
Georgia National Fairgrounds & Agricenter. Without his support this world-class
facility would not have been possible.

14

Taking Care of Business

I have a basic philosophy in fiscal management, some thing I learned while growing up and working to make a living: You can't borrow yourself out of debt, and you can't spend money you don't have. A business or a government can't do this either. My philosophy is that if you were not able to buy something, then you work until you get yourself into a position where you can afford it. You simply do without during the interval. I think we're seeing that businesses and government organizations are successful because someone is taking a lead in that kind of management.

Durable Assets

After I was elected to the General Assembly and got familiar with the state budgetary process, I realized more than ever that the funds you borrow are, in a sense, spending today for our children and grandchildren to repay tomorrow. When the government issues bonds for the funds that they are borrowing, the interest paid on that money sometimes actually costs more than the principal you are spending.

Another of our financial rules was not to spend money on projects that would not remain. For example, if you borrowed money for twenty years, that capital outlay or asset should still be there twenty years later or you should have some equity or value remaining. I've even seen attempts to borrow money for paving and repaving roads in which the asphalt would last maybe twelve years and you'd still be paying on it for twenty-five years.

Another principle that I tried to operate with was anytime you could reduce your debt and utilize additional or extra revenue to buy back or pay-off old bonds, there would be an additional savings beyond being fiscally responsible. It's awfully easy to go to the market and borrow money because the debt service that is required for repayment is only 1/20th of the total amount to be paid on that loan. You could put up a million dollars for one year's debt service and borrow ten million dollars to be repaid over twenty years. Of course, it is easier to borrow money and spend, leaving a debt for future generations, than to be fiscally responsible and manage within the available funds. It is very important to live within your means. this will prevent a problem with both your bond ratings and repayment requirements in later years.

Familiar Chords

People in 1982 were becoming aware of the growth in our inflation rate and that the value of the dollar was being eroded at the federal level. There was a lot of concern that someone manage government everywhere, not just state government. The federal government needed to be operated in a more fiscally responsible way and on a more business-like basis. We had just experienced the greatest growth in our inflation rate in the history of the United States. People were becoming quite concerned, and they were looking for someone who had the experience and expertise to manage government. This was something people could relate to— a fiscally responsible government organization, which was what I knew I had to offer.

At the time I was running for governor, the economy was slowing and people were losing jobs because the need was just not there for the goods they were producing. The unemployment rate was continuing to rise. The inflation percentage was not declining as it had been hoped that it would. There was a lot of concern about the direction the state and the country were going in fiscal management. There was a sentiment, of course, that more money had to be put into education. I still feel today that improving education is the secret to our success. As previously emphasized, this was the highest priority of our Administration and the priority that I campaigned on while running for Governor. There were as many different plans for education as there were candidates. However, I felt that the experience I had in managing the tax dollars, and the new money we'd be collecting, even though the economy might be somewhat depressed, would better serve the state in terms of getting more value out of those dollars than those candidates who didn't have this kind of experience. Some candidates were even suggesting that additional funds would have to be garnered through "other means."

Read My Actions

"Tax increase" was always a four-letter word for anyone campaigning for election. To do the kind of things that people were proposing . . . well, anyone in his or her right mind would realize that additional revenue had to be generated. But how do you generate revenue other than through growth or tax increases?

We were not projected at that point to have very good growth for the foreseeable future. However, when I took office in 1983 the collections were not coming in according to the revenue estimates on which we had passed the previous year's budget. We had only approximately $637,000 in reserve, and in reality, our reserves were depleted. We should have had close to $114 million. This meant that in our first few hours in office, we had to come in and cut the existing budget by approximately $150 million dollars just to meet the State's obligations for the balance of that fiscal year. Therefore, we had to manage our available resources as carefully as possible. I had promised in the campaign that I could operate State government for the next four years without a tax increase. I was dead-set on honoring that commitment. There was no way that I was going to go back on my word.

None of the other candidates had actually campaigned on not having a tax increase. This really was, I guess, one of the issues that started the momentum shifting in our direction and created some growing recognition of what we were doing. If I was bold enough to make this kind of statement, then what kind of experience did I have to back it up? When many people learned more about that experience, they'd say "Well, maybe he knows what he's talking about " Actually, I feel like I did, because I had studied the revenues, the rises and falls, and the projections for the next several years. Based on my own gut instinct, I felt certain that we could manage without a tax increase. However, there was another school of thought from people who didn't understand that the routine growth that the state had experienced over the years would keep new money forthcoming, even in a depressed economy. They thought that the only way you could have additional dollars through a tax increase. This meant to them that none of the education programs, and none of the other improvements that we had advocated could be possible without a tax increase. I didn't believe that.

We had tremendous growth during the first four years and continued throughout most of the second term, sometimes even into a fourteen or fifteen percent growth per year. This is really unprecedented as far as the state is concerned. And I have to say in all honesty that I never had the feelings of doubt that some did because I had lived in state government for eighteen years and had watched the growth trends and cycles. I guess I was a little naive to some degree, but I really felt in my heart that a "no tax increase" commitment would be possible for my first four years as Governor.

The news media probably posed the most serious questions about what we were doing and what we thought we were going to accomplish and kept it on the table for quite some time. But when the economy turned around and really blossomed, I never really got credit for the faith I had shown. I really felt like we could do it and that faith and optimism had paid off.

A Glass Cage

The news media is a powerful force in helping to set a direction for government and its key issues, depending on how well it is communicated to the public and how well they understand it. Sometimes the information that is being communicated is not one-hundred percent accurate. The information received is somewhat distorted and sometimes the people who are receiving it haven't the background to fully comprehend. So the message is often misunderstood. Still, the media is very powerful and can both help and hurt the public's ability to understand important issues.

We were entering into a period during my first term when the talk shows were getting a real foothold. The regular six o'clock news was moving into an hour-long segment. Then you've got a five, and seven o'clock news. Very shortly thereafter came the early morning news, with the 5:00 A.M. to the six and seven o'clock news before the *Today* and *Good Morning America* programs. You've ended up with several hours of news coverage per day, and the repetition is just tremendous. People are bombarded with the news and are constantly aware of what's happening and who's doing it. Therefore, being governor is almost like being in a glass cage. People are standing around viewing you, and a lot of times the reporters and the people who are gathering the information do not understand it themselves. The story is not completely told, because to be fair to them, they were not there long enough due to deadlines and other time constraints to do the necessary research and get all the facts. You live and die by these reports and for years, the only coverage, particularly for the state, was in the written press. Very little of it was through radio or television.

Today, the General Assembly and Governor have their own access to the cable and online networks. However, even with all the technology available today, the public still has a hard time understanding some of the information they receive about important issues affecting their lives.

Georgia on My Mind

Tourism has been very important to Georgia for many years. We have a diverse state, from the mountains to the sea coast, with rivers, streams, and lakes in-between. there are real choices here. Our state is attractive and draws people in to be a part of it. Therefore, early in our Administration we commissioned a tourism study to develop our strategy for the future. We wanted to know the attractions we had to offer and what we could do to enhance the future of tourism in Georgia. The study was completed, and the results weren't really a surprise. We didn't have the kind of "destination sites" in Georgia, such as Disney World in Florida, that people would choose to visit and spend several days doing it. Of course, we did have Stone Mountain and Six Flags and the mountains as attractions.. We also have the sea coast with its Golden Isles and various other attractive tourism venues through-out the state, both public and private. Our state parks were also attractive to visitors, but we just didn't have many places in which people might want to spend a few nights before they moved on to Florida, or maybe stop back by on the return trip.

We initiated a special effort in industry and trade and an intense advertising effort and campaign. Its title, appropriately enough, was "Georgia on My Mind." In fact, we were able to purchase the rights to our state song and make it the theme of our tourism program. The thrust of the campaign was to raise the image of Georgia as a vacation destination. Then, through the good graces of the General Assembly, and upon our recommenda-tion, funding was approved in fiscal year 1986 for the kind of money we needed to promote Georgia.

Tourism increased very rapidly, and these initiatives enabled us to build or expand destination sites such as Stone Mountain, Jekyll Island, Lake Lanier Islands, Amicalola Lodge, among others, and a number of our state Parks. Property was purchased and planning begun for a mountain resort at Young Harris, the Brasstown Valley, which is now completed. The Golden Isles are a real attraction; it has an awful lot of vacation appeal. But Jekyll Island went through several years of not doing well. Our administration helped support building a water park and several other improve-ments on the island that helped to enhance "the draw," with the revenue generated from the improvements re-paying the total cost.

As a result of this campaign, more people were attracted to our destination sites and spent more nights and more money here in Georgia than ever before. Further, we believe that our efforts helped enable Georgia to secure the Democratic Convention in

1988 and build the Georgia Dome to attract the Super Bowl in 1994 and the 1996 Centennial Olympics.

Along with our domestic efforts, tourism was promoted from the international arena. We added a person in our office in Tokyo just to help coordinate and promote travel in Georgia. Along with direct air flights of Japan Airlines, which we worked hard to secure in 1986, we were able to be a part of the success of bringing numerous Japanese tourists to Georgia and Atlanta during that time. The volume is increasing from that venture. The same is true with Canada. We became the stopover for a lot of Canadians who were on their way to Florida.

Georgia was evolving then, and still is, into a second-home site. A lot of people from Florida come to the North Georgia Mountains, and that has brought in a lot of retirement communities, which we had never had before. These were being developed and promoted through our tourism efforts.

Another part of this same study had to do with Georgia's success in the movie industry. Our involvement was expanded and enhanced with a special division in the Department of Industry, Trade, and Tourism just to promote movies and video production on location in Georgia. Film activity has continued to increase. I appointed a Film and Video Commission that was very active during our administration. It was made up of people—located in Georgia—who were in the film industry and helped promote it here. Many major films were made here over the years, and several TV series made in Georgia still continue to be broadcast. Many businesses, jobs, and opportunities developed because of those initiatives. In fact, tourism became so important for our state's economy that we added "Tourism" to the name of the Department. It became the Department of Industry, Trade and Tourism.

A Retirement Community

The demographics of the state were changing during our administration. We found that a lot more people were choosing Georgia as a place to retire and still others were selecting Georgia for their second home. The resort areas of our state were growing. When folks came here for their second homes, often they would remain. To a larger degree than in the past, people who were sixty-five and older became a responsibility of the state. This really wasn't a problem. There were a lot of blessings in a way. These people brought not only trade, business, and an increased cash-flow to Georgia, but they also brought a standard of living and expertise, which added to the cultural wealth of our state. Our commitment to them was to provide the kind of care and quality of life that they expected. This began to require additional funds and programs that we never had to fund before.

Retirement communities were springing up in the metropolitan areas, in the mountains, on the coast, and overnight they were practically all over Georgia. Many of our cities were being named as 'a top retirement community' in publications across the United States, and this just enhanced the state's popularity. Because our lifestyle is comfortable, and the cost of living in Georgia was much less than some of the other retirement areas, our state was increasingly attractive to this age group. It still is. If I ever retire, I would select Georgia.

The Geography Was Right

During our administration, over 850,000 new jobs were created, a record for the state for any eight-year period and one that we were very proud of. It was a combination of several things that enabled this to happen for our state. First, Georgia is very pro-business, and there is an attitude of support for businesses statewide, not just in the more progressive and affluent areas. Second, the geographic location of Georgia puts it into a trade area that is very attractive to businesses for purposes of expansion. Both foreign and domestic investors are always looking for expanded markets. With our location, the geography was right for distribution centers due to the large population base. Nearly half of the population of the United States can be reached in a little more than an hour's flight from Atlanta, which puts you in proximity to a large audience of people to serve. Then the transportation facilities that were available in Georgia from our interstate highways and rail system, the international airport, and fast-growing seaports in Savannah and Brunswick provided the kind of connections that were also attractive to businesses.

We also had something in Georgia that was an excellent sales tool for us—the "one-stop permit" capability. Our Department of Natural Resources could issue all the environmental and other permits that a company would need to locate within our state. Most states could not do this, and a locating industry would spend a lot of time and expense visiting different agencies, either local, state or otherwise, to get those permits. We could do all that at one stop and one place. This cut through a lot of bureaucracy and red tape with which companies would normally have to deal. Add this to the Quick-Start Training, the pro-business attitude, the work ethic of the people in our state, our past record of productivity, and one can see why our state was attractive.

Our first priority, however, was to assist and help expand the businesses of those who were already here, not chase after prospects outside the state. The majority of our new jobs came from existing industries who were already tax-paying citizens.

Education is very important. You've got to have good facilities, good personnel within your schools, and a good social climate within that community. Of course, that requires parents and families to be personally involved in the education process. When prospects came, they compared our system with the system in some other state or location. You've got to compare favorably or they're not going to select you. Another incentive that evolved and became tremendously important was our communications network, along with our other rapidly developing electronic capabilities. When you put all these together, it made a very attractive package for Georgia. I believe that my own business experience, being directly involved in the industrial development of my community, gave me a good understanding of what would be required enabling me to do an effective job of negotiating on behalf of the state. We also had a super-productive economic development team that was led by Commissioner George Berry.

A Whole New Board

I had long been impressed with George Berry and had known him in passing over the years. But I became more impressed with him as Atlanta's Commissioner of Aviation, the post from which he developed, built, and completed the Atlanta Hartsfield International Airport. The leadership he provided and the kind of person he was made me feel that he would be a valuable member of the Harris administration. He was invited to come to the mansion and talk about the possibilities. I think it was a shock to him when I offered him the opportunity to be the Commissioner of the Department of Industry and Trade.

To prepare that opportunity for him, we had to re-organize The Department of Industry and Trade, and this was one of the few times a whole state board had been wiped out and reconstituted, but we did it. Sometimes this can be a tricky political venture, but we wanted to appoint some of our people, and we wanted to bring in a new commissioner as well. We wanted a new direction and, therefore, passed the legislation that enabled us to abolish the old board and appoint a whole new board. We did reappoint some of the members who were already serving, but basically I appointed a brand new Board. Such an opportunity does not come too often in the political world.

Commissioner Berry and I were able to complement each other. We made numerous foreign trips, flying thousands of miles and made an effective presentation on behalf of business prospects for the state and took orders. George Berry was another excellent asset for our administration and for the state of Georgia.

Taking the Fall

Our first crisis was local and not international. Early in 1983 Commissioner Berry had not been sworn in officially, but the time had been set. We needed to get him on board and start things moving. He had a problem with one of his eyes (a detached retina, I think) and had been confined for several days in Piedmont Hospital. We made arrangements to go to Piedmont late one afternoon and have the official swearing-in there in a small auditorium. We arrived and were being escorted by security and some of the hospital officials down the hall to the room. There was an elderly lady at the far end of the hall, moving very slowly toward us on a walker. Her nurse was by her side, helping her make very slow steps. As I approached her, she looked up and saw me coming down the hall. When she did, she exclaimed "Governor Harris," and let go of the walker and stretched out her arms. When she did that, she began losing her balance. The nurse with her may also have recognized me as the Governor and forgot about the patient. Suddenly, the lady started falling backwards. I immediately rushed forward and tried to grab her. I couldn't stop her fall, and she continued to topple backwards. When I tried to catch her, it overbalanced me, and I fell forward. Thankfully, I didn't fall on her, but I had to catch myself.

There she was lying on the floor, looking up at me, and I was looking down at her. She said, "I bet you've never had anybody to fall for you like this before, have you?" Laughter erupted and I was grateful that she was not injured. Then the nurse quickly recovered and got the lady back on her feet and we were able to proceed on our way to swear-in Commissioner George Berry.

An International Thrust

We were cultivating both our exports and the investment in Georgia from foreign countries. It required an awful lot of my time, because prospective foreign clients are so much more protocol-conscious than we are in the United States. When you're dealing with American corporations, it is not so important who negotiates the deal with them on behalf of the state, whether it's the Commissioner of Industry and Trade or one of his representatives. Occasionally, the negotiations required that the Governor be directly involved. However, almost 100 percent of our foreign opportunities would require the Governor to be involved, either in their country, here, or sometimes both.

We also found that when you have a prospect in a foreign country, if the Governor was able to make a personal visit directly to the top people of that corporation, our success rate would be higher. On many occasions, the government of a country would be very supportive of the company's expansion plans, and the combination of visits to both of them helped us be successful. If other states were not giving this same personal attention, well, we were in the driver's seat. Therefore, we spent as much time as possible chasing those leads and going into those countries. I personally visited thirty-four different countries (some, many times) on behalf of the state of Georgia. This included almost all of the Far Eastern and European countries that were investing in the U. S., with an emphasis on those countries in which we felt we could increase our exports as well as revenues for our ports .

Since a governor is on the job twenty-four hours a day, and 365 days out of the year, I really couldn't be gone too long. If an emergency arose, I was always in close contact and available to respond officially. We tried to limit our trips to less than two weeks. Trips would be scheduled almost like a campaign. There would be as many stops in as many countries as was feasible. For instance, if you were going to the Far East, you might have a combination of stops in Taiwan, Korea, Hong Kong, Japan, or even China, all in the same trip, which saved on expenses.

There was no time for jet-lag. When we landed, we immediately went into various official functions on behalf of the state until our departure. It was exhausting and almost like a campaign for election in Georgia. You went from "can to can't," as hard as you could go, with as many stops as you could schedule.

Help from International Friends

Depending on our specific needs and purposes in a foreign country, we would meet with heads of state and high governmental officials. Most of the time They would reciprocate and make trips to the United States and be guests at the Governor's Mansion where dinners or receptions would be given for them.

Our Department of Industry and Trade and Tourism maintained offices in a number of countries. For example, we have had a longtime office in Brussels, Belgium to serve the European countries. We have had an office for many years in Tokyo to serve the Far East. In fact, we were one of the first states to locate offices representing Georgia in those two regions of the world. We also had an office in Canada.

After my first visit in 1983 I established an office in Korea for the dual purpose of serving the ports and also industry and trade because of the good potential in that area at that time. Therefore, out of those offices, we had representatives who followed up the prospects and made the arrangements when we would visit, and also helped us with questions of protocol.

Georgia does not have a state department as such to handle protocol, negotiations, and relations with other nations and other states. This was basically handled in our administration through our Department of Industry and Trade and Tourism. There were many times, however, when we were assisted by Georgia international corporations. The Coca-Cola Company, in particular, provided information and confirmation of protocol and assistance both from their offices in Atlanta and in foreign countries. Many times, their representatives were there when we landed and participated in or assisted us with official functions while we were there. Many times I don't know what we would have done without information from Coke and assistance from their representatives in those countries. In fact, I don't believe we visited a single country in which there wasn't a Coke representative already there, willing to assist us in any way. They provided a lot of background, and on many occasions they knew the people in the business community with which we would be meeting. It was very valuable to our success to have private industry support as an additional arm of our initiative.

The Crown Prince

When I became Governor, there were about one-hundred Japanese businesses in our state. We left office with over 275, plus a direct flight to Japan. I traveled to Japan every year while I was Governor. We had a lot of involvement with that country, and many Japanese were visiting Georgia particularly government officials, foreign ministers, and ambassadors. In fact, Georgia had extended a wide, warm welcome to many foreign dignitaries. They were all coming to Georgia to see what was attractive about our state for purposes of investing and visiting. They wanted to experience firsthand our Southern hospitality and be assured our welcome was legitimate.

During my first term as Governor, Crown Prince Akihito of Japan was planning a visit to the United States and was going to honor Georgia by making this one of his official stops. We were involved with his advance people as they made plans and worked out the logistics of timing and location. Of course, we invited him to stay at the mansion as we had with other dignitaries. His advance team came out to inspect it. They looked at all the rooms, surveyed the space we could make available and determined it would not be adequate for the staff and entourage who would be traveling with him.

It was suggested that maybe Elizabeth and I could make our bedroom available and stay somewhere else during that period of time, and then he could be accommodated there. The question was sent to me. It was, of course, something that had to be handled very delicately; we certainly didn't want to offend anyone. I felt that accommodations in the style that was required were certainly available in Atlanta. I didn't think the chief executive of the state of Georgia needed to be away from the mansion. Our leaving the Governor's Mansion would not have added any more to the hospitality that we could offer him during his visit. My response was that we'd help locate the proper space and make him welcome, if he scheduled the visit. We followed up with the information that space had been located at the Ritz-Carlton. They could have furnished him a whole floor and maintained the proper security. Shortly after the preparations were underway, the visit was canceled due to an illness in his family.

A little later that same year (1986), we were scheduled to visit Japan. The Japanese Consul General in Atlanta suggested that since the Crown Prince and his wife were unable to come here, he would like to invite us to visit him in Japan. This was fine with us, as a trip was already scheduled to Japan in the fall. The Consul General met us at our hotel in Tokyo and escorted us to the home of the Crown Prince. This was not the normal procedure for meeting with him. They had prepared us, however, regarding the protocol, the subjects we would discuss, and the formalities involved. I thought this was going to be a very stiff, formal meeting.

When we arrived, we had never seen a more gracious host. The Crown Prince and his wife, Princess Michiko, were two of the warmest, most cordial people you'd ever want to spend time with. They took us into what was really an informal setting and just chatted. We had a delightful time with them. They impressed us with their knowledge of our state and I think the Consul General, was surprised because the Japanese are so protocol-conscious in everything they do. We ended our meeting with good feelings and a promise that they would visit us in Georgia as soon as possible.

The Crown Prince became Emperor in 1989. Shortly after my term as Governor ended, he did make that promised visit to Georgia. Elizabeth and I met with Emperor Akihito and Empress Michiko at the mansion during a formal reception and dinner given in the Emperor's honor by Governor and Mrs. Zell Miller.

15

Facing Real Issues

During the campaign, the Martin Luther King Jr. holiday certainly was an issue that we had to face. I was in favor of the state recognizing a legal holiday to honor King and submitted the bill to the General Assembly in January 1983. It was time to acknowledge his role as the powerful and peaceful leader of the civil rights movement, as well as his being Georgia's only Nobel Peace Prize recipient. More importantly, our state needed to continue its progress in removing all of its remaining racial barriers. I felt that without the passage of this measure our strides toward equality would have been halted. This was another litmus test of our commitment to those values. Therefore, it was not only the right thing to do politically; it was the moral thing to do. It was necessary to establish the commitment of our administration right up front. The legislation was approved during the 1984 session. Of course, I signed it and helped to implement its first celebration in the state of Georgia, King's home state.

There is always resistance to any progressive move that people don't understand at the moment. Looking back, you realize that this was something that was greatly needed. I guess one of the things that makes leadership successful is that you're able to recognize actions that *are* necessary, even moving ahead of what some people might think the timing should be. This starts the process towards implementation.

The Martin Luther King Jr. holiday was one of those issues that was not popular from the start. However, it was something that the majority of the people, particularly the members of the General Assembly, recognized *had* to be done. As governor, had I not given it leadership, it probably would have been delayed for some time longer, though I think it would have come eventually. With it being part of our legislative agenda and supported by our administration, it was something we were able to move through the General Assembly with a minimum of opposition.

Minority Support

The emergence of AfricanAmerican leadership in state government is something I grew up with in a sense. I never had a problem with it because it was the proper thing, and I always felt that everybody ought to be included. This was a period in our history when the opportunity came, and the civil rights movement brought it about. I had made a campaign pledge when I ran that as governor I would make my appointments representative of the population of the state. Percentage-wise, the appointments I made while governor pretty well reflected that. It was something that I worked very hard to do.

I was able to appoint the first African American to the Court of Appeals. He was Judge Robert Benham whom I later appointed to serve on the Supreme Court of Georgia. He is now serving as the Chief Justice of the Supreme Court. This confirms that I made a very quality appointment. I was also honored to select Representative Calvin Smyre, a long-time friend, to be the first African American administration floor leader in the Georgia House of Representatives. A number of opportunities like these came up. I am very pleased that we were able to act on them and fill those positions with people who were representative of our state's population.

Two of the first employees whom my father hired when he went into the concrete business were African American. One was named Lucius Wheeler, and the other one was Tom Gainor. They were brothers-in-law who had just gotten out of the U. S. Navy. Both had served during the Second World War, had returned home and were looking for job opportunities. Tom worked in our family business for almost thirty-five years until his death. Lucius Wheeler continued to work in our family business until it was sold, and he remained, for a number of years until his retirement, with the company that purchased it.

Lucius became one of Dad's (and our family's) close personal friends during that time. He was a person who could do every single job that we had in the business. He had a wide range of skills and could always be trusted and counted on. He taught me a great deal during that period and removed, I guess, a lot of the prejudices that other people might have been subject to. I had tremendous respect for them both as children of God and as individuals. To have had that experience certainly enriched my life.

Safe Keeping

For a number of years, Georgia had not specifically ignored children's issues, but we had not properly addressed them. We initiated special programs to curb some of the child abuse, passing laws as far as reportage of child abuse was concerned, and in August 1984, a program stipulating that it's "okay to tell" about abuse and drugs, which helped to implement these programs. As First Lady, Elizabeth also chaired these groups and was a staunch advocate of the "You Can Say 'No'" campaign.

Because we were having too many children dying and too many childbirth deaths, we implemented several incentives in which we tried to address those issues—in particular to reduce the number of birth deaths. Some improvements were made, though it takes a while for that to be reflected. But we helped initiate prenatal and postnatal programs for the state. Even today, this one issue still perplexes me more than any other. Somehow, there has to be a way to reach these mothers and educate them to the need for prenatal and postnatal care.

We also had a "safety incentive" program, trying to do something about DUI's and drinking drivers. Elizabeth served as chair of that group and helped promote the public awareness venture initiated during that time. Pringle, Dixon and Pringle, an Atlanta public relations firm, designed and contributed an award-winning multimedia public awareness campaign called, "Drunk Driving is Just Murder on Our Roads!" We actually reduced the number of highway fatalities because of the improvements we had in the drunk-driving laws and the enforcement of those laws. Certainly, we didn't finish all that was needed, but it was a start in the right direction. This program attracted a lot of interest and a number of public and private initiatives were ongoing, including groups promoting this cause, trying to do something about deaths on the highway. Most of these groups fell in line with the improvement packages which we developed, including the initiatives in the General Assembly, and helped lobby for those improvements. You need that kind of support if you're going to make progress in the never-ending struggle to improve highway safety.

Healthcare Crisis

The state tried to alleviate Georgians' pain and suffering, from prenatal care all the way through to care for the elderly. We were directly involved at all levels because of the Medicaid program that we were administering and in which we participated based on the wealth of the state. This meant that as our standard of living increased, so did the state dollars required to match the Federal funds. It was costing the state big, big dollars each year and continued to grow. It was becoming almost a crisis situation because of the amount of new dollars required to match the federal funds. This was an area of tremendous concern and also required a lot of attention and involvement on our part.

We helped initiate programs in prenatal and postnatal care. As mentioned earlier, we were having too many birth deaths in Georgia, which sadly had one of the highest infant mortality rates in the nation because the mothers were not receiving proper care during pregnancy. Thus, we helped organize prevention programs and applied a significant amount of money to reduce the number of birth deaths annually. There were twelve deaths per one hundred births, and our goal was to reduce it to nine by 1990. We started the trend towards reducing birth deaths and also had initiatives to give special attention to programs dealing with adolescent and child care.

AIDS was becoming a serious issue that needed attention. Through Atlanta's Grady Memorial Hospital and the Chatham County Health Department in Savannah the very first funds were budgeted for outpatient AIDS clinics. One of the my favorite programs, one for which I handled the enabling legislation as a member of the House of Representatives in 1982, was the Community Care Program for the Elderly. This program assisted people who became partially incapacitated in various ways and allowed them to remain in their own homes rather than to go into a nursing home or some other facility. This became a very important program for the state, saving an awful lot of money and reaching many people who wouldn't have been reached otherwise. People do not want to leave their own homes or community if there's a viable alternative. This legislation enabled people to make that choice and has worked very effectively for many years.

What made the crisis in healthcare real for us was the continued escalation in cost from the provider's level to the patient. Almost annually, our Administration witnessed a compounded twenty to twenty-five percent increase. Of course, the number of people utilizing these services increased, but so were the amounts being charged. One big reason for this was there were a lot more diagnostic procedures and methods for treatment than in years past. Because of the legal liability, the physicians were not going to leave any stone unturned. Today, they are able to select from a large number of options in making diagnostic determinations for patients which, technically, they were not capable of making just a few years ago. The new discoveries in science and technology, the new drugs and treatments are really something that has only been available in recent years, but the costs of those services and new, innovative discoveries are tremendous. This is reflected in the escalation of costs that we continue to have to deal with today.

Drugs at the Source

In my first year as governor, a request came in from the federal government that someone had reported marijuana growing in the state park north of Helen, in Unicoi. They wanted permission to move in with a helicopter and spray Paraquot on that patch of marijuana. I didn't hesitate two seconds to give them permission. We were trying to stop drugs at the source, and we were trying to stop the sale of drugs and prosecute those who were involved.

The other side of the request was that there was already a group of people who were fighting that kind of enforcement all across the United States. Immediately, they accessed the press and created a ground-swell of opposition to the spraying of paraquot. It really created a minor crisis for our administration during the early years of trying not only to explain our intentions but to alleviate the fear of a lot of people that the residue of this controversial chemical might come off the mountain and get into the water systems, which would, of course, have been a serious problem. However, we received a lot of federal support and recognition because we were bold enough to take that kind of step, and in conjunction with their efforts to try to do something about the drug situation. It gained us access to additional help and support with programs which we probably wouldn't otherwise have had. Up until then, many of the key people at the federal level had never heard of Governor Joe Frank Harris. It shouldn't have made any difference, really, but after the paraquot incident, we had a real rapport with them. This began opening doors.

We initiated what we called the Governor's Drug Eradication Task Force, which was a joint effort between a number of our state agencies Natural Resources, the Department of Transportation, and many of our other agencies (law enforcement, in particular) all joined together to try and identify anywhere illegal drugs might have been grown, so that we could eradicate them. But we didn't spray with paraquot any more.

We would use helicopters in surveillance. It was amazing how you could spot marijuana plants from the air. I had no knowledge of this until a pilot who was part of that task force showed me how to identify it. You could actually just fly over and look down and see the marijuana growing, because it had a different color. But if you didn't know what you were looking for, you would never spot it. In fact, that task force is still operating today. They would go in and chop the marijuana down by hand. Some of our Department of Transportation people would assist the Law Enforcement people with vehicles and tractors or whatever was needed to get to it. Often they would travel for miles through the countryside in order to cut it down and haul it out.

During these years drugs were really beginning to be a factor in our nation. Georgia was on a direct drug route between Florida and Washington D.C. and other points North, and had become the entry point just north of Florida. They would bypass Florida and come into Georgia from coastal islands and from other countries. After I became governor, our initial involvement was to try to locate, capture, and stop the flow of drugs coming through Georgia. I believe we had an effective organization that did a good job with limited resources and manpower at least to slow it down.

It was not an overriding problem, but it was big enough to demand that we deal with it effectively. At the time I became governor, you couldn't utilize any of your National Guard or armed service units to work with the state to combat it. A little later, the law changed on the Federal level and allowed the state to utilize military equipment and personnel. We even had a number of successful missions through our National Guard. The Georgia Bureau of Investigation (GBI) was a big part of this effort, and we added additional manpower as rapidly as possible. The very capable GBI director at that time was Phil Peters. After his untimely death with cancer, I appointed Robbie Hamrick to be director. He did an outstanding job while trying to keep Georgia and our law enforcement out front.

The people who were involved in these investigations became a lot more sophisticated. It was probably the beginning of the kind of actions that have become routine all across the nation now. However, we had little or no prior experience with it then.

Almost invariably, people who were being sentenced had something pertaining to drugs involved in their convictions. The influx in arrests brought the need for additional prison space. It helped escalate our perpetual need for new prisons. When I was elected, we had a little over thirteen thousand prison spaces. When I left office eight years later, we had built, funded, and had under construction, 24,000 additional spaces, which makes space available for 37,000 inmates. The number of employees in the Department of Corrections had increased from 5,899 to 12,231 during that same period. Georgia was not an isolated case, as far as crime was concerned. It was happening across the country, even moving into the rural areas. We had never seen crime, particularly drugs, in some of our smaller rural communities. but we were finding it happening quite often.

The "Old River War"

Shortly after I entered the governor's office, I felt it was important that we commission a study on Georgia's water resources. Leonard Ledbetter, who did an outstanding job as head of the Environmental Division of our Department of Natural Resources (and who later became the Commissioner), made me aware of our problems. He convinced me that Georgia does have and will have plenty of water, but that it's not all in the right places. The abundance is here. We have an average of somewhere around fifty inches of rainfall each year. But our growth patterns were in places where new and clean water was not increasing. It has to be managed. Out of that kind of futuristic study came the determination that we were going to need some regional reservoirs, particularly in the northern part of the state. My administration made plans to develop those regional reservoirs. Even the preliminary results of the study in the local communities, which was funded by the General Assembly in 1984, concluded that we needed to proceed to develop those regional reservoirs. This later became a recommendation of the governor's Growth Strategies Commission.

The "old river war" between Alabama and Georgia over who had access to the Chattahoochee River that runs between the two states reared its head again. Alabama, with Florida's support, went to the courts and enjoined Georgia from developing any regional reservoirs until that corridor had been studied and the sharing of the river water between the states had been worked out. Much of Alabama's water on their eastern side mostly originates in North Georgia. They were fearful that anything we might impound in Georgia would limit them. Common sense tells you that you don't destroy water. You might take it out of the basin and use it but you put it back in, and it goes back in through the natural environmental process. Thus this was a political war more than a legitimate environmental war between the two states.

Our first reservoir would have been the West Georgia Regional Reservoir, which was already being planned on the Tallapoosa River in Haralson County. This water supply reservoir could have served a five county area in West Georgia and possibly some portions of the metropolitan Atlanta area. Had we been able to impound and hold back the extra flow of water during the wet season, it would really have assured those further down stream that water would have kept flowing, even in the drought.

I think there are practical reasons why the plan we had developed then would be workable today. The study indicated that, at some point in time, we may have to pump water from these regional reservoirs thirty to fifty miles to other state locations, in order to share the water we have in a responsible way.

There's not as much of a water problem in South Georgia as there is in North Georgia, where there are mostly wells, springs, and streams. Much of South Georgia's water is in huge underground aquifers with an almost limitless supply. (Even today, because of some political considerations, there's no real preparation being made to deal with this issue.)

Air Quality

Georgia doesn't have the problems of many of the other states with air quality, but we do have a challenge in managing those we do have. From the regulations that have been applied at the federal level and complemented by our state regulations, I think we are headed in the right direction—to clean up a lot of the air quality problems we have had in past years, which will prevent future problems. Our "growth strategy" venture during our second term included the Comprehensive Solid Waste Management Act. This mandated a reduction in waste disposal in Georgia. Also included were guidelines for local land use planning.

I think we enhanced the management of our environmental resources tremendously. That's not the ultimate solution, but it is something, like education, that must continue. You do not rectify all the problems at one time. Environmental problems are continual and must be dealt with on a routine basis.

Bringing it All Back Home

The Southern Growth Policies Board, the Southern Regional Education Board, and the Southern Governors' Association were all made up of the states surrounding Georgia. The Appalachian Regional Commission came from a Federal program but still involved most of our southern states, though it was more broad-based. It went on further north and even outside of the southern region to some degree.

These regional organizations basically came about because of the southern governors and the southern states having problems that were a little different from the other parts of the United States. In fact, the old Southern Governors' Association was created because of unfair freight rates—and the discrimination in shipping costs that the South was experiencing in the late 1930s and 40s. This was one of the first organizations that came together to help support needed changes, and it kept on moving from there. We had similar problems, and this forum gave us an opportunity to share some of those problems—and even seek solutions that would be common to the states that were involved.

I was fortunate during the time that I was governor to serve as chairman of all those groups, which meant that we would have their annual conventions here in our state. I remember when we had the Southern Governor's Conference down at Sea Island on the coast, which was the first time in many years that it had been held in Georgia, but to my knowledge never before on the coast. The people at St. Simons Island and Jekyll Island joined together and were just tremendous in their support of this conference.

We had to raise the money, of course, to finance it from within Georgia. I'll always have fond memories of the program, which included author Pat Conroy, entertainer Ray Charles, and the many volunteers all engaged for the purpose of showcasing "Georgia" to the Southern governors. Our annual convention was later looked back on by most of the governors who were serving during that time as being the ultimate prototype or model that all the others have tried to emulate since.

Still in Georgia

There's a feeling out in the state that everything that happens has to happen in Atlanta or in the metropolitan area. We felt that having this conference on the coast was an opportunity to reach out and share with other areas of the state. There's a very strong sentiment outside the perimeter and outside the metropolitan area that it's us against them—that all of the tax dollars and all of the good programs and services that the state might be providing are more or less concentrated in the metropolitan area, which is not true. This feeling was something we worked hard to dispel during the time that I was governor and even received criticism by some editorial writers because of it. But I have always felt that Atlanta and the metropolitan area were a very vital part of Georgia. Without it, the rest of Georgia might not survive, and without the rest of Georgia, Atlanta and the metropolitan area might not survive. I've always felt that if your capital city went down the drain, the rest of the state would shortly be right behind it. We had to work together. We're all one family, all one state. There's no fence around Atlanta. It's open for all of Georgia.

There have been many reasons for this division over the years, the county-unit system being one of the most significant. That system started some of the division, driven by the differences in lifestyle and even the economy: You've got a farming or rural economy out in much of the state on the one hand and, on the other, a different lifestyle and economy in the inner city and metropolitan area. Some resentment has built up because of these factors. You've got a more "laid-back," relaxed lifestyle further out in the rural communities with the hustle and bustle and rush in the inner city and metropolitan area. There was a study done at the University of Georgia (for the Department of Transportation), during the time that I was governor, which said there were two Georgias. I understood the study and its rationale and how these conclusions were determined and why it made certain statements. There were a lot of poverty areas out in the state, deprived areas, just as in the inner-city, even in the metropolitan area. But you can't draw a line and say, "It's the haves and the have nots." My position was that we were, of course, "a quilt of many patterns," and while there were many diversified economies and cultural elements throughout the state, we were all Georgians. We couldn't allow a wedge to be driven between us. It was our responsibility to try to remove that wedge and bring everyone together and keep working together as one state. Some of the editorial writers misunderstood my viewpoint and continued to hammer me with the fact that I couldn't recognize that we did have a second Georgia. I think that not only do we have two Georgias, but many Georgias out there and it makes up one whole, one great Georgia.

Different Styles

There's a different attitude and a different understanding of the political arena in the various regions of the state. As you travel through Middle Georgia and on into South Georgia, you find that county lines do not denote political boundaries as much as they do in North Georgia. To give an example, when you have a political campaign function in South Georgia, people will not only attend from the county where the function is being held, they come in from the surrounding counties as well. They wouldn't think a thing in the world about driving sixty or seventy-five miles to a political rally. You could have that same function in my home county of

Bartow in North Georgia, and you would not have the people from adjacent counties driving in because they would think, "That's a Bartow County function." That is, they wouldn't feel welcome to join in to the degree that they would in South Georgia. The mountains and hills tend to section off people at times because of the travel patterns.

Another thing we found in South Georgia was that all the people who were active in politics seemed to know each other regardless of the counties in which they lived. In North Georgia, you often find people in a county who might not know someone who's active in politics, even in that same county. I guess you could say they grew up in a little different political culture, that perhaps they honored their political commitments a little differently in North and South Georgia. This may be one reason that, before my election, we were unable to elect many North Georgia governors. The South Georgia politicians controlled the state capital for many, many years.

I'm not sure that I opened the door as much as it was the fact that the demographics of the state have been going through a change. There has been a shift in the population toward North Georgia. In addition, the media and television have opened opportunities and really changed the style of campaigning from what it was when I first ran for governor.

Agricenter Quest

The farming community has been the backbone of the state for many years. It's an extremely large contributor to our economy. In recent years, the family farm—as we knew it in the past— has been rapidly declining. I had resolved that if there was any way the state could assist the farming community in remaining viable and in continuing to be the economic generator that it had been, then our administration needed to do it. We worked very closely with the Commissioner of Agriculture, Tommy Irvin to try and accomplish this. While a lot of improvements were made, and a lot of new ventures to sell Georgia products were launched, we felt that

Georgia needed additional processing plants—because a lot of our raw food and fiber was being exported to other states for processing, a value that we could add here to create additional jobs. We targeted our efforts through the Department of Industry and Trade to bring this about and, in many ways, were able to expand some of the businesses here that were using Georgia-grown products. We also worked hard to increase our exports.

We opened the first trade office specifically for agricultural products in Brussels in 1985. Commissioner Irvin was there with me officially to open opened that office. In a continuing effort to introduce consumers to the superior quality of Georgia's agricultural products, we had the promotional campaign, "Georgia Always in Good Taste." Georgia was one of a few farming states that did not have an Agricenter, or a place where you could exhibit your livestock, bring the farming community together, and have a state fair. The idea began to gain momentum in the early years of our administration. We formed a committee and appointed Gene Sutherland (who operates a business at the Farmers' Market in Atlanta) as chairman. Out of that group came the initiative for the Agricenter, which was constructed down at Perry, Georgia, with the help of a $24 million-dollar initial outlay from the General Assembly.

We had wanted a site that could serve the whole state. A number of cities across the state competed for that Center. Perry was the successful site, located right alongside I-75—with a large acreage almost in downtown Perry. Thus, the Center was built, and I had the pleasure of cutting the ribbon and opening it, officially in 1990, before I left the governor's office. This was an objective that the farming community had been working toward for many years. I was glad that our administration was able to bring to fruition one of the premier agricultural and livestock exhibition centers in the Southeast. The Georgia National Fairgrounds and Agricenter includes fountains, gardens, and lakes. It is open all year for many different events.

One of the main corridors into the 628 acres has been named in honor of Governor Joe Frank and Elizabeth Harris. Martin

Dawe was commissioned to sculpt an appropriate and beautiful statue that has been erected in the nicely landscaped area. Even though I am embarrassed by such an honor, I deeply appreciate the recognition. My personal feeling and philosophy have always been that public facilities should not be named for or dedicated to people still living.

Keeping the Farm

Georgia is still an agricultural state, and there are a large number of jobs that are involved in the agribusiness community with an awful lot of revenue being generated. Our administration was committed to at least slowing down the families that were leaving the farm and to try and assist any way we could as far as tax relief and other ways that might help them stay on the land.

We had one program that was very valuable for the state and will be for many years. Georgia actually grows more pine trees than any other place in the world. Forestry revenue is very important for our state. For this reason, we had a program and a goal that for every acre of timber that was harvested, a comparable acre of seedlings would be planted. It got into the thousands of acres per year, but we did achieve that. In time, the expanded capability of the Forestry Department gave us the ability to grow and furnish the seedlings that homeowners, farmers, and others could plant. Over several years, and with the promotion of the Forestry Commissioner (Ray Shirley and, later, John Mixon), we were able to accomplish our goal.

Getting a Grip

We have been blessed in Georgia to have had a transportation system that has served us as well as it has over the years. it has been a good system. But it's not a system that can continue to accommodate the growth that we've been having and, of course, the kind of growth that we experienced during our administration: Almost a million new Georgians came here during the eight years

I was governor. This influx brought additional traffic to our roads and, of course, additional needs for an improved and expanded transportation system.

Early on in our administration, the plan to identify improvements in transportation was made through the year 2000. It was determined at that time Georgia was going to need in excess of thirteen billion dollars just to continue the improvements that we were accustomed to and the expansions that were necessary in that short period of time. This conflicted with my personal philosophy to think that you could generate this additional money from state general funds and commit it to transportation. In years past, it had been the state's policy to let the users of our transportation system pay a large portion of the cost. I agreed and felt that if such a huge amount of money was going to be needed the people who are using our roads should contribute. In fact, over thirty percent of traffic volume in our state was by people from other states who were traveling through.

We envisioned these improvements continuing and the drivers or users paying. This was one of the few times we were unsuccessful. Out of the study and the projections, we came up with what we called the GRIP program, an acronym for the Governor's Road Improvement Program, which identified the program we were proposing to not only "four-lane" a lot of the two-lane roads, where they were needed, but also to repair and improve the bridges, which were in poor condition. This was a serious problem and still is. The bridges that were good several years ago are no longer in good condition, and this pattern will continue into the future.

Politics and the DOT

We felt that an increase in the motor fuel tax was timely and was something that should happen. However, my personal philosophy over the years had been to oppose the direct allocation of fuel-tax money to the Department of Transportation. I have always felt that every state agency, DOT included, should come to the same trough and pass through the same scrutiny as all other requests. If it's a worthy expenditure or worthy request, the General Assembly is going to honor it. Knowing the politics of the DOT, I believed that if it were turned loose to compete for their budget like all the other state agencies, they would probably end up with more money than they were actually receiving through the direct allocation of motor fuel taxes. The funds that are earmarked for the DOT constitutionally, i.e., the sales tax on fuel and gasoline taxes allocated on a per-gallon basis go directly to the DOT; it does not have to go through the appropriations process. The General Assembly, however, must appropriate an amount equal to the fuel taxes collected.

Another point is that if the collections next year are less than the collections this year, then the difference must be made up in general funds. you cannot give the DOT less money this year than they received in motor fuel taxes last year. Again, this is mandated by the state constitution. Moreover, the need has exceeded the available funds by such large dollars that we have been using borrowed money, or bonds, for many years to supplement the DOT. I was looking for a way to relieve that debt service on the borrowed money and put it back into a more "pay-as-you-go" basis. This initiative was worked on extremely hard by our administration and the DOT, as well as by the people who were supportive of the road improvements which we were trying to make all across the state. Unfortunately, we were just not able to pass it through the General Assembly. we had gotten caught in an attitude by the public that "no additional taxes on transportation should be forthcoming." As luck would have it, in a sense, there was a substitution made, and instead of increasing the fuel tax the General Assembly, in its wisdom, decided to increase the sales tax. When the sales tax was increased, the majority of that money was used to fund prison construction which was already under way. Money that was absorbed in the state budget didn't have to be borrowed, and it helped offset some of the real needs that were pressing. Plus, it added some additional money in cash to the Department of Transportation.

We did have some major improvements that were completed and funded during our administration. The Appalachian Freeway, which is I-575 and runs through the North Georgia mountains, was completed. Corridor Z, which was already underway, started in Columbus, Georgia, ran through the southern part of the state, and ended up in Brunswick. Our administration finished funding it, and it was completed while I was governor. Thus, we had two major corridors that we hadn't had before. In 1985, the planning for the "Fall-Line Freeway" started. It would run from the south of Macon to the coast. A tremendous number of four lanes and passing lanes, and many bridges were improved and completed in conjunction with this Freeway.

Peachy Clean

To increase public awareness of the state's litter problem, a state-wide anti-littering campaign called "Let's Keep Georgia Peachy Clean" became the theme that originated with the Department of Transportation in 1990. Of course, we were involved in it, but there was also a growing movement among the people to discourage throwing trash out of automobile windows as well as other littering which had been almost habitual in the past. A lot of youngsters were being taught about environmental cleanliness in the schools, and this campaign helped provide brochures and materials for young people which planted the seed in their subconscious minds not to develop the same habits as their parents and grandparents where environmental litter was concerned. I think it had a positive impact.

Turnaround Trains

Much of the rural areas of Georgia were not being served by the railroads. They were actually beginning to plow under some of those areas as far as service was concerned because they were just not generating the kind of volume that it would take, as a business property, to operate those rail facilities. Therefore, the state got into the business of trying to retain some of this railroad right-of-way for the future and to actually refurbish some of the trackage. The Department of Transportation had never done anything like this. It had always been involved in highways but not rail or air. It had to become a real transportation department and look at all facets of transportation. (I think this was the first move towards making the DOT into a full-service organization, which I believe to be very important.)

The first rail trackage that was rehabilitated was the line that runs from Fort Valley to Perry, Georgia. The state moved in and allocated money to keep that line open and maintain it. Other right-of-ways were secured, and as a railroad company moved out, the state would move in and purchase the right-of-way. This enabled us to keep those corridors available until a rail line could be reestablished, if necessary. Property for future need and development remains even today because of right-of-ways that were purchased during that period, beginning in 1985.

We were able to work with the rail lines to establish what we called at the time "a sales tool for industries." Located in Georgia, it worked something like this: "Turnaround trains" would move back and forth between Atlanta and Savannah. For example, a train would leave Savannah in the morning, hauling the containers from the port to Atlanta to be distributed here at the piggyback center. Almost simultaneously, you would have a train leaving Atlanta and going South to the port, also in the morning, which meant that there would be trains going both ways, every day. Within a twenty-four hour period, if the ship brought the container into Savannah in the morning, it could be on the ground in Atlanta in a few hours and not have to be transported up the highways. We supported the rail lines in expanding their piggyback facilities here in Atlanta. The "turnaround train" concept became a real sales tool for us as far as industries that needed to import or export were concerned. The concept sounded good to our industrial prospects.

Dependent on the Rails

Our early economy came from the rails, and the state still owns the railroad right-of-way and leases of the line from Atlanta to Chattanooga. There have been moves over the years to sell this property to the railroads. When I was a member of the General Assembly, I recall that the controversy of railway leases and their renewal became issues that precipitated violent political battles during those years. There were several railroads that wanted to be successful bidders. It was a real controversy during those times, and is still very important to the state. I'm a firm believer that if the state of Georgia owns property, it shouldn't sell that property, because the value of it continues to escalate each year. The amount of money that you can generate from the private sector, for use of that corridor or that property, is worthwhile to future generations. I'm glad that these resources were not sold before our time, because we were able to enjoy the revenues that had been generated. Then, too, the leases have a built-in escalation clause that increases the rent on an annual basis—whether or not the value of the dollar decreases, or the economy increases. I think we've had some good benefits from having inherited that property.

Cartersville, my hometown, has three rail lines that serve our community. There is a rail line that comes in from Chattanooga and continued on into Atlanta, another line from Knoxville, Tennessee, and and there is a "spur line" from Rockmart to Cartersville. We have access to three different rail companies that serve the city of Cartersville. Even today, there are more trains through downtown Cartersville than probably many of the industrial cities of the world. We still have an awful lot of train traffic, going both ways from Cartersville to Chattanooga or Knoxville. It has been extremely important—just as it has been for the whole state—that we have not only proper road and highway transportation facilities, but that many of our industries that are shipping or receiving raw material or finished products have access to the rail. Then again, it's handy to have the rail for the piggyback facilities.

In Harris Cement Products, our family business, we were totally dependent on the rail, initially. Much of our raw materials, which we used in our concrete business, came to us by rail. Our white sand came from middle Georgia. The crushed stone would arrive by truck, usually from a quarry not far away. Then the raw cement would come from the cement plants that are located in Georgia, Tennessee, and Alabama. Initially, there was no way to ship the raw cement except by rail. If you weren't located on a railroad, you didn't have access to raw materials. We had to locate our plant on a rail site and were very dependent on the rail for many years. Today, all of the material, including raw cement, can be transported on our highways.

16

Back Before the People

Elizabeth's schedule was probably as intense as mine; she not only had to manage day-to-day operations at the Governor's Mansion, she had to handle preparations for all the functions that were scheduled there. These included numerous events each week, sometimes several a day. There was the "open house" time period in which the public was invited to tour the mansion grounds on a daily basis during the mornings from 10:00 A.M. to 11:30 A.M. Large groups of school children and others took advantage of this, which we were glad to see. The mansion is a beautiful place and quite representative of our state. The citizens ought to have an opportunity to enjoy it. We were pleased that this could happen, but it takes a great deal of preparation on the part of the staff and the volunteers who came to serve as hostesses for the large number of visitors.

The First Lady had that responsibility, and, in addition, received an awful lot of requests to speak and make appearances on behalf of our administration. There were many individual requests particularly for the church and other religious functions to speak and share her personal convictions. Her already-busy schedule was also affected by my requirements: many of the functions or events that I attended required the First Lady to be there, particularly if other governmental officials' wives were in attendance. She was also an important and very valuable part of all of our foreign travels, which of course included our overseas economic development missions.

In our conversations with our host government and business leaders, she was able to pick-up important knowledge and information that was useful to us in presenting the state in a proper way. Many times, because of her valuable experience in economic development strategy, she planted seeds that became helpful in our efforts to sell Georgia.

In 1985 as I considered my future political plans, I was convinced that no one in public office ever had a more effective, or more loving, family support system than Joe Frank Harris.

A Family Lawyer

My son was involved in my 1983 campaign and was just beginning college at the University of Georgia majoring in finance. He was in the Honors Program and was exempted from some of his early courses. As a part of this program, he took a business law course in his junior year and really liked it. He came in one weekend and said, "Dad, what would you think if I told you that I might want to go to law school, instead of getting a master's in finance?" I said, "Joe, this is your decision, and I support whatever you decide; but you've heard the questions that I've received on the campaign trail about whether I'm a lawyer or not. Would you mind sharing with me why you would want to be a lawyer?"

"For two reasons," he said: "One, if you're going to be successful in business today, it has become so legalistic that a background in the law would probably be better utilized than an advanced degree in finance." He felt that it would be a good extension of his education and that a lot of other possibilities could come from that, too. "The second reason," he added, "is that I'll be out of law school a couple of years before you end the second term as Governor and you're going to need a good lawyer!" My response to him was, "Joe, if I did, I would need one with experience, not one fresh out of law school." Of course, he did go to law school, and his business career became secondary. (So far, he has enjoyed his law practice.)

Momentum for a Second Term

The second term was something that many people expected, because our biggie, the Quality Basic Education Program, had already passed and was being implemented. I was two years into my first term before we were able to develop the legislation for

QBE and introduce it to the General Assembly for passage. It became law in 1985. With time now for other important initiatives, I felt we were really just beginning, and this was not the time to stop.

Knowing subconsciously that eight years instead of four was a possibility, I suppose I was mentally preparing myself for a second term. If things had not been working well and my successes had not been what I had hoped they would be, I would certainly have had to reassess whether or not to make myself available for the next four years. However, it didn't take a lot of study to realize that, we do need to continue because our popularity had remained very positive, support was still strong, and there was a lot of encouragement everywhere not to leave now; we were just getting started. The decision was "Let's do it."

Personally, after being elected Governor, I had never planned beyond the term that I was serving, because politics can be so temporary. You never know when public sentiment is going to change or something unfortunate might happen to you or your administration; decisions that you've made previously could become a disaster very quickly. Even when I was in the General Assembly, I never planned beyond the term which I was currently serving. I never assumed that I had another term assured me, nor that I was going to be re-elected before it actually happened. Then, when I did qualify for re-election, I would become a full-fledged candidate seeking that office once again, never feeling like I had earned an endorsement term just because I had done a good job. I felt the same in the Governor's office. If I continued the success that I was having, and if the door was still open to remain for the next four years and if that was again what the Lord had in store for me then I needed to be available for it. Physically, mentally, and in terms of experience, I was prepared.

Welcome Aboard

I got to know Thomas C. Lewis back when I was Chairman of the Appropriations Committee. Tom was the Executive Director of the Georgia Franchise Practices Commission, a small sub-State agency that managed this particular area. I had met him and gotten to know him when, as Executive Director of that group, he had to appear before the Appropriations Committee. I had not known him before then, because he was fresh out of college, recently married, and living in the Atlanta area. He had moved there from Union Point down in Greene County.

I saw Tom periodically but didn't develop a personal friendship with him until he applied, and was one of the finalists, for Executive Director of our Cartersville/Bartow Chamber of Commerce. He was chosen and came to Cartersville as the Executive Director.* Having known Tom in connection with Appropriations Committee business, I was one of the first people with whom he became friends when he arrived in Cartersville. He had been visiting several churches, so I invited him to our church, the Faith United Methodist Church. Tom and his wife, Patty, later selected our church and brought their family membership there. We are all still members of this church today.

We had also been involved with Tom in the industrial development programs through the Chamber of Commerce in Cartersville. After I got into the campaign for Governor in 1982, I discovered that Tom had experience in working with other politicians, including an internship with U.S. Senator David Gambrell, along with Bert Lance's campaign for Georgia governor. Tom had been a "politico," therefore it was natural for him to be involved in our campaign at the local level, which he was and, during those days, probably spent more time on our campaign than on his Chamber work.

When I was elected, there was a natural tendency to appoint the people in whom you have the most confidence and trust. Tom Lewis was, of course, honest and of high moral character. I brought him on board as one of my executive assistants and was glad that he chose to go to Atlanta with me. He headed up the Job-Training Partnership Act, which was a new program of real interest to me as

---

*The title is now "President."

Governor. In fact, this was his primary assignment, and he did an outstanding job of coordinating the program and implementing it all across the state.

In my third year as Governor, Tom Perdue, who was the Senior Executive Assistant, left to organize a bank. Tom Lewis was a natural to move up into this position, and he served the remainder of my term as what is now called the Executive Secretary to the Governor; however, in our organization it was called the "Senior Executive Assistant." Whatever his title, Tom became a real asset in the Governor's Office. He was there to 'turn off the lights' when my two terms ended.

In 1986, when I decided to go back before the people for a possible second term, I felt fortunate to have folks on board like Tom Lewis who along with Jackey Beavers, Mike deVegter, Barbara Morgan, Gracie Phillips, Rosemary Preston, Rusty Sewell, Rick Stancil, and Ponda Walker had helped us navigate successfully through the four previous years.

Smooth Sailing

Actually, we were very blessed because I didn't have a lot of primary opposition in 1986. I think we were blessed because our team had been successful, and we had accomplished a great deal during that four-year period. We still had a tremendous level of support all across the state. Polls taken by other people, and the general polls, were still very positive and complimentary of our Administration. I really didn't worry about my re-election; I felt very confident about it. However, I had enough experience to know that in politics you'd better be prepared for what lies ahead. You never take an election lightly!

We started before the primary with a few fundraisers, raising the kind of money we felt we were going to need. But I have to admit that the motivation was not there not like it was in the first gubernatorial campaign. I did not want to raise more money than we actually needed, particularly since we didn't have strong opposition. Therefore, we didn't have the number of fundraisers we could have had to raise large amounts that would not have been spent on that campaign because we really didn't need it. After we reached what we thought would be required for a minimum campaign, we delayed the additional fundraising events until later and then I felt fortunate that we didn't need them. Truthfully, I was so busy being Governor, doing the job that the people had elected me to do, I spent very little time on re-election activities. Of course, constant campaign efforts were being carried out by my campaign staff and volunteers. I was able to appear just in time for an event and, in most cases, leave to go on to some official function on behalf of my duties as Governor. (Lewis Massey, who later became Secretary of State, managed this successful re-election campaign.)

The activity that consumed most of our campaign time during this period was assisting candidates that I had appointed to fill unexpired terms, as well as those running for re-election to positions to which I had initially appointed them. One of these Robert Benham, who later became Chief Justice of the Supreme Court was running for re-election to the Court of Appeals. Superintendent of Education, Werner Rogers, was also running for re-election at that time, as was Public Service Commissioner Gary Andrews. Of course, they were all members of our team. I had appointed them and I had a responsibility to assist them in their re-elections, which I gladly did. The incentive to raise money that year was really more for them than for the gubernatorial primary.

The Democratic primary was held on 12 August 1986. Opposed by Kenneth B. Quarterman, I received 85.32 percent of the vote. The smooth sailing continued into the general election when, on 4 November 1986, I was opposed by the Republican nominee, Guy Davis. By a vote of 825,465 to 346,512, I was elected to a second term as Governor.

17

Critical Assets

On 13 January 1987 my second inaugural speech was delivered before a tremendous audience outdoors on the Capitol step on another chilly day. The platform and decorations from our first inaugural were removed from storage and used again. This reduced the expense for another traditional inauguration. As the clock down the street began to strike twelve, Justice Robert Benham administered the official oath of office to me. In that inaugural address I made the following statements:

> Just as I want all of our citizens to be fully self-sufficient, I have the same goal for all of our communities across this state. And we can achieve! We are limited only by the extent of our dreams. My dreams for all Georgia are based on what I know about our people and our land. Georgians believe in the traditional values of home, family, community, education, faith in God, hard work, and investing for the future. We are entrepreneurs at heart—inventors, dreamers, doers—stretching to outer boundaries with our ideals. We are greater than ourselves because we are bound together. I believe in my heart that our best is yet to be.*

One of the points I wanted to make as I took office for a second term was that many of the strengths of Georgia's people were rooted in our traditional values. These were critical assets upon which we could build and achieve whatever dreams and goals we might realistically set for ourselves. And as we launched upon a second term we had little idea of the seemingly unachievable dreams that would be realized.

---

*Full texts of inaugural speeches appear in Appendix B.

This inauguration had a different feeling from our first one, not because we had been through it before, but because it was really the only event to signal the official beginning of our second term. However, we did have the prayer and dedication service earlier that morning just as we did for the initial inauguration. I felt that it was necessary again to set the tone of the endorsement term with prayer.

Since I didn't feel it was necessary to burden my supporters and friends with the obligation to raise the additional money necessary for another round of parties, entertainment, and a formal ball, I made the decision to skip these additional events. The funds for all of these activities must come from private sources and not from the state.

I couldn't believe the tremendous crowd of people that came on that day. There didn't seem to be any reduction in the numbers from the first inaugural. In fact, some indicated there may have been more people for this one. The excitement and enthusiasm were just as great as before. There was a wonderful spirit and a feeling of anticipation as we looked forward to the new second term challenges.

Only Two Shots

There is much less pressure in the second term because you're more experienced in your position and you've got more confidence not only in what you have achieved, but in what you feel you're able to achieve. You've also had some successes that help to bolster that confidence. So your vision becomes a little broader.

I think it's probably good that there is a limit of only two terms. Unlimited terms would probably not generate a feeling of finality— when you realize your time's running out, you know that your objectives have to be accomplished. If you didn't have that deadline, you might feel like"We'll look at this in the third term" or "If I'm here, we'll do this in the fourth term." You've only got two shots. and it's very important to get it done. I was committed to the idea that I would not be a lame-duck governor, even though the press tries to make you one the minute you're re-elected. You've still got things to do, and you've still got initiatives that you want to develop and complete. I had determined that however I might be classified by the media, I was going to be productive right until the day I walked out of office.

I did not spend any of my time while I was in the Governor's Office worrying about what my personal future was going to be when I returned to the private sector. I would not even meet with prospects, particularly in the last year, who wanted to talk with me about some venture or position that they thought I might be interested in after I left the Governor's Office. My standard response to them was "I'll talk to you after I complete my term as Governor. If you're still interested, come back and see me then."

Growth Strategy

Our second term was dominated by the "growth strategies" legislation that was developed and passed to devise a truly responsive development strategy for tomorrow's complex economy. We had another group of people similar to our Educational Review Commission named to the Growth Strategies Commission. Joel Cowan, who had been the chairman of my campaign, as well as the voluntary Chief of Staff for the Governor's Office during my first term, agreed to chair that group. Like the Educational Review Commission, he spent many, many hours on these important issues. Again, a cross-section of people from the state came together and helped develop the plan that was passed by the General Assembly. While these recommendations did not pass unanimously, as the education bill had, they included everything from new environmental protection laws to an omnibus planning act that was included in several bills. It was not just one package but several packages with bills dealing with solid waste disposal and reducing the amount of solid waste that the cities and counties were creating. It was mandated that within five years after the bill was passed, the solid waste generated across Georgia had to be reduced to ninety percent of the total generated at the time of the bill's passage. The counties and cities are under this mandate today.

I was honored to receive national recognition from the American Planning Association with the 1990 Distinguished Leadership Award for an elected official for our successful effort to develop the new "Growth Strategy" for our state. At the award presentation ceremony in Denver, Colorado, on 24 April 1990, Stuart Meck, president of the American Planning Association said:

> Governor Joe Frank Harris bucked the political odds by advocating statewide land-use planning in a conservative southern state and won a stunning victory. He startled Georgia's political community by launching his second term with a proposal to move toward state planning, and is the first Southerner to receive this award. . . .

This was truly a proud moment for me to realize the whole nation recognized the hard work by so many dedicated individuals to develop a plan for our future that attracted national attention.

A University System to Compete

While campaigning for Governor most of the attention from the public and press was focused on needed improvements in our public education: kindergarten through high school (K-12). However, I would always make clear that my goal was to also provide the funding and academic initiatives necessary to build a strong university system to compete with best system of higher education in the nation. There was no way I could have imagined the tremendous growth that occurred during our eight years.

Our enrollment bucked all the national trends at the time and increased over 44,343 students (thirty-three percent growth rate) for a total of 180,307 students. Officials of the university system at the time indicated the enrollment increased because of the "educational culture" fostered through QBE, a growing public school enrollment and a new awareness of the need for higher education.

Our goal to fully fund the Regents Formula was achieved for the first time during the 1986-87 school year and continued every year—an historic milestone for the university system. It had never been achieved before.

Even with the large number of new faculty that were required for the growth of new students that averaged over 5,542 per year, I was proud to provide funds to increase the average faculty salary six percent per year for a total of forty-eight percent, while the total budget for the university system was increased over seventy-eight percent during the same period.

Microelectronics

In 1983, the first year I was Governor, we were competing with a number of other states for a large microelectronics research center, which eventually went to Dallas, Texas. However, we were in competition with other states and wound up being one of the finalists for that microelectronics center, which represented a tremendous financial investment. Dr. Joseph Pettit, the president of Georgia Tech at the time, worked with us on our proposal and even visited Chicago with me to make a presentation before the selection committee. In spite of all of our efforts and hard work, Georgia was not chosen.

We tried to reassess what we had to offer, why we were not chosen, and what the other state had and how they came to be selected. We brought together a group of people, creating the Georgia Research Consortium Group, which began a concept that continues today. Originally, we received some financial support from a private foundation that enabled us to fund a study by The McKinsey & Company. The study came back with recommendations that if we were going to be competitive in these kinds of ventures we had to have more research capabilities and facilities, particularly in microelectronics. In order to do that, we were going to have to put some big money in those facilities and in our local colleges and universities.

I came up with the program advocating that we raise half the money on the state level, if the schools would raise the other half. Our first project was the microelectronics center at Georgia Tech. It was supposed to be a thirty-million dollar expenditure: they were going to raise $15 million and we were going to raise $15 million. Tech had a good initiative going and immediately raised over $17 million dollars. It was through that aggressive fundraising effort from Georgia Tech that we were able to show the General Assembly that "this initiative is possible" and were able to get the $15 million out of the next year's budget in a very dry budgetary year to start the Georgia Research Consortium program. With this program, we raised, funded, and built over $213 million in research facilities at Georgia Tech, the University of Georgia, Southern College of Technology, and even Emory, a private university.

We participated in a research facility at Emory University that brought them into the consortium, and it is being shared with the university system today. This was a first for the state and a lot of good has come out of their working together. The program continued into the succeeding administration under the name of The Georgia Research Alliance.

Governor on the Line

You're programmed probably as intensely as you can imagine during your working day. My schedule operated on fifteen-minute increments during the time that I was in the office. I tried to schedule people within those fifteen-minute increments as much as possible. Sometimes spending a little more time would be necessary. There were constant requests for meetings in the office with legislators, state officials, and private citizens. If you could be in the office for twenty-four hours a day, I believe you could schedule appointments for every minute.

I think a lot of people who entered the office thought you had a trap door, and that if they didn't finish their business within a certain amount of time, you'd push a button and they'd fall through to the bottom floor of the Capitol. It didn't work quite that way. I'd have to give my staff an awful lot of credit for moving the tremendous numbers in and out as rapidly as we did. Ponda Walker, my personal secretary, along with Judy Thompson and Morene Whitworth, my schedulers, worked with people to prepare them before they entered the office, informing them about how much time they had. Senior assistants or staff would meet with many of the people and sometimes even accompany them into my office. They would help to work through a lot of the 'fluff ' that would be necessary to get to the basic reason for the appointment as quickly as possible. I would usually receive a briefing or a memo, giving me some information about the appointment so that I could be familiar with the matter and make the proper response or decision.

Some days would have fewer meetings than others because you'd be out in the state or you'd be attending an official function away from the Capitol. You'd try to utilize your time at the Capitol with as many people as you could accommodate, but even then, there were many others that you really couldn't schedule. One of my senior staff persons would try to handle their problems when possible.

Another real problem had to do with important phone calls that came in while you were meeting with others. Usually, you couldn't interrupt a meeting to take those calls. Of course, people want their calls returned. I've tried for many hours on end to return calls. Actually, six to ten calls an hour are about as many as you could return. This sounds like very few, but it takes time to get a person on the phone, go through the pleasantries, get down to the point of the call and then on to the next one. You really can't return a lot of calls in a short amount of time. You try to catch them in-between appointments, and if one ended a little early, you'd use that time to return calls. You were constantly scrambling, trying to do justice to the volume of your schedule.

Who Shall Enter First?

When people came into the Governor's Office, I could often sense that they were intimidated because some of them had never been to the capitol before. We used to refer to some of the visitors as doing "the entry shuffle" when they came to the Governor's Office with several in their party. Just before entering, as they stood in the small anteroom outside my office, usually the person leading the charge would come up to the door and then step aside and invite someone else to go in first. Invariably, you'd have a rotation of people saying, "You go first," "No, you first . . ." and then some brave soul would step forward to lead the way.

Some of the staff would watch the entry shuffle and try to pick who was actually going to be the leader when they got up there. Many times, the person who made the appointment and was in charge would often step back—and not totally out of courtesy to the people with them. They just didn't want to be the first person to enter.

Night Vigil

I have been in the Capitol in my office many times all night long, particularly when the General Assembly was in town and a conference committee on the budget would be meeting. Sometimes, the phone would ring all night. I imagine people thought the Governor's Office was open twenty-four hours a day. Whenever I could, I liked to answer the phone myself, though most of the time that wasn't possible. I did on occasion answer my own phone, particularly if it was after hours. Usually, it was a total shock to whomever was calling; I'd hear a long pause, and sometimes I'd hear that same pause when I dialed someone direct, which I liked to do.

It never occurred to me to answer the phone by saying, "This is Governor Harris." I would always say "This is Joe Frank Harris." Sometimes people would say something like "Aw, no, it can't be." Or "You're kidding." I had a lot of fun with that. This always brought a smile. (It happens even today: Quite recently, the phone rang at home and when I answered it, there was a long pause, and the man asked me again to identify myself, "Are you really the former Governor?" "Yes." "Well, I didn't expect you to answer the phone.")

I did have a direct line that came into the Governor's Office to which only Elizabeth and my son had access. No matter how many hours I spent there or what I was involved in, I felt it was important that they be able to reach me. Sometimes, my son would call and just ask "What are you doing?" Even though I may have had very important people there in my office, I never wanted my wife or son to feel there was anyone more important to me than they were.

During the legislative session, if the General Assembly was meeting on the budget, I was not about to leave the Capitol. I learned this important lesson from having been a member of the Budget Conference Committee, the General Assembly, and particularly as chairman of the Appropriations Committee. In those days, we would do our most "damage" to the Governor's recommendations when the Governor was out of town or unavailable. Occasionally, he would be gone for whole weekends, and we'd be meeting. There was something about knowing the Governor was away that would incite you to do things that you might not have done if you knew he personally cared enough to be close at hand and was on the job with you. Therefore, from my personal experience, I knew that if the Conference Committee was meeting on the budget, I was going to be at the Capitol, on-site in the Governor's Office, many times all night long.

No Ideal Schedule

People like to feel that they've got access to a governor, that they can be heard, and that they can talk to the governor. I tried to make myself available, just as much as was humanly possible. Sometimes, I attempted more than I was really able to do, but I still tried to do it. Again, I will have to give our staff extremely high marks, because they shared my feelings. We tried to find ways to help people, rather than to find reasons why you couldn't help them, or shuffle them off to some other place.

I would average sixty requests a day just to speak around the state. That sounds like a large number, but if you multiply 159 counties times all the cities and all the civic clubs and all the various special events that communities would be holding that would like to have the governor attend, it could have been a larger number. In fact, it would keep my staff busy just declining those invitations properly—and communicating back to those requesting your appearance. Of course, you never knew if all the phone calls with invitations to speak were legitimate, and our policy was to request that the caller write a letter and give the particulars. That's how requests, particularly speaking requests, would be received and processed. We'd get a letter and then call back to confirm the information that we had received.

I guess if I had one real disappointment—out of all the things that one could have been disappointed about—it might have been that I couldn't honor all of the many requests for making speeches and appearances that I received. Elizabeth felt this way, too.

The lieutenant governor does not relieve the governor's schedule because the governor does not share any of his authority with the lieutenant governor. That is, the constitution does not provide the lieutenant governor with official responsibilities other than the legislative authority to preside over the Senate. As many times as possible, particularly for ribbon cuttings and functions the governor cannot attend, of course you would ask the lieutenant governor, and, to the degree that his schedule could accommodate, he would represent the state at as many of these events as possible. Lieutenant Governor Zell Miller and I had a good working relationship in that respect. But as far as most appearances, speaking engagements, and appointments were concerned, people wanted the Governor, and, whenever possible, it was the Governor that they got.

18

Weathering Some Storms

On the Sunday morning a few days before my son's state bar exam, I got a call at the mansion from my brother, Fred. He said that my aunt, Allie Roper, had just been discovered dead; she had been murdered the night before (February 11, 1989). 'Aunt Allie' had been very active in our church in Cartersville. She was in the florist business and had always brought fresh flowers to the church on Sunday mornings. She would arrive early, set up the flowers, attend Sunday school, and then sing in the choir. When she didn't arrive, someone suggested that maybe she had gotten sick or something, and they would try to call her. When they couldn't reach her on the phone, they went to my sister, Glenda, and her husband, Bill, who were at the church. They rushed to her home which was only a few miles away.

In the meantime, Aunt Allie's daughter Saralu, son-in-law Barry, and grandson Christopher, were contacted, and they met at her home about the same time. Her home was still locked, and they had to crawl in one of the windows. That's when they discovered her body. She had been assaulted and murdered in her home. Of course, the authorities were called in and started their routine investigation. They were able to pick up some fingerprints *and* footprints—where the door had been kicked in. It was a very brutal murder, including sexual assault. She had been exposed to the kind of ordeal that you just wish no one would ever have to endure, particularly someone as kind and gentle as Aunt Allie.

The day of the funeral, the news reports of her murder included the fact that she was an aunt of the Governor of Georgia. Of course, a lot of publicity was generated, as well as the crank phone calls, which you expect being in a public position. When we drove up for the funeral, our security people had gotten several threatening calls—and not knowing who the murderer was or whether it was a group of people, or why this had happened, they had to take all the necessary security precautions: Extra security people had to be sure that the church and the cemetery were protected during that time, all because these threats were made. It was very distasteful and a very sad occasion.

Amazingly, a quick arrest was made with the aid of new fingerprinting equipment and technology that had been requested by the Georgia Bureau of Investigation (GBI) early in my administration. (During a tight fiscal time, we had been successful in funding this crime and detection process, and it required over seven million dollars to establish such a system in Georgia.)

The discovery of the suspect in my aunt's murder was the very first time that an arrest warrant had come as a result of the new equipment. The fingerprints had been placed on file somewhere in South Georgia—for two misdemeanor charges there. When they put them through the Automated Fingerprint Identification System (AFIS), it required only twenty-two minutes to identify the suspect, who turned out to be a young man from the Cartersville area. He had apparently randomly selected a house, and investigators determined that he had no previous contact with my aunt.

It was almost unheard of in our community for someone to be murdered. It was alleged that drugs may have been involved. It was extremely traumatic. Many people had never locked their doors before. Now they realized that they had a problem as well and that doors had to be locked. Some had never had burglar alarm systems before, and they went to the expense of installing those alarms. People who had never had blinds and shades installed them along with other expensive security measures.

Today, we are really living a different lifestyle, trying to maintain the personal freedom that we used to have and enjoy. However, this tragedy confirmed that all of my efforts as governor to combat crime in Georgia were not enough. More had to be done. We had to be prepared on several fronts. Of course, the state had to have additional funds for law enforcement and an increase in the number of jail cells and correctional facilities. But it also had to expand the prison and rehabilitation programs and initiate programs that would get into our schools to try to prevent young people from being involved in criminal activities. It was a constant need and priority during the full eight years.

Our son Joe had all this additional stress to deal with at the time he was taking the most important exam of his life, the state bar exam. If that weren't enough, the day he was supposed to report for the exam, we had a serious storm that knocked out all of the electrical power, and all the traffic signals were out. We didn't have power that morning at the mansion, and fallen tree limbs had to be removed from the driveway before he could leave. In spite of all this, Joe passed the exam the first time around and remained focused during a sad and stressful time for our whole family. Elizabeth and I were extremely proud of him, for we knew the press would have reported it in headlines if he had not passed it on his first try.

Praying for Rain

Our church membership remained in Cartersville at Faith United Methodist Church, but our church home actually came to Atlanta with us and we attended Peachtree Road United Methodist Church. We also attended the Northside United Methodist Church and St. John's United Methodist Church, depending on our schedule. Usually, we attended the early church service because the afternoons were often occupied with cutting ribbons on libraries, schools, or some other requirement out in the state. While we usually attended church in Atlanta, we visited a lot with other congregations, such as the Roswell Street Baptist Church in Marietta. The Reverend Nelson Price, the pastor there, has always been a warm personal friend.

When our state was experiencing a terrible drought in the summer of 1987, we attended a special day of prayer at Roswell Street Church. In fact, I had issued a proclamation requesting all the congregations in our state to hold a special day of prayer on this Sunday because of the statewide drought. It was a serious situation for our entire state, since we had been a number of weeks without any measurable rainfall. The water reservoirs were being depleted and the creeks were drying up. We had a number of cities with wells that could no longer pump water. The cattle were dying, and the farmers didn't have hay or grass to graze them. Hay had to be hauled in from other states. We didn't know what our next step was going to be, and the only answer seemed to be divine intervention. That's when I issued the proclamation calling for a statewide Day of Prayer. It was being honored that Sunday, and I had already been scheduled to attend with Nelson Price at the Roswell Street Baptist Church. When kneeling for prayer on that Sunday morning, you could feel the spirit of the Lord; we knew our prayers were going to be answered.

Immediately after the service had ended, the press had all gathered and were waiting for me at the entrance of the church. As I walked out of the church, the microphones were stuck in my face, the cameras were rolling, and the question was asked, "Do you really believe those prayers for rain are going to be answered?" My response was "I have faith to believe that the Lord is going to answer this prayer today. I believe in prayer." There were witnesses there who can attest to the fact that, as I stated this, big drops of water fell on the sidewalk outside the church. I pointed to the ground and said, "Well, look down. It's already raining right here."

It didn't rain very much then, other than to provide a confirmation that the rain was coming and our prayers were being answered. The forecasters said that it would probably take many months before the water table would get back to the normal level, and the drought was going to be extended. But the rain came, and the water table started rising. Pretty soon the calls began coming to the governor's office, saying, "You prayed to turn the water on, now pray to turn it off."

They were looking for a reversal; however, before the fall was over, the water table was back to normal. This incident really was a physical confirmation that prayers are answered. It reinforced my belief in prayer once again and proved God is still in the prayer-answering business.

Entertaining the Democrats

The 1988 Democratic Convention was an opportunity not only to showcase Georgia but to move into the major leagues where the convention trade is concerned. It was the first time the Democratic Convention had been this far South. We put together an attractive proposal and traveled to Washington to make the presentation before the Democratic National Committee. Of course, a number of other cities were competing, and the experience was one we would use later for both the Super Bowl and the Olympics. We made the presentation and later received visits in Georgia from members of the Democratic National Committee who would make the decision. We felt we properly entertained, lobbied, and showed them what we had available. The Committee met later and made its decision.

Our main disadvantage was that the Omni Complex was really smaller than they desired. They wanted a larger place, and we didn't have one. However, this was a bit of a catalyst for us to move on the proposal for the domed stadium. If we were going to attract events of this kind and travel in the big leagues of conventions and sporting events, Georgia had to be prepared to compete; therefore, we were able to use that situation in order to showcase our need for a larger facility.

We were notified that the National Democratic Committee was meeting and that, whatever city was chosen, the phone call was going to come during that hour. I invited Mayor Andrew Young and the chairman of the Fulton County Commission, Michael Lomax, both of whom had worked on our presentation, to join me in awaiting the announcement.

I'll always remember waiting for that phone to ring. We had assembled in the governor's office and had the speaker phone ready for Paul Kirk, the chairman of the National Committee, to make the decision of the Committee known. When the call came, he made the announcement that the 1988 Democratic Convention was, in fact, coming to Atlanta. We had won; Georgia was finally on its way.

We knew we would have to raise a lot of money—over $15 million dollars in fact. We also realized that we were going to have to provide the required accompanying activities and events. Of course, several of those events were to be held at the Governor's Mansion. In our proposal, we made the commitment that we would entertain the big Democratic contributors at the Governor's Mansion not realizing that the total was going to be in excess of eight-hundred people. We had also promised that we would entertain the Democratic governors at a luncheon at the mansion. In addition, we had several smaller events that were to be scheduled there during that week. The cost for all of these activities was covered with the funds we raised from the private sector.

Mayor Andrew Young, Commissioner Michael Lomax, and I served as co-chairs of the Atlanta '88 Committee, Incorporated. (Bobby Kahn served as President.) This private, nonprofit corporation had to be established to manage the convention and make it all happen, including the collection of the contributions. (Out of that committee would come a working relationship with the state, city, and county, and a process that we would later utilize in our efforts to build the Georgia Dome.)

After the timing of activities was all set and the various functions were all scheduled and ready to go, the fund raising got serious. Happily, the business community, the Democratic establishment in Georgia and surrounding states, and even some national Democratic party members supported the effort in overwhelming numbers that made this a winning effort.

Someone to Ask the Blessing

The events that were held at the mansion will always stand out in my mind. On the Thursday before the convention was to begin on Sunday, I received a call that morning from T. W. Wilson, an assistant to evangelist Billy Graham. He reported that Dr. Graham, being non-partisan, always liked to attend the conventions. Graham had just returned from a foreign crusade that week and T. W. indicated that if we could find housing for him, he would be available and would attend some portion of the convention the following week. This was an exciting idea to me to think he could be available to perhaps bring a spiritual attitude and atmosphere into the convention. I certainly welcomed the possibility, and my hopes were that we could find a way to get him to come.

That evening I was back at the mansion late, discussing the schedule for the next week. We were having to put up some large tents to accommodate the receptions and functions we were to have there. Elizabeth was handling the planning of the functions at the mansion, and because there were so many events, she had to have added staff to support her: the planning of the meals, their preparation, the service, and the people to provide all the necessary arrangements had to be coordinated.

We were going over the format for the various meetings there, and when we got down to the Governor's Luncheon, which was to be scheduled the next week, I inquired about the program—whether there were any scheduled speakers and whether or not I was to preside. She indicated that, as usual, I was to be the host and should welcome them when they assembled in the state dining room. Then she asked, "Could you call on one of your fellow governors to have the prayer?" which was our custom before all meals. Joking with her, somewhat, I said, "I'm not sure I'm going to be able to do that; I don't know any Democratic Governors who can pray," adding, "I know some Republicans who can, but they won't be here." Then quickly, I said I had a better idea: "Why don't we invite Dr. Billy Graham to come and ask the blessing?" Without missing a beat, she said, "Sure, and let's invite the Pope to do the benediction."

When I told her later that I'd had a conversation with T. W. Wilson that morning and arrangements were being made for Dr. Graham to be here and, in fact, give the blessing she really didn't believe it. He did come on that Sunday, stayed most of the week, and attended every single event that we had at the mansion and was invited to pray over the convention. (I'm not sure whether he was praying for a Democratic or Republican victory, because the Democrats were not successful. I do know he prayed for the Lord's will to be done.) We were blessed that he was a part of the proceedings and we enjoyed his being a part of our family during that week. He stayed at the Marriott Hotel, but he came to the mansion for all the events. The Marriott was very generous in making space available for him and accommodating him during that week. Personally, for our family, spending this private and special time with Billy Graham was one of the high points in our eight years of life in the Governor's Mansion.

Only the Press Kicked

For the big spenders function for the Democratic Party, there were over eight-hundred guests. Several tents were erected on the terrace, and the activity spilled out into the garden areas. Flowers and food were abundant and planned to truly show off the Southern way of enjoying life. It's probably worth noting, too, that we did not serve alcohol at any of those events. In fact, at no time during our stay at the mansion did we serve alcohol. Even so, we were able to entertain at not only these kinds of functions, but also those involving foreign dignitaries, heads of state, and visitors from around the world at a high standard, which I think was reflective of the highest caliber our state had to offer. Never, ever did we personally receive criticism from anyone except the press. Surprisingly, we often received compliments (on our policy of not serving alcoholic beverages) from people who came to the mansion and expressed such sentiments as "I admire what you're doing." or "We appreciate the stand you're taking and the message you're sending that you practice what you preach about drinking and driving."

This was one of the reasons I think our message was so effective when we launched a real campaign to reduce the number of drunk-driving deaths in our state. Elizabeth was chair of the Governor's Safety Council. It was exciting to see some reductions in the overall deaths on the highway during my time as governor, due mainly to the award-winning public relations campaign, done without charge by Pringle, Dixon and Pringle, amid other volunteer activities. Then, too, I would have hated to think that because we served alcoholic beverages in the Mansion that someone who left there had struck or injured someone or had been killed in an accident.

A Battlefield Commission

In planning for these events for the 1988 Democratic Convention, we were very fortunate that Elizabeth had a lot of friends and acquaintances who worked in the hospitality and food industry in Atlanta. They not only helped provide a nice variety of fare, which included a Southern regional menu, but they came to the mansion to do it. Paul Albrecht from one of Atlanta's leading restaurants, Pano's and Paul's, came in with Pano's blessings and supervised the preparation of the plates that were being presented for the Governors' Luncheon. The food was truly outstanding, and the presentation was excellent. All Georgians, I think, would have been proud of the image being conveyed of their state.

Since the Convention was in the summer, we controlled the heat with fans under the tents that kept the air moving. Iced tea was in abundance; I really don't think anyone was too uncomfortable. There were, of course, an awful lot of parties in the hotels and hotel ballrooms and in a number of other venues all around town. Most businesses and corporations entertained special guests at their own hospitality suites, and we were invited to attend as many of those as we could, or at least drop by and pay our respects.

It was a busy time for us all, but this was a major responsibility for Elizabeth. There were space needs to be fulfilled, which were paramount; the proper menu and ingredients were needed and skilled people to serve the event: It all had to be hot or cold, on time and in place. And afterwards, everything had to be cleaned up; supplies that had been borrowed or rented had to be accounted for and returned. (Perhaps it was best not to know what we were getting into.)

It was just a huge management undertaking. Elizabeth really earned her "stars and bars" during that convention though it was more like a battlefield commission, because she was in the field being "shot at" before she had time to really learn what was required. She had to oversee all of it. Fortunately, she had an excellent group of people supporting her over the years—a mansion manager and office help whose services were invaluable. In fact, two individuals who were of enormous help were Linda Meir, the mansion manager, and Julie Kerlin, who served as Elizabeth's administrative assistant during that time. Nancy Newman, one of our friends from Cartersville, worked part-time and was a very valuable help to us during our eight years. A number of other friends and volunteers would come in and supplement, but we depended on the key management people and the regular staff at the mansion.

Probably, more individual events were held the week of the 1988 Democratic Convention, requiring more entertaining than at any other period during my time as governor. Every minute was filled: numerous breakfast meetings, luncheons, caucuses and seminars. The evenings were particularly full of activities.

When the Red Carpet Tour banquets were held in the mansion ballroom, we'd entertain and seat over 250 people. There were also the legislative functions in the beginning weeks of the session as well. It always seemed like there was so much going on that you were either attending one function or preparing for the next. It was like operating a sizable hotel and convention center. We had the same accommodation requirements as a commercial establishment with an added responsibility to create a positive impression of our state for our visitors.

The mansion has security around the clock, and people were admitted at the gate by invitation only. Any potential problems were mostly eliminated at the gate. A lot of problems again were eliminated because we didn't serve alcohol; people would attend the function and leave in an orderly fashion. Never once did an event get out of hand.

A Smokin' Backpack

I was a delegate to the 1984 and the 1988 Democratic National Conventions. Of course, I was there both times to participate in the convention as chairman of the Georgia delegation. You've got to be sure your delegates are all assembled at the proper time, though we did have staff people who worked with us on the logistics. I was the person with the responsibility to announce the Georgia vote of the delegates, a task in which I had had some experience. The first convention I had attended, as leader of the Georgia delegation, was the 1984 Democratic Convention in San Francisco.

I guess we were biased, but we felt that we had a better convention in Atlanta, and that the delegates enjoyed it more here perhaps because our Southern hospitality made a difference. We did have a good time in San Francisco, though we were unsuccessful with our candidate that year as well. The San Francisco convention was an educational experience for all of us; we had never before attended one. Similarly, many of the people who were delegates at the Georgia convention had not been delegates before either, though there were a few of us repeaters.

Having had that experience, I think we had some working knowledge about what to look for, and this helped us prepare our people to be delegates at the 1988 Atlanta convention. It also helped us accommodate delegates who were coming here from other places. We tried to make available here some of the things we would liked to have seen in California.

My unforgettable moment caused me to receive a lot of kidding while I was on the floor at the 1984 San Francisco convention. There are always several votes taken during the course of the convention and we were in the process of voting on the nomination of the presidential candidate. Connie Chung happened to be one of the news people there on the convention floor. She was in the early stages of her career with one of the nation's top networks. In those days they wore some kind of battery pack around their waists to power a transmitter—a little crude by today's standards.

Ms. Chung came up to interview me as chairman of the Georgia delegation, and all of a sudden, while she was interviewing me on live TV smoke started curling up her back. There was a malfunction or short somewhere, and it overheated. My few minutes of national fame really created a commotion. The delegates from Georgia accused me of giving her some "hot answers" during that interview. Connie Chung proved she was a professional, really handled the situation beautifully and all ended well. (If I had to pick a reporter to "light up," I think I made a great choice.)

Difficult to Support

Traditionally Georgia Democrats have been much more conservative than the National Democratic Party. There were so many issues and positions in the 1988 national platform that Georgia voters were unhappy about they were just not going to support them in that election year. The same thing happened in 1984. Some of the candidates for the Georgia General Assembly just kept a steady stream to the governor's office, saying, "We can't endorse the national ticket" and "Please, don't you endorse the national ticket" and "Give us a break or a buffer, because if we endorse the national ticket, it's going to defeat us."

Many Democrats had a very hostile attitude about it and just didn't want to support the national candidate at all. It was a little tough because I was trying to be sensitive to the political feelings of the people of Georgia and also accommodate the national candidates, the visitors campaigning in our state, and even the National Democratic Convention in the year Governor Michael Dukakis was nominated. It was a pretty stressful time. I was expected to support the national ticket because I was governor of the state and titular head of the party, and yet I could not.

A few weeks after the conclusion of the Democratic Convention in Atlanta, which we had worked so hard to secure, it became evident that Dukakis's positions on the dominant issues were not popular with the average Georgian. Later, when the Republican nominee, Vice President George Bush, successfully used the Willie

Horton affair to paint Michael Dukakis as an ultra-liberal who was not strong on keeping criminals in prison, it was evident that the Democrats were in *real* trouble.

During meetings of the National Governors Association I had always sat next to Governor Dukakis. I was thus able to develop a personal friendship with and respect for him despite our many differences in political philosophy. Because of this friendship, it was painful not to openly support him. When he or his campaign staff visited our state, however, I always made sure they were provided the proper courtesy for a national candidate.

19

To Build a Dome

The Georgia Dome was viewed early on in our administration as a problem and an opportunity. For me, I wasn't sure which it was going to be, but I was sure it was going to be one of my biggest challenges. In looking back now, I see very clearly that it was one of the best accomplishments of our Administration.

The primary reason the Dome was so important was that some of the large shows that were coming into the Georgia World Congress Center needed additional space. During our administration, the size of this facility had doubled. I was a member of the Appropriations Committee of the House when the original money was appropriated for the first phase of the Georgia World Congress Center. While I was governor, the need was there to build the second phase, which was funded by our Administration and built. Even before it was completed, a number of the largest shows using the facility indicated they needed even more space. That was of course a factor that had to be considered. Furthermore, the Atlanta-Fulton County Stadium Authority had a study about that time indicating that the existing stadium needed repairs and renovations. Finally, there was a possibility that we might lose the Falcons, the Braves, or both, because their leases were going to be expiring in just a few years. All of this started stirring up a lot of talk among 'the powers that be.'

Needless to say, it would have been a serious blow to Atlanta's and Georgia's economy if either of our major league teams had left. This was something that had to be carefully considered. The worst thing that could have happened would have been for these franchises to move to another city and leave that void. Therefore, I knew that building the Dome or an additional stadium was going to take a major administrative initiative, if it was attempted, and that I would have a major role to play in it.

Worst Possible Time

This was in early 1984, the year after I had taken office, and the political climate at the time was such that many other important initiatives were on the front burner, among them, education reform, prison overcrowding, transportation problems, agriculture, and the many other improvements that we were working toward. Also, the economy was not very good. It was recovering, but there were a lot of budgetary and financial problems that had to be dealt with. The timing was just not good. In the city of Atlanta, for example, there was almost a property tax revolt brewing because the local option sales tax had just recently been approved and committed to a property tax reduction. Disgruntled citizens felt that it had been absorbed in the budget and that the property tax roll-back just didn't happen. There were a lot of hostile attitudes and mixed emotions about taxes, and I knew right off that there would not be additional revenue raised locally to build a new facility.

Also to be factored into the equation was the poor performance of the Braves and the Falcons, neither of which had a very good record in those days. Still worse, they carried a lot of high-salaried players that people questioned. Even the personal problems of some of the players in those days were diluting the incentive for people to be interested in building a new facility for them. There was yet another factor: the personal wealth of the owners of the teams. Ted Turner and Rankin Smith were viewed in many people's eyes as owners who were wealthy enough to build their own facilities. Many felt that this was not an obligation of the city, county, or state government.

It was without a doubt the worst possible time to consider a project of this magnitude. According to public sentiment, the problems with the existing stadium were being overblown by the stadium's leaseholders who were trying to leverage their lease renewals against their continued tenure there, which discounted somewhat the necessity for a new stadium. There were also a lot of people who felt that the traffic and infrastructure costs associated with a new stadium would be too costly and just make things even more congested. Overall, the climate was just not great. And it was risky for our administration because it was only one year before my re-election effort.

All these things had to be taken into consideration: It's certainly not politically wise to generate a highly controversial project that could become a debatable item during an election year. In addition, the local officials with whom we had to work were suspicious almost to the point of paranoia thinking that the state was going to get into the stadium business. They were already in it through the Atlanta/Fulton County Recreational Authority and thought we were going to displace them and their involvement. So much turf was being protected.

New Proposals and Vested Interests...

A study by the Atlanta/Fulton County Recreational Authority was made in 1984 and came up with four alternatives: One was that the existing stadium could be renovated for baseball only and a new football stadium built for $84 million dollars. The second proposal was to renovate the existing stadium for both sports for a little over $36 million dollars. A third alternative was to renovate the existing stadium for football and build a new stadium for baseball at a cost of $82 million dollars. The fourth, involving the largest numbers, was to demolish the existing stadium, use that for one site, and then build another stadium nearby for either football or baseball. We could build these two new stadiums for $120 million dollars. This was not taking into account a domed stadium nor the purchase of new property, since we would be utilizing property that was already there. Therefore, the cost of any of the alternatives was much less than the actual cost of the new domed stadium, when it was finally built.

At that time, I felt that neither Fulton County nor the city of Atlanta, or a combination of both, had the financial resources or desire for such an undertaking, particularly in the political climate that existed. Furthermore, the bonds on the existing stadium was not scheduled to be retired for eight more years. They still had a number of years running on that obligation, but the Falcons' lease was supposed to have been up in 1990. Had the Falcons left without renewing the lease, then the Atlanta taxpayers would have had another three years to generate the funds to pay on that property and the bonds, without having the income from the stadium attendance.

About that time, John Aderhold, who was the chairman of the Georgia World Congress Center Authority, came to me with the idea that a combination convention center and sports stadium complex would be an excellent extension to the World Congress Center that would add needed space, plus house the Falcons or the Braves (we didn't know which at that time). This was a very logical idea and it would be a good addition. So a vision was born but neither of us had any idea how to fund something like that, or how to get it off the ground, or whether it was even a feasible project. Could the kind of revenue be generated that would be necessary to fund such a project?

I called a meeting in the Governor's office on 19 March 1985 with all of the people who we felt would have a vested interest in a domed stadium, or even an open stadium, particularly with a view toward adding it to the World Congress Center complex. At that meeting was John Aderhold, chairman of the Georgia World Congress Center Authority, Andrew Young, the mayor of the City of Atlanta, Marvin Arrington, chairman of the Atlanta-Fulton County Recreation Authority, John Clendenin, president of the Atlanta Chamber of Commerce, Gene Dyson, president of the Georgia Chamber of Commerce, and Dan Graveline, director of the Georgia World Congress Center, Michael Lomax, chairman of the Fulton County Commission, and Justus Martin, vice-chairman of the Fulton County Recreation Authority were all in attendance, as were Georgia Tech Athletic Director Homer Rice, Falcons owner Rankin Smith, Braves owner Ted Turner, and Dan Sweat, president of Central Atlanta Progress.

All these people met in my office. We talked about the dilemma, each of their needs and interests, and, of course, renewal of the leases of facilities with the owners of professional sports teams that were already here. We decided at that initial meeting, and it was a consensus, that we form a study committee and receive commitments from the participants for underwriting the costs of having conducting a feasibility study. The study should show: number one, the estimated cost of the facility, a market analysis of what kind of shows and the estimated attendance; two, site evaluations, i.e., would the Georgia World Congress Center site be feasible, or should we look at other sites? In fact, we did look at several sites in and around Atlanta. It was not a *fait accompli* that we were going to build it at the World Congress Center.

The cost estimate was to include revenue and expense forecasts for the facility, if it was to be built, as well as what would it cost to operate. Then, above all in importance, what kind of profit could it generate? All of these projections would be forthcoming from the consultants that we would select. The feasibility study would address such issues as a financing plan: Where can you generate the revenue to offset the building costs? An implementation schedule: Can you have it built before the leases for which the teams are already obligated run out? How soon can they move in? My directive to the feasibility study group from a governor's perspective was that we seek the ultimate solutions that would best serve the needs of the entire metro-area and the state as a whole.

Heard it Through the Grapevine

When I made the decision that the feasibility study was going to be made, and that the state was going to have to be responsible for the bulk of its $150,000 cost, I knew that I had to brace myself for the brush fires it was going to generate. Because the legislature had just ended its regular session, none of this information had been shared with the members of the General Assembly, the Speaker, or Lieutenant Governor Zell Miller. The Capitol "grapevine" operates very effectively and very quickly. Before I'd had an opportunity to call and meet with Speaker Murphy, and let him know what we were doing, he had already heard the rumor. He came storming down to the governor's office to question me: "What is this I hear about you building a domed stadium in that gulch over at the World Congress Center? If that's what you're going to do it will be over my dead body."

Well, the "gulch" he was speaking of was an abandoned piece of kudzu-covered property adjacent to the World Congress Center that the railroads still owned. There, on the property, was an old smokestack that was part of a gas plant that had operated there in years past and was a vestige of the early history of downtown Atlanta.

On several occasions over the years, the State had considered building an office complex to serve the Revenue Department and other state agencies somewhere outside downtown Atlanta, possibly near the perimeter. First, it was believed you could build it cheaper there. Second, parking would be more available because you could build a large parking lot. And it had to be near MARTA (Metropolitan Atlanta Rapid Transit Authority) where it could serve the people who would come from the inner-city to work there. Third, there were not a lot of good sites available that met these criteria that could be purchased at a reasonable cost. You'd think there would have been, but our requirements just didn't fit into the property that was available. I'll always remember Commissioner of Revenue Marcus Collins promoting the idea, because he desperately needed additional space. If the state had a complex of that nature with an office building and a giant parking lot to serve the office building, it would be a natural to build a stadium nearby and utilize that parking space for the stadium facility; it would serve a dual purpose.

The Speaker would have preferred a complex of state offices, plenty of parking, including a new stadium at another site. My reaction to Speaker Murphy's initial opposition to the Dome and its location was not one of having to battle him as much as it was to have a chance to explain the entire concept and potential of the plan. I felt that if he knew and understood all the options, along with the long-range possibilities, he would be supportive. Later in the process, he caught the vision and was very supportive and helpful.

We had to go through the General Assembly on two separate occasions with legislation to enable the building and the financing of the project, as well as the necessary increase in the hotel/motel tax that required legislative approval. It was a good idea and I had to try to convince the Speaker that it would work. I think about it a lot now, when I pass by there and see that beautiful Dome serving the whole state. Furthermore, the Speaker's not dead, and the Dome has been built. It was an interesting time . . . .

Getting it Built

The chronological sequence of the establishment of the Georgia Dome began in 1984 with the first idea. To show how slowly the government works sometimes, it was eight years before the Dome was actually opened (August 20, 1992). But It takes a lot of time to accomplish something like this from the time the idea is conceived until its actual completion.

The initial "Dome Group" first met in March 1985. In June, after their informal study had been completed, John Aderhold, chairman of the Georgia World Congress Center, on behalf of the State, began conversations with business and government leaders about the stadium and started the informational push for a stadium. Next, Leventhol and Horwath, a consulting firm, was hired in July to conduct the feasibility study. The preliminary study of the Fulton County/Atlanta stadium that was already underway was completed in September of that year. It indicated very clearly that they could not renovate the existing stadium properly for both football and baseball. It was pretty well accepted at that time that another stadium for one of the sports was going to have to be built. The Atlanta Falcons felt they needed it more than the Atlanta Braves, because the fifty-yard line seats, which should be mid-field and your prize seats, were further from the field than in most of the other stadiums across the country. The Falcons needed more seats along with additional suites. The football team seemed to be the one that was pushing the most to get a Dome constructed. The Braves didn't really want to play under a roof anyway.

In June 1986, a re-election year, the consultants came back with their final recommendation that a domed stadium needed to be built and could pay for itself and that it should be built adjacent to the Georgia World Congress Center as a part of that complex. Their estimate, not including the land, was $154 million dollars. That turned out to be low, but there were some additional considerations: The total cost was actually over $200 million dollars, plus the amount paid for the land, when it was completed. Thus I knew that when the results of the study were made public I would have to deal with it and defend its recommendations. I felt that I was prepared to do this.

In December 1985, the Falcons stated that they were absolutely not going to renew their Atlanta-Fulton County Stadium lease beyond 1990, unless they had a new stadium in the Atlanta metro area to move into; otherwise, they'd seek a new location. This statement, with media headlines, really poured fuel on the fire. There were no negotiations on-going at that time by anyone. The question was where would they go? Of course, cities outside the state were looking for professional teams and even communities around the metro-area were looking for opportunities. Cobb, Gwinnett and DeKalb Counties had business people who were ready to put together proposals to build a stadium.

The Private Sector

Finally, in 1987 I felt there was politically no way that the General Assembly would build a domed stadium at that time, because a crisis really hadn't developed to generate the needed support. People were just ho-hum about it; this wasn't a constituent need that the General Assembly members were enthusiastic about. The study had just been completed the year before, and enough information had not been developed for the political homework to be done. The government simply does not operate as fast as in the private sector; thus, a private group was formed. We felt that a private group made up of business leaders would be the best way to keep it moving, and maybe the state could participate with them and keep it going.

In July 1987, ten Atlanta businessmen joined together and put up one million dollars as seed money to explore the possibility of private financing. The formula they proposed was for them to raise seventy percent of the money and for the State to provide thirty percent. I felt that with the land adjacent to the World Congress Center that we were already in the process of buying and with in-kind services, we could come up with our thirty percent without much problem. While we didn't have the land at the time, we were negotiating for it.

The Georgia Stadium Corporation was born, and these ten business leaders in the GSC had the following roles: One, they would serve as developers of the project. Two, thy would market the project. Three, they would secure the private financing that would carry their part of the project. Four, they would construct the stadium. Five, they were to manage the leasehold and the investment for the next fifty years.

A Cat with Nine Lives

In September 1987, with my appropriations experience and background, I began the planning for the state's portion of the money, so that if the private group raised their seventy percent we could match it with our thirty percent. The next month the leasing of the private luxury suites was ready, and then the vehicle to finance them was announced by the Georgia Stadium Corporation. In January 1988 we had a deadline for raising the private financing and marketing the two-hundred luxury suites that were going to be available. The deadline came and only half the suites were sold, which meant only half the money was raised. Previously, we had worked out an agreement with Mayor Andrew Young and Commission Chairman Michael Lomax that we could use part of the hotel/motel tax, which would require legislation, for the government's thirty percent of the investment. That would be our share, and we were ready to go. I had to ask the General Assembly for the money to buy the property, even though we agreed that it would be a year or so before that amount would actually be needed.

The General Assembly honored my request by appropriating fourteen million dollars to buy the property. Now with this approval and funds available to purchase the site we started more intense negotiations with the CSX Railroad. Thus, in June of that year, the project was rescued momentarily.

The Dome was like a cat with nine lives. It would get on track, move along for a few days, and then die a sudden death. Since the seats and suites were not sold by the deadline, the project was rescued by a fifty million-dollar package from the banks to complete the private financing. The Georgia Stadium Corporation could finish selling the suites and seats later.

In July 1988, the Democratic Convention came to Atlanta. The members of the General Assembly and others were suddenly very aware that the Omni was just not a large enough facility to fully accommodate an event of that type and serve Atlanta's future needs where events of this magnitude were concerned. Timing is everything and the experience we had with the 1988 Democratic Convention could not have been a better push for the Georgia Dome.

We used all of our ingenuity to accommodate that event. It was very successful and lived up to everyone's expectations. But the Omni Coliseum was not as adequate a facility as it could have been or should have been, particularly in terms of future needs. This was a major factor in moving the domed stadium idea along a little further. Then in August the Atlanta City Council and the Fulton County Commission approved the Dome plan with the caveat that a ten-million-dollar housing-trust fund be set up to assist the residents of Vine City who would be displaced.

At that time, it looked impossible to put together this kind of financial package. Word leaked out that the Falcons had opened up intensive talks with some private investors in Gwinnett County about building a stadium there. In September 1988 the Falcon talks moved on from Gwinnett County to Jacksonville, Florida, which was openly courting the team. It appeared, at that moment, that there was no way to put the private group together on a seventy-thirty basis. This was compounded by all of the other problems hammering out a negotiated contract that would not only build the stadium but one the General Assembly, along with the city and county governments, could approve. Then a lease had to be secured with the Falcons. It was at this point, I felt the state had to get up front and take over the project, a decision I resolutely made in late September of that year.

I declared the public/private stadium corporation a failure, and that the state would now take the lead and operate on a "fast track." We had to move very quickly because the Falcons' lease expired in two years. I knew it would take almost two years to build the project, even if we were ready to go right then. However, in December 1988, we were able to reach accord with CSX Realty, which was an extension of CSX Railroad that owned the land. Seeing this as a sign that we meant business, the Falcons agreed to wait on the Dome until 1992. But as fate again would have it, two weeks later, Rankin Smith, owner of the Falcons, balked again at the state's financial deal and the Georgia Dome, in reality, was dead again.

Striking Another Accord

I felt this was another temporary delay, and our efforts didn't stop. We had negotiations that were ongoing all during that time. With all these scenarios taking place, the number one issue was the Falcons' lease; that had to be finalized. We had to work out something satisfactory with them. Other critical elements were the negotiations involving the leadership and membership in the House and Senate, because the matter had to go, once again, to the General Assembly for their approval. We were also negotiating with the Georgia World Congress Center Authority, the property owners, and the individual homeowners in the area. Regrettably, some of that property had to be condemned, which was a problem that needed resolution. Negotiations were also ongoing with the financial institutions for approval of the bonds that were to be sold; and, of course, Attorney General Mike Bowers was finalizing the contracts to be submitted to them. We had to work with the Atlanta Mayor and the City Council, and the politics of that body, along with the Fulton County Chair and the County Commissioners. There were also ten churches represented in this area from small storefront churches to a couple of larger ones that had to be dealt with in a positive way.

My staff and I spent an enormous amount of time on the project. Rusty Sewell, my attorney on the senior staff of the governor's office, was my liaison who negotiated and represented me in many of these matters and did an outstanding job on my behalf. While a good deal of personal involvement was necessary, he was the key person on my staff who attended countless meetings, made thousands of telephone calls, and kept me briefed to help bring all of this to a successful conclusion.

In spite of the withdrawal of the Falcons in December of 1988, a day or two after the General Assembly convened in January, we were able to strike another accord on 14 January 1989 and it was back alive again and moving. We agreed on a twenty-year lease for the Falcons. The funding for the lease would include our offsetting some of the additional costs that the Falcons were going to incur by remaining in the existing stadium until they could move into their new domed stadium a year after their old lease had expired. That was part of the consideration that we would help to compensate them for an additional year in the old stadium.

In February 1989 the legislature not only approved the Dome concept but they approved an additional two cents for the city and county to raise the hotel/motel tax. The additional two cents was already being collected to offset the costs of the 1988 Democratic Convention so it didn't really raise the amount. It just transferred the money (that had funded the Democratic Convention) over to the domed stadium and provided the income source that would offset the requirements to retire the indebtedness over the twenty-year period. The majority of the funds would come from visitors to our state and users of the facility. The financing mechanism that we finally developed was the most innovative of any strategy for financing new stadiums anywhere in the country. There would be no other tax dollars required.

Community Concerns

In April of that year, the state and local governments devised a plan for the minority-owned businesses to participate. This was agreed upon by the city, county and state governments. We were able to agree upon the ten-million-dollar trust fund, but negotiations broke down at that time on other issues. These were issues such as who was going to get the concession contracts, who was going to be employed at the Dome, and who was going to be the general contractor. A lot of personal and political turf got involved at that time.

On May 24 another stumbling block fell from the sky: The president of the City Council, Marvin Arrington, for some reason, called a press conference and promoted building a second stadium, an altogether different concept from the Dome. I'm not sure whether that was an effort to buy some time for the City Council members or whether he was sincere about it and felt that we were not going to be able to make it and somebody needed to move. As I recall, at this press conference, he had a press release of several type-written pages, bringing forth his proposal and plan for a new stadium. Once again, this slowed things down and created a lot of press coverage and questions about what we were about to do and how we were going to be able to work it all out. This amounted to another delay.

In June, having overcome that setback, we were able to get final approval from the County Commission, as well as the City Council, and we were back, alive again and moving. In July Heery International was chosen as the lead architect and brought together a group of architects to produce the stadium drawings. This had to be a fast-track project. Beers, Incorporated was selected as the construction management firm, and the general contractors became a joint venture of Beers and H. J. Russell & Company, Holder Construction Company, and Barton Malow Company.

Even though things seemed to be finally moving, glitches appeared to be cropping up again. The churches near the Dome complex still had concerns. Their main concern was the traffic congestion we were going to create, particularly on game days, parking, the noise abatement issue, i.e., the noise level at games in the Dome when the churches have some program going on, and, again, their loss of revenue. Were their members going to attend a function at the Dome and not come to church and not bring their tithes and offerings as they should and as they had always done? If you miss a Sunday, you can't make the offering up as far as most churches are concerned.

When we had the official groundbreaking, in order to voice their demands, the Concerned Black Clergy led a demonstration that was becoming disruptive to the ground-breaking ceremony. Mayor Young, who was in attendance, was able to negotiate with them with a promise that their concerns would be taken care of. At the time, we didn't realize that it was going to take additional money to take care of their problems. The State was already concerned about the amount of money that the churches in the area were already being offered, particularly some of the store-front churches. They were demanding additional money above and beyond those sums. There was no legal way for the state to pay more than the appraisals that had been made and the amount that would have been available for condemnation. Now we were left searching for some way to alleviate another obstacle, move on with the Dome, and also honor the requests of the Concerned Black Clergy plus finding a solution to honor the commitment that Mayor Young had made to them that day.

It was discovered that we were incorporating and taking over a street that belonged to the city of Atlanta inside of the area where the Dome is now built. One of the streets actually ran beside one of the churches that we were buying. Rusty Sewell, in his legal research of the matter, found that we could compensate the city for that property whatever the appraised amount might be and then the city could, in turn, compensate the churches. That was a procedure that was worked out to get the project moving again and get the Dome underway. The cat did have nine lives.

Super Bowl Silver (Minus Fiasco)

Then in May 1990, in Dallas, Texas, we competed with New Orleans, Tampa, and Miami to host the 1994 Super Bowl. I made a proposal on behalf of the state and was joined by Mayor Maynard Jackson for the city of Atlanta.

During our presentation before the National Football League, we thought our efforts had been sabotaged when our professional video presentation "blew up." Ted Sprague, President of the Atlanta Convention and Visitors Bureau, was the master of ceremonies. Just as he completed the introduction of our short video that was to show the highlights of the dome-to-be-built and the great things we were offering the sound system went crazy. It became so loud it almost pierced every ear drum in the room.

In spite of the fact that Ted Sprague had arrived a day early and had gone over every detail with the sound engineers and even tried the very tape that was to be used, something happened. We were all prepared to cover important points in our remarks that were rehearsed and timed to the minute. However, in all the confusion and embarrassment, Ted reversed the order of our appearance. Mayor Maynard Jackson was prepared to open the presentation with proper greetings, then discuss what the city of Atlanta could do if we were their choice. My remarks were to have been last and include the state's offer along with the proper conclusion asking for the order.

As the introduction began, I knew I was in big trouble because I was being presented instead of Mayor Jackson. After the earlier glitch, there was no way we could start over again. Quickly, I had to change my speech on the way to the podium, because my prepared remarks were not appropriate now. Mayor Jackson had to do the same thing, although he did have a few minutes longer to think about it than I did.

In spite of the confusion and our feelings of failure, amazingly Atlanta was selected. Our prayers were answered. In the meantime, there was a lot of speculation about what had happened. Blame was given to everything and everybody including the devil. We will always believe that one of our competitors arranged to change the settings on the sound system, hoping it would sabotage our efforts since it had been rumored Atlanta was the favorite.

Even though we negotiated the contract on behalf of the state, the new stadium was just now being cleared for construction. Finally, in June 1990, the actual construction of the primary structure was begun. We already had the contract with the Super Bowl before it was ever started. . . . Now if this wasn't an act of real faith. . . .

Olympic Gold

In September, 1990, we met in Tokyo for the competition for the 1996 Olympics. I had made a proposal and a presentation to the International Olympic Committee on behalf of the State, as had Mayor Maynard Jackson on behalf of the City, and as had Billy Payne, president and CEO of the Atlanta Committee for the Olympic Games.

The International Olympic Committee members who came to Atlanta could see the Dome construction; we could let them fly over in our State helicopter or view it from the World Congress Center . . . as the site was being prepared. I'm sure it had an impact. They could see that we were able to move forward on sites for the venues. In November of that same year, the revenue bonds were issued by the Georgia World Congress Center Authority.

A sound proposition . . .

In February 1991, just as I had completed my term as governor, the cable-supported roof center tension trusses were in place.

Then, in February 1992 the roof was completed. The Dome had risen to 275 feet, which would be equal to a twenty-seven story building. It doesn't look that tall; but if it were up beside some of our downtown skyscrapers, you would see how tall it really is. On 31 August the Georgia World Congress Center Authority officially accepted the title to the Dome. It was on-time and actually within the budget that had been allocated.

Looking back, the consultants who did the feasibility study indicated very plainly that the kind of revenue that could be generated by the Georgia Dome in conjunction with the World Congress Center, as additional square footage space, would make the World Congress Center probably the second largest complex at that time in the United States. The combination has been very valuable, and the two have complemented each other very well. It has been utilized and rented for many more days per year than we had ever anticipated. From the first year, when the Dome was opened, it has generated revenues to operate the entire facility in the black. It has never had a deficit and what a sound business investment this proved to be.*

The one point that the media never understood, and what most of the public still does not understand, is that the Dome is an excellent, sound business proposition. The only money that the state invested in the total project was the $14 million dollars that was paid for the property, which I negotiated with the chairman of the Board of the CSX Railroad, John Snow, for the agreed-upon price. Actually, we would have needed to buy that property anyway to protect the World Congress Center for additional expansion and parking. This tract would have been needed, if not for the Georgia Dome, then in future years for further expansions. It was a good investment. In fact, the revenue that has been generated from the seats, suite sales, and the concessions, with the small increase in the hotel/motel tax, that is generated by conventioneers, has created a revenue stream that has been well in excess

---

*The Georgia Dome was selected for a second Super Bowl for the year 2000.

of the needs of the project. The money was borrowed for twenty years, and the debt probably will be retired before the end of twenty years. Moreover, the State will continue to receive the revenues at a profit after that time. There has been an additional revenue windfall generated in sales tax by the people who attend events, stay in our hotels, eat at our restaurants, and spend time as tourists in Georgia.

The First Event

A part of the Dome that was of personal concern to me was my hope that when it opened, its first event would be a Billy Graham crusade. I had always felt that we needed a facility like the Dome that could accommodate the religious community along with the sporting community. It was my personal hope that Graham could come and hold a crusade as the first event. He was unable to schedule it, but he did promise us that he would come and do the formal dedication ceremony, which he did. I'm very grateful for his being there on 20 August 1992 for that dedication.

While Billy Graham was here for the dedication, we were able to have a Leadership Luncheon of business, political, and church leaders. During this luncheon, a formal invitation was extended and later accepted by him for "The Atlanta Billy Graham Crusade" for October 26-30, 1994.

When the invitation was given to those present with spiritual needs, at the close of the first message by Dr. Graham, I was seated as his guest on the platform. This gave me the opportunity to view the thousands of people who came forward to make their commitments and accept Jesus Christ into their hearts. This was another touching and great emotional moment for me when I realized that all the pain and problems of the Dome were truly worth it all. The Atlanta Billy Graham Crusade set a Georgia Dome record for single-day and cumulative attendance. More than 78,000 people attended the crusade on October 29, 1994, and over 330,000 persons attended the five-day event. A commemorative plaque was placed at the "Gate E" area in the Dome by the Georgia World

Congress Center Authority to document this record. The Atlanta Crusade also had the highest average daily attendance of any Billy Graham crusade ever held in North America.

20

Billy Payne's Vision

Back in 1987, Billy Payne made an appointment through Gracie Phillips who was a member of my senior staff. Billy's dad, Porter Payne, and Gracie's husband, Barry Phillips, had been friends and played football together at the University of Georgia. Billy had known Gracie since his early childhood. Gracie came to me and said that Billy Payne wanted to talk to me about "making a proposal for the Olympics." I was willing to give him an appointment because Gracie had requested it. However, I was a little skeptical about talking about making a bid for the Olympics; it seemed kind of a far-fetched idea. Even though it was nine years away, I knew something as big as that would require a good bit of time: Our experience in working with getting the Democratic Convention and other major conventions coming to Georgia made us know that these events don't just fall out of the sky and are always scheduled years in advance.

Billy Payne arrived at the governor's office, and we exchanged the normal pleasantries. I had met him in passing on a few occasions and had known who he was even before that. Seeing him that day brought back a lot of memories from watching him become an All-American football player at the University of Georgia, and then, after college, a successful lawyer. I had known and respected his family and background. After hearing his reason to see me, my question to him was simply: "Why do you think we could put together a successful bid for the Olympics here in Georgia?"

He covered the salient points of why it would be feasible, but the most compelling argument was less factual. He indicated to me that this campaign for an Olympic berth was a personal thing with him. Billy had a heart attack and open heart surgery before he was forty years old. I imagine when you go through a life or death situation like that it makes you reassess where you are, where you've been, and where you're going. He had these things in the back of his mind, and he indicated to me that he needed to look for another place to be involved, where he could "give something back."

Billy had been the chair of a committee that had raised the funds to renovate their church sanctuary. When the job was completed, he had realized that he had personally felt a lot of satisfaction out of that accomplishment. Somehow or other, he had the vision of an Olympics in Atlanta, Georgia. As far out as it might seem, he felt that with the mobilization of the Atlanta business community and with some of the venue sites such as the Georgia Dome already in place or underway, it would be a natural. (I'm sure that had Billy understood then what he has had to go through since, he might have had second thoughts.)

Moving Mountains

After listening to Billy make his pitch, my commitment to him that day was this: "I will support you with the full resources of the State if you can raise the money." The big attraction to me was that this would be a multi-million dollar investment in improvements and would generate millions in revenue but wouldn't cost the state or local governments a dime. He assured me that a committee would be organized to raise the money and put our proposal together.

The numbers kind of boggled my mind. I had been involved in state appropriations for years and had talked billions of dollars many times on the state budget level. However, raising that kind of money from the private sector and building all of the necessary facilities and having the large numbers of international people involved and coming to Georgia without it costing the state any money—well, naturally, I was all for it.

Billy tells the story that when he came back later to talk about some of the needed improvements, he indicated that the lake at Stone Mountain (one of the proposed venue sites) wasn't quite big enough and that we needed to "move the mountain just a little" to make it larger. He said that I replied "Well, which way do you want to move it, right or left?"

I know Billy felt my commitment was that strong and that we would provide whatever support was within our power at the state level. And we did. We entertained, visited, lobbied the guests that he invited to Georgia, and hosted many events at the Mansion. Elizabeth helped arrange and put together souvenir gifts; for example, a copy of *Gone with the Wind*, bound in leather, which was presented to the International Olympic Committee to remind them to keep "Georgia on their Mind." Most of them were acquainted with the movie *Gone with the Wind* and were pleased to have the book. Out of some eighty voting delegates on the International Olympic Committee list, I probably visited with two-thirds of those personally (either in Georgia or in their native countries) during the course of our bidding efforts.

"You Might as Well Get Ready"

One of the memories that was especially meaningful not only to Elizabeth and me, but also to Mayor Young and Billy Payne was something that occurred when we invited a number of the International Olympic Committee members, and their wives, to the Mansion for a Southern breakfast. It had always been our custom to pray before each meal, which we were planning to do that morning. When Mayor Young arrived, Elizabeth mentioned to him that we knew some of those attending represented many different religions from around the world. Since he knew most of them personally, we wanted him to know that it was not our intention to be offensive to any of them when we had a Christian prayer at the Mansion that morning; but if there were any problems, we knew he would handle it and make them aware that this was our custom. He assured Elizabeth that there was no problem, adding that we should do things as we always had and have the prayer.

That morning I called on Elizabeth for the prayer. I have always felt that if anyone could get a prayer through, Elizabeth was the person who could do it. Even back in our campaigns when we would have a special event, we would assign the weather to her. She would deliver, and that morning, as she prayed, you could just feel the spirit of God in the room. If there was such a thing as reaching up and taking the hand of God while you pray, she did it.

After the breakfast was over and we were bidding the guests goodbye and seeing them out, the wife of the I.O.C. member from Nigeria came up to Elizabeth and said, "While you were praying, the Lord spoke to me and told me that the Olympics were coming to Georgia. So, you might as well get ready for it."

This was the first real confirmation that this might actually happen. Elizabeth's conversation with this lady in the fall of 1989 proved quite prophetic. There had been a lot of prayer, not only from us but from a lot of people in many of our churches, asking that if it was the Lord's will for these people to come from around the world to our doorstep, then our prayer was that it be made possible. This was a meaningful occasion and one that we will always remember. I conveyed the Nigerian lady's words to Billy Payne, and the lady herself conveyed them to Mayor Young. She was right and I will never doubt that the Lord did speak to her.

Billy Payne was the keynote speaker for our Chamber of Commerce annual banquet in Cartersville in February 1996, and I mentioned this incident as I introduced him. While I was telling it, he indicated to Elizabeth that he had just received word that the lady from Nigeria had died unexpectedly two months before. It was sad to know that she would not be able to attend the event that the Lord had spoken to her about.

The Logical Choice

We all knew that our chances of bringing the Olympics to Georgia were very slim in the beginning. Most cities in the past that had hosted the Olympics had competed for it over a number of years and had gone through several four-year cycles before they received a bid. This was our first attempt, and I have to be honest with you: Even in Tokyo, when we were there to make our presentation to the International Olympic Committee just before the decision was made I'm not sure I really believed in my own heart that we would be successful. Billy always had my total commitment and support, but I would never have told him that I felt it was an exercise in futility. I felt that we needed to do our best in order to gain experience for the next opportunity to be considered in four years. This was, after all, the hundredth anniversary of the modern Olympics, and Athens, Greece was, of course, the birthplace and the first Olympic site. We all thought they were the logical choice, and felt they had the inside track, with historical sentiment on their side.

Until the vote was announced, there was no real indication that we would be chosen. Along the way, a few I.O.C. members indicated to either Mayor Young or Billy Payne, in general conversation, that they felt Georgia looked good and that they were going to support us. However, it was impossible to project just who our actual supporters were. There were several ballots and cities continued to be eliminated. It got down to the final ballot and I recall thinking: If we had not been the first choice of those who voted for their cities on the first ballot, and they lost on that ballot, then they might convert to Georgia. However, some of the commitments that were made earlier didn't materialize for various reasons and, as always, that's part of politics. But I really believe what worked best in our favor was not only did we have the venue sites and the ability to put them together the Georgia Dome was already coming out of the ground and could be seen. There was so much momentum and enthusiasm and great things happening in Atlanta, Georgia, and this excitement was contagious. I think these delegates could feel that. They wanted to be where the action was, and among those with whom we were competing that year they knew that the action was here in Georgia.

Jumping That High

One of the most exciting moments in my eight years as governor was the announcement on 18 September 1990 by the

President of the International Olympic Committee, Juan Antonio Samaranch, that the Olympics would be "awarded to the city of Atlanta."

There was kind of an echo in the large hotel ballroom where it was being presented. For a moment I thought I heard him say, "to the city of Athens," which of course, was the sentimental favorite. The group from Athens, as I recall, was seated to our right, in the front of the ballroom. I had them in the corner of my eye as I watched the announcement being made. Some of them started to rise and cheer, and, almost immediately like someone had stuck a pin in a balloon—deflated—and suddenly pandemonium broke loose with all of the Georgia participants jumping to their feet, including Mayor Maynard Jackson, who was seated to my right, Billy Payne, seated to my left, and Andy Young to his left. It was an exciting time.

Horace Sibley, an Atlanta attorney and usually an unemotional person, was part of the original group that put the bid together. I'll always remember that Horace was seated behind me; and when we all jumped up, I looked around, and I thought Horace Sibley was going to jump over all of us. I've never seen anybody jump that high! I think he could have gone over a seven-foot high jump. We could see, on the closed circuit TV, that people back in Atlanta were jumping too. It was a tremendous emotion, never to be forgotten.

It Can Happen

Billy Payne was a master at presenting a unified assurance of the solid support of all Georgians. I think it was really a miracle that he was in this position and able to bring together something of that magnitude. When you look back on it, I guess, you would have to question the credibility of anyone who thought they could do something like this. I've used his effort at winning his Olympic dream many times as an example: If you believe in something and you've got your heart in it, and you work hard enough, it can happen. Anything is possible.

There was, to be sure, an awful lot of hard, grueling work involved in bringing the Olympics to Atlanta. You just can't imagine the hours, the travel, the planning, and the preparation. Ginger Watkins, Linda Stephenson, Cindy Fowler, and Charlie Battle kept me busy with a steady stream of Olympic dignitaries visiting in my capitol office. I would also make calls on some of the international Olympic members when I would be in their countries representing the state, though I didn't travel to their country for that specific purpose. Mayor Andrew Young did a herculean job and deserves a great deal of credit for his untiring support of Billy Payne and the way he balanced and complemented Billy's efforts. They were a great team.

A Ticker Tape Parade

The Atlanta Organizing Committee was trying to bring every single member of the I.O.C. to Georgia and almost did during the course of about eighteen to twenty-four months. They would make arrangements for those people to come, put together a series of events to entertain them while they were here, exposing them not only to our Southern hospitality but to what they could expect should Georgia be selected. There is no doubt in my mind that our hospitality was a real, positive factor in helping us recruit the support for Georgia. Our visitors felt both comfortable and accepted by all Georgians. That's not to say they don't feel the same in other states, but I think that there's a special feeling here in Georgia, and I hope we never lose that touch of making others feel welcomed.

Elizabeth and I were not able to return from Tokyo with the Georgia delegation, because I had to remain in Japan for several more days to visit some economic development prospects for Georgia. Those returning enjoyed a repetition of the excitement of that special moment when they landed at the Atlanta Airport: fire trucks out on the runway, pumping water up in the air as the plane pulled under it and then another gigantic outpouring of people at the airport. However, we did get home in time to participate in the downtown parade, which was another exciting time and one of the few ticker tape parades I've witnessed in downtown Atlanta. There was a massive amount of paper and a great deal of excitement.

Winning the '96 Olympics was really a festive period for our state and one that, I think, created numerous benefits. Foremost among them was the geographic exposure brought by the 1996 Olympics, which helped people from around the world know just where Atlanta and Georgia was on the map. It also established the international credibility for our state that we had been working for so many years to bring about.

No Limitations

In 1990 I was optimistic that people were going to participate in the 1996 Olympics in such record numbers that it was going to be one of the best of all times. Indeed, there were more countries, more events, and more visitors than had ever been to an Olympiad. Athletic records were set and the whole event was tremendously successful.

However, there was some criticism during the first few days concerning the bus transportation, the information system, and lodging in the Olympic Village. Billy Payne and his staff moved swiftly to address these problems just as they did with the tragic bombing of Centennial Park on July 26. They were not able to satisfy some of the I.O.C. criticism concerning the street vendors that were licensed by the city of Atlanta. Maybe this was the reason President Samaranch's comments at the closing ceremony were not as complimentary as we would have liked. He said the games were "exceptional" rather than the "best ever."

I take personal issue with his assessment. Since this venture was totally funded from the private sector and ended with a surplus, I would say they were not only "exceptional" but also the "Best ever." I'm not really sure that even those of us who've been involved in some way or other, particularly during the time since its inception, really understood the magnitude of the games and how many people were actually coming, or how much money the

Olympics overall would bring to Georgia. It's something that you have a hard time comprehending. It really set a standard for our state. If Georgia was able to accommodate and handle something of that magnitude—the number one event in today's world so far as press coverage, participation, and the numbers involved—then there are no limitations to what our future can be.

21

Leaving Atlanta

When I originally ran for this office, I made the commitment that I could be governor on the first day I took office, which I did. My previous experience had prepared me for that. When I ran for a second term, I had made a commitment to my staff, and others, that this final four years would not be a lame-duck period. Also, I was committed to the idea that I would function as governor until my last day in office. I didn't intend to take a sabbatical, or be on call, or wind down several weeks before the end of my term, even though my successor had been elected and was in the process of putting his administration together. The business of the state went right on. Someone had to be in charge and run the store. That's what I had intended to do, and that's what I did.

Neither was I going to use any of my remaining time meeting or talking with people about my plans upon leaving office. My standard response, when such a question was asked, was that my office will be ending on January 14th, 1991, and I will be glad to talk with you after that date. But until then, I'm still occupying my time being governor. I guess, subconsciously, I didn't want to feel like I had infringed upon the responsibility I had in office by using that time to plan my personal future. Maybe, looking back, I should have, but I didn't. I spent my time attending to the final business of the administration and working on a smooth transition, which we had. I'd had a smooth transition coming into office. Governor George Busbee had given us the full benefit of his office and his people. In fact, we kept most of them. We offered the same consideration to Governor-elect Zell Miller. He kept a lot of our people also and made a smooth transition. I don't think the state of Georgia missed a beat during either transition.

I'll have to admit that the closer the time comes to the end of your term and you know there's an end in sight, you become concerned about being sure that you don't make a mistake or trip on something that's going to embarrass you or your administration or create a problem that's going to reflect negatively on the successes you've had. I really think you buckle down in the saddle a little tighter and maybe work a little harder to be sure that every 'i' is dotted and every 't' is crossed and that no one jumps traces on you. It becomes a period of more intense management, actually, because you want to be sure that everything is left intact and there are no problems. We were blessed during that time and were spared critical or unavoidable circumstances that would reflect negatively on our administration. We were able to walk out with our heads held high and look back with a lot of pride.

A Whole Package

We had to be able to train workers for the high technology period that we were entering. Furthermore, we needed to create a climate in which people who were seeking opportunities in our state, and their families, would feel comfortable, not only in education, but also in matters of security, healthcare, and recreation. There's a whole package that you've got to put together, and it must be recognized as being in place and working or you're not going to be competitive.

I feel that the kind of things that we were able to do, and the improvements we were able to bring about, were reflected in the over 850,000 new jobs that were created during that period of time, and that had never happened before during an eight-year period. We'd had educational reform, almost a *seventy percent* increase in teacher's salaries, and built 143 new libraries; that had never happened before either. There was new money in education that we had never had before.

Our international development in numbers had been *three times* greater than it had ever been before in the history of the state. The number of new companies from abroad that had located in our state had grown from a little over 500 companies when I was elected to nearly 1500 when we left office.

We were particularly successful bringing in Japanese companies. We added over 175 new facilities, leaving a total of over 275 and secured a direct flight to Japan, which we were able to negotiate with a Japanese airline. There were a dozen foreign banks represented in Georgia when I was elected. we left with a total of *thirty-six* foreign banks within the state when my term ended. Every area of state government had been improved and that made me feel blessed. Most of all, I felt like the state had been blessed.

A Few Regrets

I think the big regret that I have, in looking back at my eight years as governor, was that we were not able to use the additional money that we recommended for corrections and prisons for education. Had we been able to do that, it would have resulted in another big advance and made even more of a difference in improving education. We had a little over thirteen thousand prison spaces when I was elected. I funded and had under contract for construction or contract another twenty-four thousand additional spaces. That made a total of thirty-seven thousand prison spaces.

In all the years of Georgia's history until 1983, we had only built thirteen thousand spaces. Then, in eight years, because of overcrowded local jails, we had to add twenty-four thousand more spaces. We had to add nearly six thousand more employees in the prisons. We had over five thousand employees when I was elected and had to add over six thousand more. The budget went from a little over $150 million to over $500 million in an eight-year period for prisons alone. If we could have taken that $350 million dollars and added it to teacher's salaries, classrooms, and to other needs in education it would have had a powerful and lasting influence. Since that was not possible, it lingers as one of my major regrets.

We were living in a period of time when the drug traffic was affecting the crime rate. Of course, keep in mind that the population of Georgia was growing, too, so the criminal population became larger. When I became a member of the General Assembly in 1965, the total population of the state was less than four million people. It had grown to over 6.6 million people by the time I left office. This necessitated additional space for criminals.

There's an attitude that I support, along with the majority of citizens in the state, that a person who commits a crime should pay a penalty. You can't penalize without having a space to put them. There's another factor: If you've got the space, the courts will provide the prisoners.

Meeting the Press

My personality and style of operation are a little different from the average politician because, basically, I don't care who gets the credit as long as the job gets done and the program gets completed. A lot of times you get more accomplished in politics if you let other people take the credit, though sometimes this puts you at a little disadvantage with the press. they often don't understand a person who will allow this. They think a governor is supposed to jump up on every stump and take credit for *everything* coming and going. To them you are supposed to brag about what you're going to do and then brag about it after you've done it. Many times, when you brag about something in which you've been successful, even those who helped you accomplish it realize that they're not getting proper credit. They'd think, and rightly so: "I didn't do it for him. I did it for the state, and he's taking credit." So, this can create ill feelings and cause some resentment, and I tried to prevent that. Sometimes this would cost me credibility with the media, because I didn't communicate all the ongoing daily working relationships and negotiations that I was having with members of the General Assembly, or even some of the agency heads or others people with whom I was working. I couldn't risk exposing them in whatever issue or action that we were considering at that moment because of the possibility of misunderstanding. In looking back and seeing what we accomplished in those different steps along the way, I believe I had the right policy. And frankly, this approach was more a part of my nature. I was trying to be what I was and not something else.

Winding down

During the time that I was governor, I still felt inside like Joe Frank Harris. But people from my hometown, and other friends from across the state, because of their respect for the office that I held, as much as their respect for me, seemed different in the way they would address me. But I always realized that this was temporary either four or eight years at most, if I was lucky. It wasn't something that I would be privileged to be involved in for a lifetime. I had to return to the "real world." I wanted to keep that mental attitude foremost in my mind so that it wouldn't be too much of a shock going back. Time was winding down, and we had lost our lease on the high-priced "public housing" where we lived for eight years. We had enjoyed living in the beautiful Governor's Mansion.

I have to say in all honesty I didn't have any specific plans beyond serving as governor. That eight years of serving as Georgia's governor totally consumed me twenty-four hours a day, seven days a week, 365 days of the year. Maybe I should have planned beyond, because life does continue. I felt that I would find a place back in the private sector. The Lord had provided the opportunity to be in the governor's office, and the Lord would provide other opportunities; or, there would be other places where I could use some of the experience I had gained during those eight years. If this was back in Cartersville, fine. We still had a home there and at least had a place to go.

Amazingly, I'd never spent a night back in Cartersville during the time I was governor. Of course, distance was not really a factor, being only forty-two miles from Atlanta, but the demands were so great until I just didn't feel I could take the time off. When I was on the job, whether it was at the Mansion or at the Capitol, I was busy. (I would visit my parents back in Cartersville, then return to my duties in Atlanta.) But we did keep our home, and after we ended our service as governor, it appeared that the path the Lord had provided for us was to resume our residence in Cartersville.

A Window of Opportunity

I remember quite clearly that the last day was an emotional time. I'd spent twenty-six years of my life in state government. Now, it was near the end. Now, it was time to step aside.; someone else is going to take over. The power of the governor's office will not leave with you. That's something that remains, and someone else would assume that power as of noon on Inauguration Day. It was a very solemn time for me.

I guess it was really a prayerful time for me in two ways: I had a lot of thanksgiving for the Lord who had stood by me and had allowed me to accomplish the things that I had accomplished and had provided safety for the many thousands of miles that I had traveled over those years, allowing me to get from one point to another without injury or other major problems. Also, He had provided me with a window of opportunity to accomplish many goals and improvements for Georgia that had never been achieved before.

My second prayer was that the administration taking my place achieve success, and that the state continue to move forward. The Bible instructs Christians to pray for our leaders anyway, and I was praying for those who were assuming the positions of leadership and responsibility.

I left a gift that day for my successor, Governor Zell Miller. On his desk I left him a Bible. I had written in the Bible the following:

To Zell Bryan Miller, 79th Governor of Georgia, Inaugural Day, January 14, 1991.

May God grant you the courage, patience, and wisdom to meet the challenges you will face in the days ahead and may prayer be your source of strength.

Then I referred him to Psalm 37:5. It was a private gift that I hope he had an opportunity to utilize many times while he served as Governor. I know what a source of guidance my Bible is for me.

A Ride Home

We left the governor's office and traveled to the Inauguration of Governor Miller, which was held at the Alexander Memorial Coliseum, located on the Georgia Tech campus in Atlanta. Once again, it was back to an indoor arena, a pattern that we had broken when we returned the inaugural ceremonies outdoors to the historic Capitol grounds almost eight years earlier. Governor Miller had made the decision to return the ceremony indoors and had selected the Coliseum.

The day came all too quickly and suddenly I was there, participating as an outgoing governor. The "power" was transferred, and Governor Zell Miller made his inaugural address. Even though I sat through the Governor's and Lt. Governor's speeches, my thoughts continued to reflect back on how full my life had been as the seventy-eighth governor of Georgia.

As we left, I was standing outside in the cold, waiting. The security that had been assigned to us was ours no more as they, too, had been transferred to the new governor. There was some friendly kidding about my leaving the inauguration that day. A senator friend of mine from Augusta later said, "You know, I saw you standing outside Alexander Memorial Coliseum after the inauguration and you looked sad. I'm not sure that there wasn't a tear in your eye." I said, "Well, Senator, I probably was sad, and there may even have been a tear in my eye. But it wasn't because I was leaving the governor's office. It was because I wasn't sure if I had a *ride home!*"

Elizabeth and I were waiting for a ride to Cartersville. Lieutenant Jim Dixon, who became head of our security when Captain Jerry Wheeler was selected as the Director of the Victims Assistance Program a few months earlier, arranged for Jerry to take us back to Cartersville. He let us out at the door where he had picked is up over eight years earlier when we left for the Governor's Mansion in Atlanta.

22

Life After the Ride

Prior to leaving office we had decided to return to our home in Cartersville. We had enjoyed living in Atlanta, and our son Joe and daughter-in-law Brooke were living there. He was practicing law with the Atlanta firm of Kilpatrick & Cody, and we would have liked being close to them. In fact, Elizabeth had looked at a number of houses in and around Atlanta that were on the market. Compared to our place in Cartersville, none of them really fit our established criteria, nor were in a range our pocketbook could afford. Time was running out.

We had certainly always been comfortable at our residence in Cartersville. Some renovations were needed on our home there. Elizabeth supervised and organized the subcontractors in accomplishing the things that were needed in preparation for our return. When we arrived at the door of our home, we had the realization that we really were back to being private citizens and back in the real world again. We thought the renovations were going to be minor, with just a few repairs. One thing led to another, however, and we ended up having to put in a new heating system and a new roof on the house. Other repairs were needed. Kidding Elizabeth about it, I said, "Well, really, nothing is the same, except the brick on the outside and the paneling in the den inside." But everything we did was needed and worthwhile.

In the meantime, we had a lot of giant pine trees in the back of our home. Elizabeth had contracted with someone to remove thirteen of those trees, because they were so tall and could have been a hazard in an ice or snow storm. It really exposed the back area. At first glance, it looked almost bare when I walked out in the backyard to view "the damage."' Our backdoor neighbor, one of the local physicians, Dr. Bob May came over to the fence, which separates our property, to welcome me back to the neighborhood.

"You know," he said, "they were talking about you over at the drugstore this morning." "Well, that's not unusual, " I said. "What was the conversation?" "How you'd gone from the big house to the outhouse all in one day." he quipped.

I thought this pretty well described the topsy-turvy nature of the transition. In one day, you go from the number one, most important position in the state, living in the beautiful Governor's Mansion, back to being a private citizen after twenty-six years of public service. That's pretty drastic.

Elizabeth has been a tower of strength. You can imagine the pressure when you leave the Governor's Mansion where all of your meals were prepared, and a staff helped you accomplish all of those daily things you needed done. You were really busy, but you were not cooking the meals, washing the clothes, and cleaning floors of the Governor's Mansion; someone else did this.

Upon returning home to Cartersville, Elizabeth assumed her household chores: cooking, washing, ironing, and cleaning. However, I'm still her "yardman." I was once asked what I thought had been the greatest invention during my lifetime. I guess they thought I would mention some advanced computer application or some other technical innovation. I said I thought the greatest invention in my memory was the weedeater. Anybody who has ever done yard work will realize how valuable a weedeater really is. it's the handiest tool you can have for yard trimming. I used a weedeater and the lawnmower prior to entering the governor's office, and when I returned home I didn't have to re-learn how to mow the grass or operate the weedeater.

Didn't You Used to Be . . .?

It probably would have been easier, in some respects, to have stayed in Atlanta, because we would have been absorbed in a totally new neighborhood and just gone on with our lives. But when you go back to your hometown, people still drive by and pull up into your driveway (particularly when you're cutting grass).

They'll stop and say, "I saw you out in the yard and wanted to speak to you and find out how you're getting along."

We appreciate that people still remember us. Regardless of where you go, whether it's in Cartersville or even a foreign country, people recognize you because you've been so totally exposed for eight years as governor. Not long ago, I was getting gasoline and two young fellows were sitting on the curb as I entered to pay for the gas. They looked up as I walked by, and I felt like they may have recognized me. When I came out, one of them stood up, Coke in one hand and a cracker in the other, and said, "Didn't you used to be Joe Frank Harris?" "Yeah, I sure did," I replied. "And I still am."

People have been very warm and kind. Over and over again, when I've encountered folks all across Georgia leaving restaurants, or other public places, or just walking down the street, they'd come up and tell me that they prayed for me while I was governor or, "Our Sunday school class prayed for you." Of course, I've always let them know how much I deeply appreciated it, because I'm such a believer in prayer. I also tell them, "Don't quit now, keep praying for me. We all need it."

The People of Cartersville

I think we were probably prepared for the transition, as much as anybody could be. Subconsciously, we always knew that if we were fortunate enough to have a second term at the end of eight years, it was all over. My name had been on the ballot every two years for nine terms as a member of the General Assembly, and for the two terms as governor a total of eleven straight elections. I feel fortunate that my candidacy had never been rejected. We never had to experience a defeat in the twenty-three times our name was on the ballot (eleven primaries, eleven general elections, one runoff). However, we always knew that there was going to be a "hereafter." In looking back, there is a life after politics. I've discovered that you can survive.

During my initial campaign for governor, the people of Carters-ville provided us with more volunteers than we could actually manage. People were writing notes to their friends all over Georgia. in fact, we encouraged our home folks to use their Christmas card lists. We had cards printed with photos of our family on it and asked them to "write your friends and tell them this is someone you would like them to support." We also asked them to give us those addresses, and later we would follow up with other commu-nications or literature from the campaign. We had over 250,000 contacts that were generated by people in Cartersville who just wrote their friends, family and people with whom they were associated, in organizations and clubs, along with other statewide contacts that they had. This really formed the nucleus of our campaign. These same people manned our campaign office there in Cartersville and put in long, long hours every day. Groups traveled in a campaign Winnebago that was painted up with "Joe Frank Harris for Governor" signs. I never rode in it, but I followed it to communities all across the state.

People in Cartersville would join together in teams and go blitz a neighborhood, a shopping center, or a community where we were not able to personally reach and keep the interest going. Those kinds of teams were constantly being formed locally. We were overwhelmed with the support we received from the local people of Cartersville. I couldn't have asked for anything better than that, and I wish I could list everyone's name, for each one was so important to winning the election.

When we returned home after eight years in the Governor's Mansion, well, the residue of all those campaigns, kickoffs, and other activities was still there; but it's a little different. I guess the thing you probably miss, and the sense of loss that you feel has to do with the fact that you can't really go back where you were, even though you return to the same home and neighborhood. You are not viewed in the same light as you were when you left, even by family and friends. Even though they are extremely respectful and still our family and friends, there's a separation caused by my becoming known by almost everyone in the state of Georgia. The recognition factor really prevents you from being able to return to life as you left it. Eight years is a big chunk of time to be away. I think anyone several years down the road from leaving their home and then trying to return to it will find real differences in places and people. Time changes everything.

Above all, we are very fortunate and grateful and blessed that we had our own place in our hometown of Cartersville to return to. Our loyal friends there believed in us and supported us all those years, helped us be in the position to be elected, and then worked very hard to elect us. When we came home, they welcomed us back with outstretched arms and their continued friendship.

Hundreds of New Faces

We are still members of the Faith United Methodist Church that evolved out of the old Atco church of my childhood and the one Elizabeth's dad pastored in the 1960s. It's not a large congregation. However, we're growing and in the process of building a new facility at a new location. Our hometown of Cartersville is a growing area, and all the churches are experiencing new growth. After our marriage in this church, over the years, we had assumed all areas of church responsibility: Elizabeth had filled many of the positions from Sunday school teacher to pianist, organist, president of Faith United Methodist Women, lay speaker, and even the Rome District President of the United Methodist Women.

I had been chairman of the board of trustees and served on the administrative board and many other leadership positions within the church. We didn't want to go back to claim our old positions because we had been gone for those eight years; and almost a year or so prior to that, we were traveling the state and not active in Cartersville, other than to spend the night there. There was a tremendous time-gap in which we were essentially out of the community. With all the new people moving in, there were hundreds of new faces and families there that we had never met. So we felt like we couldn't go back to Cartersville and say, "Well, here we are. We are back to take over full responsibility again." It was quite different for us in this respect.

New leadership was already evolving, and we certainly knew our place was to support those leaders and their efforts, at least not get into anybody's way. We were there to help them continue to move the church and community forward.

Limited Only by Time

Of course, I had to make a decision on what my next challenge would be. Prior to running for governor, we sold our family concrete products business. and most of my other investments in industrial property and real estate had been placed in a blind trust during most of the time I was governor. Even some of that had been sold. I really didn't have a job or a business to return to, other than the old Harris Georgia Corporation, which was an industrial development business I founded after we sold our concrete products business. I still remain as chairman today, even though I spend very little time with it, because my activities are more in other directions right now, serving on some corporate boards, as well as my duties at Georgia State University.

My first priority is anything pertaining to my church or religious invitations that I receive, such as lay speaking and even filling pulpits on Sundays as a layperson. Elizabeth and I both are invited to do a lot of that. We still feel that the Lord has places where we can witness and be used. We're very reluctant to refuse anything, because we believe that may be the place the Lord needs us to be. we feel we're almost under obligation to go.

I am a member of the board of AFLAC, Incorporated, which is the number one supplemental insurance company in the United States and Japan based in Columbus, Georgia. Listed on the New York stock exchange, the company insures more than forty million people worldwide. This was a good fit for me because of the experience I had dealing with international business during my time as governor. I've thoroughly enjoyed working with AFLAC's Chairman, Paul Amos, and the President and CEO, Dan Amos.

Since I became a member of the Board in 1990, under their leadership, the assets of the company have tripled to over $25 billion.

I also serve on the board of directors of Bankhead Enterprises, Inc. The chairman of that board is Glenn Taylor, a longtime friend and one of my initial supporters. I 've already told the story of how he was really the catalyst that kept me in the governor's race. It has been my pleasure to be associated with someone for whom I have so much respect. Glenn Taylor founded and built a tremendous business as a heavy equipment manufacturer, railroad maintenance contractor, and asphalt producer.

Since leaving the governor's Office, I've had more demands on my time than I have had time to serve. I have been forced to use a little discretion in terms of the number of outside activities that I've taken on. Even today, I still receive a large number of invitations to speak or appear on programs or to visit where a ribbon is being cut or a dedication is being held. You could spend full-time just doing those kinds of things. I try to prioritize what I do, based on the demands of the boards I serve on and, of course, my responsibilities at Georgia State University.

Involved in Academia

Perhaps my most fulfilling new challenge came when I was offered the opportunity to become Professor of Public Affairs at Georgia State University. I lecture at the graduate level of the Department of Public Administration and Urban Studies located in the School of Policy Studies. I've enjoyed being in the classroom as much, if not more, than anything else I've done. Elizabeth, who was a teacher for the first years of our marriage, had warned me that teaching would be very challenging and exciting. I have even enjoyed the commute.

Tom Lewis, my senior executive assistant during the time I was governor, became the Vice President for External Affairs at Georgia State University. He made me aware that Georgia State wanted to get more involved in public policy and move in some new directions. Being located so close to the Georgia capital, actually as next door neighbors, Tom felt there would be some educational opportunities that might be interesting to me.

"You've never been involved in academia from the teaching side," he said. "But you might want to try it and see if you'd enjoy it. ." He went on to suggest that students would benefit from the knowledge and experience which I had gained over the years, along with my fortunes and misfortunes. I agreed and started teaching part-time in the old College of Public and Urban Affairs as a visiting professor. It was the best of both worlds: I didn't have to grade papers, but I did have the opportunity to visit various classes from budgeting, to public administration, to leadership and ethics. The professors invite me accordingly, and we schedule a time when I lecture to their classes. Usually, these graduate-level classes are over two hours long. That's a pretty good volume of information to absorb and keeping students interested and awake, particularly late in the day, is quite a challenge in itself.

I learned very quickly that there's a gap between where textbooks end and where practical experience is actually applied. That's a very compatible situation for me, because I've been involved in that "gap area" for many years. And I've enjoyed the opportunity of answering the students' questions or telling them, for example, the political and financial ramifications of how the Georgia Dome was built and how we were able to pass QBE through the General Assembly without a single dissenting vote, a historic event for the state. We've even talked about the concept of "taking power" as governor. I let the class know right quick that I did not 'take power' as governor, that anyone who moves into a position at that level of responsibility and magnitude has to earn that power. You may have the opportunity to occupy the position, but no authority is granted to you. The authority really belongs to the people. You're given the opportunity to exercise that authority effectively.

On 1 December 1994, Dr. Carl Patton, President of Georgia State University, appointed me to be the University's first Distinguished Executive Fellow. The Fellowship is sponsored by

Truett Cathy, founder of Chic-Fil-A, and Deen Day Smith and the Day Foundation.

Make the First Step

The transition back to Cartersville and the adjustment was much harder on Elizabeth than it was on me. I was preoccupied with finding a new challenge along with a way to make a living. I was out of work and off any payroll, and had to find some meaningful employment somewhere that would generate at least grocery money. Soon the opportunities came to be a member of several corporate boards, and later, my appointment at Georgia State University. Elizabeth felt that because she had been busy with so many activities, and so many official responsibilities, that there might be a new challenge waiting, something she could move into immediately, a new opportunity. Nothing really materialized. Like many of us, she thought that if the Lord had something definite and in mind, He was going to lay it at her feet. With the passage of time, however, she's been able to look back and see that the Lord did have some things for her to do. It just wasn't what she had envisioned.

Elizabeth serves on a number of boards, Wesley Woods, State Botanical Gardens, the Commission on Colleges for the Southern Association of Colleges and Schools, and has served on the LaGrange College Board for years. She was involved in their recent Capital Campaign, and that required a lot of her time. She was also a member of the presidential search committee that located Dr. Stuart Gully when the former president, Dr. Walter Murphy, retired. In addition, the invitations she receives to speak to various religious groups consumes much of her time.

She also served as a member of the Billy Graham Atlanta Crusade Committee, which raised the funds for a successful crusade in October 1994. She was invited to speak and give her personal witness prior to Dr. Graham's message during the Friday evening service.

This may have been the highlight of her public speaking career, a chance to speak at the Georgia Dome to over seventy thousand people. Even so, it was a very difficult time for her, because my father had undergone emergency surgery that morning. He became ill the day before, and we took him to Crawford Long Hospital in Atlanta for gall bladder surgery. We remained there with him practically all night. As it was the night before her speech, she kept trying to get her thoughts together, and concentrate on what she was going to say and the message God wanted her to give. Finally, we sent her home to do that, and I stayed with Dad at the hospital. Later, I met her over at the Georgia Dome, just prior to her speech that evening. Naturally, she was very nervous because this was the largest group that she had ever stood before. She certainly didn't want to say or do anything that would not give Jesus Christ honor and praise, or limit the success of the crusade.

I'll always remember that as we were seated on the platform by Henry Holley, our longtime friend and assistant to Billy Graham, I noticed that there was one step up to the podium. Many times, when you are introduced as a speaker, you're really not that conscious of your surroundings. You just think about getting to the podium and not tripping over something on the way. I whispered to Elizabeth, "When you're introduced and stand up to speak, don't forget there's a step there." I could just see her tripping on that step and falling through the podium and tumbling out into the audience. As she was being introduced, I took her hand again and squeezed it so she would know I meant what I said and added, "Don't forget the step. Make the first step."

She did make that step and did a beautiful job as speaker. I would have to say I was extremely proud of her. She has a natural gift that I really wish I had. Her ability to relate to an audience, and the sincerity with which she comes across are just amazing. She's had many opportunities to witness and to be involved, and her support of many initiatives have been invaluable to people over the years. And today, her schedule is as full as mine.

Something Unusual

My joy and excitement at holding Joe as a newborn baby for the first time and I guess any parent would feel this way is a memory I'll always cherish. I never thought that I would relive or replay that moment again until our little granddaughter, Catherine Elizabeth, was born on July 30,1995 in Atlanta's Piedmont Hospital.

Immediately, there in the room where she was born, Elizabeth and I were allowed to enter along with Shirley and Tom Gurley, Brooke's parents. Then each one of us had a chance to hold the newborn baby, only a few minutes old. I'll always remember Catherine Elizabeth reaching up at that time and grasping my finger. I thought, well, this is really something unusual and perhaps a sign that young people really are looking for something to hold onto, some security, somewhere. That was the kind of thing that was always on my mind as governor.

I had spoken many times of a Georgia that would be something for our children and our grandchildren. We've had our child. now, here was the grandchild I had spoken about: the child who, twelve to fifteen years from now, would be in the middle of her school career. Will there be a quality education for these children? In the 1980s, we tried to establish such a program for the young people of today. I hope education will be improved on the foundation we helped build, and I feel strongly it will be.

There's nothing like a new birth to establish new directions. We were very blessed finally to become grandparents. Joe had moved his law practice to Cartersville. He and Brooke moved there in the fall of 1991. Happily, we have an opportunity to baby-sit quite often. We are grateful for those opportunities, and it helps Joe and Brooke because of their many activities. Joe is involved with the community and served as chairman of the Cartersville/ Bartow County Chamber of Commerce, which raised over $1.5 million dollars and constructed a new modern office and meeting facilities on Main Street downtown. He was chairman of the Salvation Army Board during the expansion of their services and facilities in our area. And in 1995, he was selected a member of "Leadership Georgia." In fact, we traveled to Bainbridge during that time, when Catherine was only a few weeks old, to baby-sit while they attended one of the Leadership Georgia functions.

The same kind of situation occurred in our family when Joe was a baby. I had qualified to run for office when he was two months old, and because I was involved in the General Assembly and all the extra- curricular activities, he had grown up in a loving atmosphere of grandparents. With the pressure of Elizabeth and me away at meetings, it was my Mom and Dad who baby-sat him and really instilled in Joe a lot of the qualities and characteristics that I'm not sure he would have gotten just in our home. we were very grateful for that. Many of the religious convictions and the values by which he lives his life came from his grandparents. We are hopeful that we are able, along with Brooke's mom and dad, to instill the same kind of principles and values in our grandchildren that our parents helped instill in our son.

No Boundaries

I'm still very optimistic about our future, even though sometimes when you read the papers and listen to news reports and watch TV, you feel like we're headed for trouble—that everything is going to be 'doom and gloom.' But when I visit with students at Georgia State University, and listen to some of their aspirations and goals, I realize how much of that 'gloom and doom' atmosphere is being created by a small percentage of the total. I'm renewed in my belief that there is a future for America, a future for Georgia, and a future for our children.

The difference, I feel, between the time when I was a youngster just starting out, and more contemporary times, is that my world was as big as the state of Georgia. When our son came along, his world was probably the United States. It had grown that much. Catherine Elizabeth's world is international. There are no boundaries.

A Defenseless Posture

Something that continues to amaze me is the many people who are interested in, or running for, statewide office who have contacted me and wanted my advice. I would never, ever discourage anyone from running for an elected office or serving in a public position, because we desperately need good, qualified, dedicated people who want to serve. I think the overall scrutiny that a person, and his or her family, receives from the media and opponents can be severe and terribly cruel, especially the negative mode which political campaigns have recently gotten into. If anyone has skeletons in their closets, they're going to be exposed. Or if they don't have them, they're going to be accused of it anyway and have to defend that also. Understandably, many people do not wish to subject their families and their financial futures to this kind of scrutiny and exploitation.

The majority of people with whom I served, and work with today in Georgia, other states, and even in the national arena are totally honest and dedicated to serving the people who put them there. I think there's a real misunderstanding on the part of the voting public about elected officials, particularly as it relates to expectations of those who serve in the legislature. People expect you to be able to vote correctly (from their viewpoint) on every issue. They're unforgiving. yet, in many instances, they just don't have the information needed to fully understand an issue that you might have voted either for or against. They will label or judge you based on maybe one or two votes out of a thousand in a session and either support you or try to defeat you because of your position on one issue. It would be helpful if people were more understanding at times and would realize our Democracy is based on reasonable compromise. sometimes it's a victory to make small changes, a little at a time.

The legislative arena is a compromising situation. It's a boiling pot into which you bring all the ideas and measures and then try to extract the best of what's presented. There's no way that you can go in and come out with one-hundred percent of everything you've asked for. If you're lucky, maybe you can get eighty or ninety percent. However, because you can't get one-hundred percent, some people will be unforgiving. They would say, "You didn't hold out, you didn't get it all."

It was the same with the appropriations process. You couldn't get every dollar for every program that you'd like. Oftentimes, you could get enough to keep the program alive, keep it going. but people don't always understand that. They think that their project or their appropriation is just as important as some of the others and "you didn't support what I wanted, so I can't support you."

We've also got a problem today with the saturation of the media subjecting both candidates and those serving to such a degree of scrutiny and exposure that they are left, on most occasions, in a defenseless posture. You don't have the opportunity of explaining your actions or the reasons behind a statement that you make. It's all in sound bites. the media extract what they want to use and, oftentimes, so much is chopped up or taken out of context.

More often than not, my experience was that they would send a camera crew out and record everything I said. Lo and behold, when they told the story on TV, the news anchor would give his slant or interpretation of my statements, never playing back a word of what I had said. You would see me speaking in the background, but the person giving the report would be interpreting what I had said. Sometimes it would come across accurately, with the proper inflection and proper meaning. But most of the time, it just kind of fell flat or failed to convey what and how something was said.

In a Heartbeat

The magnitude of the money issues was as large when I first ran for governor as it is now, but the cost during the course of our initial campaign, as compared to the cost today, was not as great. We had to raise (and spent) over four million dollars; back in 1982, that was a huge amount of money. The style of the campaigns today are just different. I'm not sure you could run and win a campaign today like we ran in 1982. Times have changed with the media becoming such a significant part of any campaign. You've got to raise an ungodly amount of money to access the media. Your opponents are doing it, and you've got to either outmaneuver those opponents in other ways or raise the money to compete with them through the media.

All in all, without reservation, if this were 1982 again, and the conditions were similar to what I had at that time, I would have no hesitation in running for governor again. I would do it in a heartbeat. It was a place I felt I could serve and make a contribution. In looking back, I have no regrets. None.

Writing in the Sky

When people ask me if I'll ever run again for public office, my standard response is that "we never say never." You never know what the Lord might have in store for you or where He might want you to serve. This was the commitment Elizabeth and I made early on in our marriage—that we would be available wherever the Lord could use us. And this has led us to some unusual opportunities, including the honor of serving in the highest position in the state.

At the moment, I don't see any future political service, but then again, my age and physical ability are not something that's limiting me if that opportunity came along. People will sometimes say, when a political vacancy comes up, "I wish you would run. ." I'll get phone calls and letters at times saying, "You ought to consider running."

When Senator Sam Nunn decided that he was going to retire, naturally the phone cranked up. I simply registered that the calls were from people just wanting to compliment me or make me feel good. One friend in particular started calling and was very insistent about my committing to the race. Elizabeth inquired as to how I answered people who were this insistent. "If anybody calls, and wants to know if I'm going to run," I said, "tell them that if the Lord writes in the sky where I can read it, and the message says

'Go run for the Senate,' then I'll run." She told him this the next time he called. He responded, "You tell Joe Frank to get out in the yard. I'm getting a skywriting plane, and we're heading to Cartersville." I replied, "That's not the Lord. That doesn't qualify."

Winning and Losing

High school sports made a tremendous impression. No matter how hard you train, or how hard you apply yourself no matter how hard you try, there's always someone out there who possesses superior skills. Giving one-hundred percent is just not enough. Sometimes it's going to take one-hundred and ten percent if you're going to be successful and win. Of course, winning was always our ultimate goal; you just couldn't live with yourself as a loser. You had to be a winner at whatever you did.

That attitude, I think, was instilled in me: Whatever you do. do your best and give everything you've got. When it gets down to that fourth quarter, you're not only going to be winded and tired, you're going to be able to compete and finish the game. Once you are committed to a task, stick with and give it all you've got.

Of course, there's always going to be a loser, and you must have compassion for the loser. I don't think that you have to win at all costs. You're only required or expected to do your best. My prayer was always that the Lord would help me be prepared and give me the strength and wisdom to be able to perform to the limit of whatever abilities I might have. I don't think that in all the competitions I've had and in all the races that I've run that my prayer was for the Lord to let me win. We're all God's people. I don't see any conflict at all in God's people wanting to be winners or survivors. Most of all, you've got to have humility and compassion for the person who may not be successful today, for they may prevail at another time in their lives when you won't be successful.

You've got to be as prepared to lose as you are to win and to accept both outcomes. I don't think concern for either outcome has ever lessened my desire to try to perform to the best of my abilities in whatever test might have come my way.

The Task Before You

As I was growing up, Dad always worked from early in the morning to late in the evening. He would leave chores for us to complete at home. We always had a tremendously large garden, even sold some of the vegetables to people in the Atco Goodyear cotton mill village for our church building fund.

We raised and sold live chickens. Back then, we didn't have the frozen chickens that people are accustomed to today. We would do a lot of work, plus keep the grass mowed and the corn hoed. Those assignments would often be left with Mom when Dad left for work in the mornings. He would instruct my Mom to make sure my brother and I had completed our assigned chores. We knew that if you had a chore assigned, it had better be completed by the deadline. There were no other alternatives or excuses. As a child, this kind of training made an impression on me that followed me into my adult life. Whatever you start, finish it; don't do something halfway. Do it right, complete the task that is before you, and move on to something else.

In Church Somewhere

I feel fortunate to have been brought up in a Christian home with church-going parents. I didn't have to make the decision as to whether I wanted to go or not. It was just natural and always has been. On Sundays we are going to be in church somewhere, wherever I may be. Even when I was governor, around the world and in other countries, we always attended church on the Sabbath. Usually, when visiting in foreign countries, there was an English-speaking church in most of the larger cities that you could locate. But in some of the countries in which we happened to find ourselves on Sundays, either the cities weren't large enough or we couldn't find a church in which English was spoken. We would attend church anyway and listen to the songs and join in when we could, even though not a word of English was spoken. But we nevertheless could feel that the spirit of the Lord was there. It was all a part of what has been a lifelong commitment for me that still stands today.

During the years after I accepted Jesus Christ into my heart and life, I didn't always honor that commitment. There were times in my life that I did things that I shouldn't have done. But a person can renew that commitment and ask for forgiveness again, because we serve a forgiving God. I've had to do that several times over the period of my lifetime. One should always keep that commitment updated and current and that's something I've always tried to do. Life is a constant test. We are always exposed to new challenges, pulled between what's right and what's wrong while trying to maintain stability within our lives. One must realize that there is a foundation in God. You've got roots—and they connect you to a higher power. That has to be maintained over the years. The way you do that is through your own personal prayer life through praying and communicating with God. I believe in prayer.

A Family Altar

I think it's very evident that through the faith that we shared, and our religious commitment made shortly after we were married, that Elizabeth and I were willing to go and serve wherever the Lord might call us. Our family altar was not something formal or even a tangible fixture. It was any place in our home around the kitchen table, in the den or at night in the bedroom where we selected to pray together on a daily basis. Kneeling around the bed became our most convenient place and it was a place that could travel with us wherever we were around the world, even into the Georgia Governor's Mansion. After we established this time to pray each day, we were not only committed to each other, but Elizabeth and I prayed daily for our home, our family, our business, and later, our politics. Through this prayer time we both totally re-committed our lives to Christ. We prayed for the Lord to provide the opportunity for us to witness and be used. Our favorite verse of scripture became: "Commit thy way to the Lord. Trust also in Him, And he shall bring it to pass." (Psalm 37:5)

We did commit and trust that the Lord would show us ways where we could make a difference. I never felt a call to preach or to a foreign mission field . But I have felt called to be a Christian businessman, and Elizabeth has felt called to be a Christian school teacher, wife, and later mother.

As we struggled with giving it all, or being willing to accept the Lord's will for our lives, I had a very difficult time because I was fearful of a call to a be a missionary in a foreign land. I didn't want to go. It took a little time before I could finally say, "Lord, I am willing if that is where you need me to be." The moment this commitment was made, there was a real peace in my heart and a feeling of anticipation.

Never in our wildest imagination could we have dreamed of the opportunities the Lord provided us. Never could we have envisioned the prayers we would see answered. Never could we have believed the miracles that we would be a part of and have the opportunity to witness, that day of commitment.

While I was fearful of a foreign call, I did not dream that my assignment would be in the state Capitol, only forty-two miles from my home in Cartersville. It was a miracle that the Lord could take this cotton mill kid from the Goodyear Mill in Bartow County to the Governor's Mansion and then to thirty-two countries as the governor of Georgia.

This family altar, or prayer time together, included our son Joe while he was growing up and at home. Now that he is married and a father, he continues this practice in his home with this wife Brooke and daughter Catherine. This is a daily family time. No matter where we are we can pray together, not only for the personal needs we have as a family, but also for the Lord's guidance in every decision facing us, the state, nation, and our world. It is reassuring to know that you have God as a resource to turn to, that God's power is there to guide you, and that the Lord is with you in *everything* you do. "For with God, nothing shall be impossible." (Luke 1:37)

Appendix A

Election Results, 1982 and 1986

The 1982 Gubernatorial Democratic General Primary was held on August 10. There were ten registered candidates. The results of that Primary Election were as follows:

Candidate	Votes	Percentage
Bo Ginn	316,019	35.11
Mildred Glover	8,958	.99
Joe Frank Harris	223,545	24.84
Tom Irwin	1,855	.21
Henry Jackson	2,706	.30
Billy Lovett	62,341	6.93
Mac McNease	2,545	.28
Buck Melton	20,052	2.23
Norman Underwood	147,536	16.39
Jack Watson	114,533	12.72

Total votes cast: 900,090

The election results of August 10 required a Primary Runoff Election that was held on August 31, 1982. The results were as follows:

Candidate	Votes	Percentage
Bo Ginn	410,259	45.03
Joe Frank Harris	500,765	54.97

Total votes cast: 911,024

The General Election for Governor of the state of Georgia was held on November 2, 1982. The results of that election were as follows:

Candidate	Votes	Percentage
Bob Bell (Rep.)	434,496	37.2
Joe Frank Harris (Dem.)	734,090	62.8

Total Votes Cast: 1,168,586

The 1986 Gubernatorial Democratic General Primary was held on August 12. The results of that Primary Election were as follows:

Candidate	Votes	Percentage
Kenneth B. Quarterman	89,759	14.68
Joe Frank Harris	521,704	85.32

Total Votes Cast: 611,463

The General Election for Governor of the State of Georgia was held on November 4, 1986. The results of that election were as follows:

Candidate	Votes	Percentage
Guy Davis (Rep.)	346,512	29.49
Joe Frank Harris (Dem.)	828,465	70.51

Total votes cast: 1,174,977

Appendix B

Inaugural Addresses

The following Inaugural Address for Governor Harris's first term *was delivered on January 11, 1983:*

This day began as a venture of faith for me and my family many months ago. Being Governor of Georgia is a tremendous honor and an awesome responsibility that with God's help I accept. Seventy-seven distinguished Georgians have preceded me in taking this solemn vow, and it is with humility and a strong faith in the future . . . and in my God that I assume the challenge of this high office.

To my family and to the many other Georgians who worked so tirelessly to make this moment possible, I thank you from the bottom of my heart. I pledge to you that I will spend the next four years striving to be the kind of Governor that you will always be proud that you worked and voted for. I will need your continued support and your prayers in the days, months, and years to come. As I stand here before you today . . . the seventy-eighth Governor of the great state of Georgia, I am keenly aware that at this very moment and on this very spot . . . the past meets the future. In preparing for this moment, I read many of the inaugural addresses given by Governors before me and what is so immediately apparent is that every man who has served as Governor of this state shared a common hope and desire to make Georgia a better place to work, to live, and to raise our children. I am like all of my predecessors in that I, too, cherish that dream for Georgia. But like each of those individuals, I hope my personal experiences and abilities will make that dream come true. I am a believer in the lessons of history, and I am a believer in building on a solid foundation. I'm also a believer in the people of our state. We in Georgia have a history of *sound* State Government, especially in recent times . . . and I intend to build on the solid foundation which has been left as a legacy to us by previous Governors and previous General Assemblies.

I am taking office during a time of economic uncertainty, and I am not so naive as to try and paint a picture of financial bliss in the State Government. I am only too aware that the realities of the economy will limit the scale and the scope of my Administration, but I am prepared by determination and personal experience to make the most of the limited resources at our command—for the time being. I am committed to stringent and responsible management of the State's fiscal resources, to getting the most service for every tax dollar, and to the principle of better government, *not more* government.

While I fully intend to see that State Government is managed and operated within its means and with no tax increase for the next four years, let me hasten to point out that my commitment does not require State Government to operate without dreams, nor does it mean that those dreams cannot—or will not—be fulfilled. Georgia will not stand still during our Administration.

Present accomplishments and present achievements were once only dreams to those who came before us. Without dreams, a boy-child born forty-six years ago in a cotton mill village in North Georgia would not be standing here before you today—taking a solemn oath of office to serve as the chief executive of this state for the next four years. I am following in the footsteps of a long line of outstanding Governors who were both dreamers *and* doers, men who dreamed of new industries and jobs, men who dreamed of better roads and highways, men who dreamed of improving public education, men who dreamed of a better quality of life for all Georgians and worked to make it happen.

The men who preceded me left long lists of accomplishments and achievements, but as best I can tell from the history books, no single Governor was ever able to fulfill all of the dreams he held for this state. In four years, some may review the record of the Harris Administration and say we did not achieve enough . . . but *no one* will ever be able to say that we did not have dreams and that we did not exert every possible effort to achieve those dreams. I know the results of hard work, the results of prayer, and the results of being committed to the completion of a task.

During the next four years, I will be striving to instill one principle ingredient in every aspect of State Government . . . and that ingredient is *excellence*. I am committed to achieving excellence in education, to the expansion of the state's economy, to provide jobs for Georgians. I am committed to the enhancement and enrichment of our human service delivery-systems, to the improvement of our system of transportation, and to the strengthening of our criminal justice system.

To best describe the way I am feeling about these next four years, I can only refer to the first time I held my newborn son. All of my hopes and dreams for him and his future came together in that one emotion-filled moment. Every parent I know has experienced that same feeling. My greatest goal as Governor of this state is to be the kind of leader who can help make Georgia the place where children have the opportunity to fulfill their parents' dreams for them and a state where children have every opportunity to reach their full potential.

There will not be a single moment in the next four years when anyone in the Harris Administration will have the luxury to stop and reflect on our accomplishments, because our job will not be completed until the next Governor takes the oath I have just taken today. I am a dreamer, but I am also a builder. I want the history books to reflect that the State of Georgia was a *better place to live* because of the Harris Administration. I want my Administration to be characterized by openness, honesty, fairness, and—above all—a burning commitment to excellence as we serve the citizens of this state.

I ask the members of the General Assembly, and all those who serve the State Government, to join with me as we shape an Administration to achieve this singular goal. I pledge to each and every member of the House and Senate—and the people of Georgia—my total cooperation and my total efforts so that as partners we work to build a state where all citizens can indeed be afforded the opportunity to fulfill their dreams.

To fulfill my commitment and to achieve my goal, I ask all Georgians to extend their hands to me—and give me counsel and support. I ask God for strength, for His guidance, for Divine Inspiration, and for His blessings on the people of Georgia, for with God's help, *all things are possible!*

The following Inaugural Address for Governor Harris's second term was delivered on January 13, 1987:

Four years ago. . . on a bitterly cold January day, I stood here and accepted the reigns of government that you accorded me. Today, I humbly accept the challenges for a second time and renew my vow to work even harder in serving as your Governor.

These four years have been marked by unusual experiences and matchless memories, great progress and real achievements, difficult times and tough decisions. But with your support and your prayers, Georgia has prospered!

In 1983, our state was faced with economic uncertainty. Public education was crying for improvement. Reserve funds were depleted and the budget had to be slashed . . . and many Georgians were in need of jobs and increased governmental services. I was committed to stringent and responsible management of our state's fiscal resources by getting the most service possible for every tax dollar . . . and giving better government, not more government, and by operating within our means, *with* compassion and *without* a tax increase. Above all, I pledged that State Government under the Harris Administration would work to instill *excellence* in every area. Because of your help, the General Assembly's hard work and support, and our State Employees' dedication and loyalty, those dreams became reality—and gave birth to a record of great accomplishments.

Today, Georgia's reserves are filled, and we are not faced with a shortage in the existing budget. We have become a national leader in education reform with the passage and implementation of the Quality Basic Education Act. Our economic growth has been unprecedented, setting new records for capital expansion, foreign investment, and new jobs. State Government is reaching out with more efficiency and effectiveness to more people than ever before. A new business-like approach to State Government and a solid team concept are in place among the members of the General Assembly, constitutional officers, state agencies, and local governments.

These experiences and lessons give me tremendous hope, optimism, and excitement as I look to the future. My faith in the people of Georgia is greater today than ever before, because I have seen what we can achieve. I'm convinced that we can realize our full God-given potential by continuing to work together.

My enthusiasm, as I look toward the future, is based on my belief in you. I am eager for the challenges ahead because you continue to be the catalyst which makes great things happen. Reflect on our achievements with earned pride, but rest not. Today I am more concerned with the future. We cannot and must not become complacent. Georgia has yet to reach its best. Our competition is world-wide, and we must be prepared!

Being your Governor has made me acutely aware that this office will always belong to the people of Georgia. State Government exists only to serve your needs and help solve your problems while seeking a better tomorrow. *Every Georgian must have the best education possible.* Education is the avenue to make our youth both dreamers and doers . . .and to reach our adults with better means of meeting a changing world. Education is a process which begins at birth and should never end. Those adults who missed opportunities before will be given a brighter pathway out of the darkness of illiteracy. For the first time, education will provide the chance to assume with confidence the rights and responsibilities as a citizen and find fulfillment in life. Just existing is not enough. Georgians must be at their best. Having access to health and medical services will enable them to be strong and to avoid illness and problems which limit or cut short their potential.

Greater efforts must be made to prevent problems, such as teenage pregnancy, infant mortality, birth defects, child abuse, alcoholism, and drug use *before* they occur, instead of dealing with them as crises afterwards. Stopping this demeaning, *deadly* cycle, which links these problems, is the challenge we face in restoring our citizens' hope and faith in themselves.

All Georgians must feel safe in their homes and in our streets—being protected from the criminal element and knowing that if crime occurs, justice will be done. Lawbreakers will be caught and punished.

Every Georgian should have an opportunity to work in a chosen field, hold a meaningful job, one which recognizes your contributions to the economy and pays you well enough to take care of your families and plan for the future.

We must continue efforts to diversify our economy, to provide a buffer from economic uncertainties, which are beyond State and local control. However, diversification does not mean abandoning support for our traditional industries, such as textiles, nor our historical economic base, agriculture. All of these are necessary for a vibrant, sustaining economy.

Georgia is blessed with a dynamic community, from small business men and women to top corporations and foreign investors, which sends a progressive business signal across our nation and around the world. Coming generations must have the same opportunity to build businesses, rear families, and develop communities. Therefore, the responsibility is great to protect the natural resources God has given us. Our existence is linked to the future of our land, air and water. We must manage these sacred resources with care and foresight.

A "growth strategy" for the future *must* be developed to insure that improvements to our infrastructure are wise and productive. Local government officials who are closest to the stresses and strains must help to meet *this* economic development need.

Just as I want all of our citizens to be fully self-sufficient, I have the same goal for all of our communities across the state. Providing our cities and towns with strong assistance is vital to put them clearly in charge of their own destiny. Today is our future, and we *can* achieve! We are limited only by the extent of our dreams.

My dreams for all Georgia are based on what I know about our people and our land. Georgians believe in the traditional values of home, family, community education, faith in God, hard work, and investing for the future. We are entrepreneurs at heart—inventors, dreamers, doers—stretching to outer boundaries with our ideals. We are greater than ourselves because we are bound together. . . a team . . . as partners . . . sharing, caring, and working.

Above all, we are a state reaching out together for God's blessing. I believe in my heart . . . our *best* is yet to be. I am not afraid of tomorrow, because we have weathered yesterday, and *God has given us* the greatest gift of all; he has given us *today.*

Let us once again join together . . .in our prayers and in our efforts . . .to make today Georgia's best. May God bless each one of you, and may *God bless out state!*

Appendix C

Personal and Political Chronology

Feb. 16, 1936   Joe Frank Harris (JFH) is born in the cotton mill village of Atco in Bartow County, Georgia. He is the second of three children born to Franklin Grover Harris (born in Gilmer County 9/17/11) and Julia Frances Morrow Harris (born in Newton County 11/9/11 deceased, July 22, 1996).

JFH is the grandson of Kimsey S. Harris (born June 27, 1884, married Aug. 12, 1906, in Gilmer County; died, October 23, 1913 in Johnson County, Texas) and Alice L. (Hice) Harris (born January 6, 1888, in Gilmer County; died June 28, 1970); and of Amos J. Morrow (born November 3, 1882, in Henry County), married December 25, 1906, in Newton County, died April 30, 1958 in Bartow County; and Sara R. (Turner) Morrow (born Nov. 21, 1889 in Butts County), died October 6, 1943 in Bartow County.

1942   JFH attends Cartersville public schools.

1944   Accepted Jesus Christ as personal savior. (He states: "...The greatest thing that ever happened in my life.") Joined Methodist Church.

1953   JFH joins the Georgia Air National Guard and remains an active member until 1958.

June 1954   Graduates from Cartersville High School. Attends Asbury College for a year.

1955   Enters University of Georgia as a sophomore

1958   Receives a BBA Degree (bachelor of Business Administration) from the University of Georgia. Member of Lambda Chi Alpha fraternity.

Serves in the U.S. Army on active duty.

Begins service in the U.S. Army Reserve which lasts until 1964.

Takes the position of secretary/treasurer for Harris Cement Products, Inc.

Joins the Georgia Chamber of Commerce; serves as Chairman of the Industrial Development Council; remains an active member until 1983.

JFH is a member of the Masonic Order, Shriners, and Lions Club (served as President).

June 25, 1961   JFH and Elizabeth K. Carlock are married. Born in Whitefield County on January 29, 1940, she is the daughter of an United Methodist minister, taught science in the Cartersville public school system, and received a degree in Secondary Education from LaGrange College.

Her parents are Ernest D. Carlock (born February 8, 1906, in Rhea County, Tennessee); married September 26, 1928, in Hamilton County Ohio and Minnie E. (Kehm) Carlock (born December 24, 1899 in Carnegie County, Pennsylvania).

March 22, 1964   Son, Joe Frank Harris, Jr., is born. Son attended the University of Georgia and graduated from the University of Georgia School of Law in 1989.

Nov. 3, 1964   Running for public office for the first time, JFH is elected to the Georgia House of Representatives for his first two year term. He is reelected for eight consecutive terms, serving eighteen years. JFH's career in the Georgia House of Representatives is as follows:

1965-1966   128th Session: District 14 (Bartow County); 1966-Dist. 14, Post 1; Education Committee; Industry Committee; Temperance Committee (Subcommittee, Secretary of Domestic and Foreign Wines).

1967-1968   129th Session: District 14, Post 1(Bartow County); Highways Committee (Subcommittee, Highway Authority), Local Affairs Committee, Secretary; (Motor Vehicle Committee Subcommittee, Vice-Chair of Motor Carriers).

1969-1970   130th Session: District 10, Post 1 (Bartow County, part; Cherokee, Dawson, Pickens counties); State Retirement System Committee, Secretary; Highway Committee (Subcommittee, Highway Authority) Motor Vehicles Committee (Subcommittee, Motor Carriers).

1971-1972   131st Session: District 10, Post 1 (same as above) Appropriations Committee, Secretary; Highway Committee (Subcommittee, Highway Authority);   Motor Vehicles Committee (Subcommittee, Motor Carriers).

1973-1974   132nd Session: Dist. 8, Post 1 (Bartow County, part; Cherokee, Dawson, Gilmer, part; Pickens counties). Appropriations Committee, Secretary; Highways Committee; Motor Vehicles Committee (Subcommittee, Vice-Chair, Motor Carriers).

1975-1976   133rd Session: District 8, Post 1 (same as above); Appropriations Committee, Chair; Highways Committee (Subcommittee, Vice-Chair, Interstate Highway System); Motor Vehicles Committee (Subcommittee, Vice-Chair, Motor Carriers); Ways and Means Committee.

1977-1978   134th Session: District 8, Post 1 (same as above); Appropriations Committee, Chair; Highways Committee (Subcommittee, Vice-Chair, Interstate Highway System); Motor Vehicles Committee (Subcommittee, Vice-Chair, Motor Carriers); Ways and Means Committee.

1979-1980   135th Session: District 8, Post 1 (same as above); Appropriations Committee, Chair; Highways Committee (Subcommittee, Vice-Chair, Interstate Highway System); Motor Vehicles Committee (Subcommittee, Vice-Chair, Motor Carriers); Ways and Means Committee.

1981-1982   136th Session: District 8, Post 1 (same as above); Appropriations Committee, Chair; Highways Committee (Subcommittee, Vice-Chair, Interstate   Highway System); Motor Vehicles Committee (Subcommittee, Vice-

Chair, Motor Carriers); Ways and Means Committee.

1966   JFH is named the "Outstanding Young Man of the Year"

1967   JFH is named the "Outstanding Young Man of America"

JFH is member of Board of Trustees of the Kennesaw College Foundation;

JFH is member of the Board of Trustees of Reinhardt College;

JFH is the President of the 7th District Legislative Association;

JFH is a member of the Board of Governors of the Mercer University School of Medicine;

JFH is the Chair of the Bartow County University of Georgia Alumni Association;

January 1975   JFH is appointed Chairman of the Georgia House of Representatives Appropriations Committee, a position he holds until 1983.

An active member of Faith United Methodist Church of Cartersville, JFH holds the following positions: Lay Leader; Chairman of the Board of Trustees; Administrative Board Member.

1978   Named Outstanding Business Alumnus of the University of Georgia

1980	JFH sells the Harris family business, Harris Cement Products, Inc. and founds the Harris Georgia Corporation, a diversified industrial development company of which he is the president.
1981	Receives Honorary Doctorate from Woodrow Wilson College of Law.
March 1982	JFH declares his candidacy for the position of Governor of Georgia.
Nov. 2, 1982	JFH is elected Governor on November 2, 1982, with 63% of the vote. At this time, he resigned his office as president of the Harris Georgia Corporation.
Jan. 11, 1983	JFH is inaugurated as the 78th Governor of the State of Georgia.
Jan. 14, 1983	Governor's car was stolen.
Jan. 15, 1983	JFH introduces a bill to make Martin Luther King's birthday a state holiday.
May 27, 1983	Announces plans for the development of $30 million Georgia Research Consortium. Funded over $213 million for new Centers of Excellence at University of Georgia, Georgia Tech, Emory University, and Southern College of Technology.
June 27, 1983	JFH receives the Georgia Key Citizen Award, the highest award granted by the Georgia Municipal Association.

June 1983	Receives Honorary Doctorate Degree, Asbury College.
Dec. 6, 1983	Receives an honorary Doctor's Degree from Morris Brown College and is named Georgia's 1983 Man of the Year.
Feb. 11, 1984	JFH commissions the U.S.S. Georgia (Ohio-class Trident submarine).
Mar. 28, 1984	JFH names Attorney Robert Benham to Court of Appeals, first African American on the Georgia Appellate Court.
June 1984	JFH named Lead Governor for Economic Development for Southern Governors Association.
Aug. 17, 1984	JFH becomes Chair of the Southern Growth Policies Board.
Aug. 27, 1984	JFH announces the "It's Okay to Tell" campaign to help prevent child abuse.
Oct. 18, 1984	JFH names Judge Dorothy Beasley, first woman on Court of Appeals.
Nov. 12, 1984	JFH announces the completion of the work of the Governor's Education Commission (established in Jan. 30, 1983) and plans for the development of the Quality Based Education program QBE).
Nov. 29, 1984	JFH chosen Co-Chairman of Appalachian Regional Commission.

Jan. 17, 1985   JFH announces plans to develop the Agricultural Exposition Center in Middle Georgia.

March 1985   JFH announces the Georgia Business Retention and Expansion Program and the Georgia Strategic Community Program.

April 16, 1985   JFH signs the Quality Based Education Act QBE which passed House and Senate without a single negative vote.

June 28, 1985   Appointed nine members of Georgia Agricultural Exposition Authority.

July 18, 1985   Announces $1 billion investment of Fort Howard Paper Company the largest single capital investment in state history.

May 3, 1986   JFH announces his intention to run for a second term as Governor of Georgia.

May 29, 1986   JFH is named "Southeast Father of the Year." In 1986 he served as Membership Chair for the state PTA.

Sept. 26, 1986   JFH receives the Richard B. Russell Public Service Award.

Nov. 4, 1986   JFH is elected to a second term as Governor of the State of Georgia.

Nov. 14, 1986   Names Thomas C. Lewis Senior Executive Assistant.

1986-87   Chairman of the Southern Regional Education Board

Jan. 15, 1987   In his State of the State address JFH announces the release of the "Water Resources Management Strategy Document," and the development of the "Growth Strategies Commission."

Feb. 12, 1987   JFH introduces Dr. Billy Graham, the speaker for the Governor's Prayer Breakfast.

Feb. 14, 1987   JFH receives the Tenth Anniversary Big Heart Award.

June 1987   JFH appoints members of the Growth Strategies Commission. Receives Honorary Doctorates from LaGrange College and Mercer University.

Oct. 22, 1987   JFH announces the Drug Abuse Awareness Campaign by creating the Governor's Commission on Drug Awareness and Prevention.

Dec. 31, 1987   JFH announces the formation of a Human Relations Commission.

1987-1988   Chairman (Sept. 1, 1987) of the Southern Governor's Association; Vice-Chairman of the Committee on Energy and Environment; Member of the Committee on Transportation, Commerce, and Communications of the National Governors' Association.

July 19. 1988   JFH addresses the Democratic National Convention.

Nov. 2, 1988   JFH endorses the Growth Strategies Commission report with the statement: "I want to assure each of you here today that I mean business."

April 18, 1989	JFH signs Growth Strategies legislation and announces his Community Energy Conservation Program.
Nov. 22, 1989	Official Ground-Breaking for the Georgia Dome.
Jan. 18, 1990	JFH named to U.S. Intergovernmental Trade Panel by U. S. Trade Representative Carla Hills.
May 1990	American Planning Association awards JFH the 1990 Distinguished Leadership Award.
Sept. 18, 1990	Atlanta is selected to host the 1996 Olympic Games. JFH made presentation before the International Olympic Committee in Tokyo.
Jan 14, 1991	Is succeeded as Governor by Zell Miller. Returned to Cartersville, GA.
1991	Chairman, Harris Georgia Corporation; Elected to Board of Directors: AFLAC, Inc., Bankhead Enterprises, Inc., Law Companies Group, Inc.; Co-Chair, Third Century Campaign—University of Georgia: raised over $150 million.
December 1993	Invited to lecture as part time professor in College of Public and Urban Affairs, Georgia State University.
Nov. 30, 1994	Named First Distinguished Executive Fellow

at Georgia State University by President Carl V. Patton.

October 8, 1997   Bronze bust of JFH unveiled Georgia National Fairgrounds and Agricenter in Perry, GA. The "Governor Joe Frank Harris and Elizabeth Harris Boulevard" is dedicated.

March 5, 1998   Received the Japan American Society of Georgia's "Mike Mansfield Award" as the 1998 Distinguished Georgian.

For Further Reading

Cook, James F. "Joe Frank Harris, 1983-1991." In *The Governors of Georgia*. Macon: Mercer University Press, 1995.

Harris, Joe Frank. *Addresses (1982-1990)*. Preface by Max Cleland. Privately published, 1990.

Harris, Joe Frank. *Governor's Policy Statement, 1990*. Atlanta: Office of Planning and Budget, 1990.

Walker, Tom. "Gov. Joe Frank Harris." In *Planning*. American Planning Association (March 1990), 13.

Index

Massey, Lewis (Secretary of State), 164
May, Dr. Bob, 227
Mayo Clinic (Rochester, MN), 57, 58
McKinsey & Company, 169
McNease, Mac, 76, 247
Meck, Stuart, 168
Media, 73, 79, 182, 222, 239, 240
  costs, 47
  power of, 124
Meir, Linda, 184
Melton, Buck, 71, 76, 247
Mercer University, 18, 261
Methodist Church
  Indian Springs Holiness Camp Meeting, 31, 33, 57
  North Georgia Conference, 17
  Northside United, 177
  Peachtree Road United, 177
  St. John's United, 177
  Temple United, 33
  United Methodist Women, Rome District, 56
MFPE (Minimum Foundation Education program). *See* education
microelectronics, 169
Middle Georgia, 71, 76, 148, 157
Miller, Andrew (Commissioner Salvation Army), 92
Miller, Governor Zell, 104, 135, 174, 193, 219, 224, 225, 266
Miller, Shirley , 105, 135
Mixon, John (Forestry Commissioner), 151
Moore, Ray, 73
Morgan, Barbara, 163

Morris Brown College, 18, 263
Morrow, Amos J. and Sara R., 257
Murphy, Tom (Speaker of the House), 54, 55, 88, 91, 92, 113, 193, 194
Murphy, Dr. Walter, 235
Murray County/Chatsworth, GA, 15
Murray, Steve, (Gibbs Landscaping), 107

National Guard, 26, 93, 143
Newman, Nancy , 184
North Georgia, 71, 145, 148, 149
Nunn, Senator Sam, 241

Old Cile Hotel, 47
Old Green Door Committee. *See* Green Door Committee, Old
Old River War, 144
Olympics, U.S. (1996), 179, 209-17
  Atlanta Committee for the Olympic Games, 204
  Atlanta Organizing Committee, 215
  Centennial Park, 216
  International Olympic Committee, 204, 211, 212, 214
  See also Payne, Billy
Omni Coliseum and complex, 179, 198

Pano's and Paul's, 183
Parker, John I., 48
Patton, President Carl V., 234,